WHICH SIDE ARE YOU ON?

Thomas Geoghegan

WHICH SIDE ARE YOU ON?

Trying to Be for Labor
When It's Flat on Its Back

THE NEW PRESS

NEW YORK
LONDON

Chapter 10 originally appeared, in somewhat different form,
in The New Republic.

First published in hardcover by Farrar, Straus & Giroux, New York, 1991
This paperback edition, with a new afterword,
published in the United States by The New Press, New York, 2004
Distributed by W. W. Norton & Company, Inc., New York

ISBN 1-56584-886-1 (pbk.)
CIP data available

The New Press was established in 1990 as a not-for-profit alternative to the large,
commercial publishing houses currently dominating the book publishing industry.
The New Press operates in the public interest rather than for private gain,
and is committed to publishing, in innovative ways, works of educational,
cultural, and community value that are often deemed insufficiently profitable.

The New Press
38 Greene Street, 4th floor
New York, NY 10013
www.thenewpress.com

In the United Kingdom:
6 Salem Road
London W2 4BU

Printed in the United States of America

1 3 5 7 9 10 8 6 4 2

To my mother and my father

Contents

Acknowledgments

Thanks to Linda Healey. Not just for teaching me how to write a book, but for telling me, yes, I could even write one about organized labor.

Thanks to Michael Kinsley of *The New Republic*: friend, editor, patron saint of the second career, who even ran "Confessions of a Practicing Catholic," and who assured me, as he began to edit it, "Tom, I'll look out after your interests in this world and the next."

Thanks to Dorothy Wickenden, managing editor of *The New Republic*. She told me to be concrete.

Thanks to my friends Tony Judge, Joel Brenner, and Dan Swanson, for the reading of some early drafts—and for the drinking of some later draughts.

Thanks to Cara Smiddy, who, when I dithered, grabbed the manuscript away from me and typed it.

Thanks above all to Leon Despres . . . who showed me how a lawyer, sometimes, in a single life, *can* bring justice to the city. And not even Lincoln could have done it with as much grace.

WHICH SIDE ARE YOU ON?

CHAPTER 1

Solidarity

"Organized labor." Say those words, and your heart sinks. I am a labor lawyer, and my heart sinks. Dumb, stupid organized labor: this is my cause.

But too old, too arthritic, to be a cause. It was a cause, back in the thirties. Now it is a dumb, stupid mastodon of a thing, crawling off to Bal Harbour to die. How did it outlive George Meany? Sometimes, as a mental exercise, I try to think of the AFL-CIO in the year 2001. But I cannot do it. The whole idea is too perverse.

U.S. manufacturing has gone down the drain, and with it, it seems, the entire labor movement. Just 16 percent of the work force now, down from 20–25 percent ten years ago. Maybe it will drop to 12. Once it drops to 10, it might as well keep dropping to zero.

I still read in the press about "Labor" and "Business" on Capitol Hill, fighting over policy, and I think, *"Labor?* What are they talking about?" I look at other labor lawyers around town, none of us with much business, all of it shrinking faster and faster. One day I will wake up and the unions will be gone, completely gone, and the other lawyers will be calling on the phone and saying, "It's over now, really over. I'm going into workmen's comp."

I look in my open grave and see a future of workmen's comp. I see old skulls, old bones of workers.

I know what I feel, what the other lawyers feel. Call up the client and say, hysterically, "Organize, organize." Yet we, of all people, know it is impossible to organize. The NLRB, the National Labor Relations Board, almost operates to prohibit it. And, of course, the clients know that, too. They have tried it a million heartbreaking times. Labor cannot even organize the people who want to join.

Labor gives off now an almost animal sense of weakness. Concessions, de-certs, shutdowns. It's like the Italian army in 1918: cars breaking down, baggage getting lost, officers getting fired on by their own troops. I joined organized labor, and we just started retreating.

It must seem odd for someone my age, who grew up in the sixties, to be in "organized labor." I live near Lincoln Park, on the North Side of Chicago. I eat pasta, I jog, I do all that is required of me, and I pass like anyone else. I could pass as a management lawyer.

But I am not: I do not know what I am. I belong to another world, too. It is the anti-world. The black, sulfurous, White Sox anti-world. The South Side. The secret world of organized labor. Now it is passing away, and I am in a panic. But how do I even discuss it?

Business agents, arbitration. I never mention it at parties. It sounds goonish even to me. I am embarrassed. My mother says, "Just tell people you work for the poor. It makes it all simpler."

A labor lawyer once told me, "To people outside it, labor's just another interest group. For us, it's part of the structure of the universe." Yes, to us, as it was in the thirties, now and forever. The locals, the districts, the federations, they are the real world, beneath the world of appearances. Labor *is* part of the structure of the universe, part of the secret essence of things. Business agents, stewards, to me, are the unacknowledged legislators of the world.

Once I knew nothing about labor. In college, I went to a seminar, "Labor and American Politics." I saw, onstage, union staffers who were from IAM, IOE, and IUE, which could have been, to me, the names of radio galaxies. They were fat, fleshy, middle-aged men: one was in a windbreaker, one was in a leisure suit. But they were so blank, so bureaucratic, with such an unenchanted connection to things, that even right then in the 1960s I could look at them and know, "*This* is the real counterculture."

Yes, there is a certain macho appeal to it. For years, I smoked cigars, Antony and Cleopatras, until I developed sinus problems and had to give them up. Once, at the Mineworkers, I even chewed tobacco. I made a fool of myself, running to the wastebasket, drooling into it. I loved being a labor lawyer, all the little pieces of stage business. Yet this was never the true appeal.

No, it was the appeal of stepping into some black hole in American culture, with all the American values except one: individualism. And here, in this black hole, paunchy, middle-aged men, slugging down cans of beer, come to hold hands, touch each other, and sing "Solidarity Forever." O.K., that hardly ever happens, but most people in this business, somewhere, at some point, see it once, and it is the damnedest un-American thing you will ever see. Two or three days later, you will not even believe you saw it. I had to see it twice before I could believe I saw it once.

Labor thinks of itself, consciously, as American as apple pie. But it is not. Go to any union hall, any union rally, and listen to the speeches. It took me years to hear it, but there is a silence, a deafening Niagara-type silence, on the subject of individualism. No one is against it, but it never comes up. Is that America? To me, it is like Spain.

Individualism is for scabs. This country is set up for scabs. Crossing a picket line, making your own deal. America is the land of opportunity. And a strike, if nothing else, creates lots of opportunities.

Since the eighties, it has been insane to go on strike. Every strike ends in disaster. The members go out, roaring mad, like in the old days. Then they watch the "crossovers" add up, day by day, watch until they reach the magic number, tip the balance, and the company can start up, nonunion, and bust the strike.

Our guys stand there, disbelieving, with picket signs on their shoulders, like batters looking at called third strikes. They stand there with their little buttons that say, in capital letters, "SCAB

HUNTER," under the barrel of a gun. But the buttons do not scare anyone. People breeze right over the line. In America, people scab on everyone: Americans even scabbed on the pros, their darlings, in the pro-football strike.

Labor began as a criminal conspiracy. Since the eighties it's felt like more of a conspiracy than ever. It seems strange to feel that way in Chicago. People think of Chicago, at least, as a union town. But I have no sense of where, in the city, labor really *is*. The old union neighborhoods are gone. Now labor is in suburbia. But it is thin, spread out, invisible even to itself. People relate to each other secretly, like Freemasons.

Out there in suburbia, labor is very, very still. The rank and file sit in front of the TV, corrupt, stupefied, like the rest of the country. Except they know that the rest of the country is gunning for them: for their cars, their RVs, their Chicago Bear tickets, their big, high-wage, high-pension jobs. After all, this is America, and there should be no "working class," with people making $40,000 or $50,000 a year. There should just be one big indeterminate middle class, like in *Les Misérables*.

A union movement in America will always be a scandal. It is an outlaw culture trying to play golf at Burning Tree. The idea of a *union*, of solidarity, is becoming less and less acceptable. Even in labor it is becoming less acceptable. The heading on a letter used to be "Dear Brother." Now it is "Dear sir and brother." It is a complex fate, in labor these days, to be "sir" *and* "brother."

The subversive thing about labor is not the strike, but the idea of solidarity. The whole thrust of organized labor is to . . . well, not socialism. But something. What does labor want? We want . . . we do not know what we want. But, at the very least, we want to be cut in on the deal. Even now, we still want to be cut in on the deal. As if it's still not too late. That's why Lane Kirkland is still playing golf at Burning Tree. We still think that somehow business, government will decide finally, "Let's cut them back in on the deal."

Believe me, in labor today we don't talk about socialism. Or solidarity. We talk about survival. In the after-dinner speeches I used to hear at labor events, someone would always say, "America will always need a free and independent labor movement." I sure hope America will always need us. But lately, in the back of the room, some of us have begun to wonder.

Even liberals, even progressives, do not seem to need us. At least, organized labor, I think, is incomprehensible to them. In some ways, American liberals, even American radicals, have more in common with the Reagan right than they do with us. All of them, the whole bunch, are middle-class, Emersonian individualists. Emerson, Thoreau, all of these guys are scabs. Lane Kirkland is outside the American consensus in a way that even Abbie Hoffman never was.

Back when Meany was alive, a friend of mine, a labor radical, said, "You know, I feel much closer to Meany, whom I despise, than a lot of the liberals. He may be right-wing, but if the crunch really came, you could count on Meany, like you couldn't count on any liberals . . ." Most people in labor feel that way, at some deep, paranoid, primal-scream level.

Actually, the crunch *did* come, and the liberals never lifted a finger to save us. Maybe I am unfair; everybody on the left had problems in the eighties. But you meet other activists, go to their meetings. They understand each other's causes, but have no sense of yours. Of course, they expect labor to fight for their causes. They always want labor to help *them*. Sometimes I think, "Hey, how about helping us?"

Look, I support the ACLU. But, seriously: give those people everything they want, the whole Bill of Rights, and it would not cost the country a thing. It would be no big deal. But give labor anything it wants, even a lousy ten-man machine shop, and every drop of it is blood. It all comes out of a bottom line.

I often meet people who, when they find out I am a labor lawyer, say, "Gee, I know nothing about labor." And I want to say, "Would you like to?"

The other day, I saw a friend, a journalist, who used to write about labor. Now he writes about something else. He said, "A few years ago, when labor was dying, that was interesting. But now it's dead, and it's been dead. People want to hear about something else."

Maybe I should do something else. Every year, I still go to the Debs-Thomas dinner, put on by the Democratic Socialists of America, the late Michael Harrington's group. I go, not because I am a socialist (I am not), but to see all the labor people in town. Even the hack, conservative labor people show up. Maybe we go because, as labor people, we think we should be socialists, even though we are not.

Solidarity. Dear sir and brother. The little rituals of a nineteenth-century criminal conspiracy. The whole thrust of labor is to . . . well, not socialism (I said that). Anyway, none of us would know what socialism means. The very idea of it is gone, blanked out, from the disconnected halves of our labor union brains. No wonder we are weird. Labor shambles around like Frankenstein, half its brain gone, scaring the culture of narcissism, and really, all we want is a little love. Solidarity. Union. It is the love, the only love left in this country, that dare not speak its name.

Chapter 2

Mountains of the Moon

I should start by answering a question.

"How did you become a *labor* lawyer, when you're just like the rest of us, i.e. you grew up suburban and middle-class and wouldn't have known a union from an onion at least until you were in your twenties?"

Basically I was unlucky in love. It was the closest thing I could find to the French Foreign Legion.

O.K., here's what really happened:

Although I went to college in the late sixties, I was a "student moderate." While other kids were taking over buildings, and exams were being canceled year after year, it never occurred me to go on "strike." And away from campus, it's possible that the only picket line I ever saw was one of transvestites in Copley Square; I think a restaurant wouldn't serve them.

Actually, back then almost everyone was a moderate. The truth is that in the sixties you never had to do anything. You could be "political" just by sitting in your dorm room, and that would be your witness to History. While other kids your age would be burning down ghettos or small villages in Vietnam, you could just sit there in your room, and be paralyzed, and listen to the small-arms fire. And then, later, for the rest of your life, you could walk around like characters in a Hemingway or Fitzgerald novel and say, "I really lived through something." What it was, was not exactly clear, and trying to name it all the time is what drives people my age a little nuts. We can never say what the damn thing *was*. It was, I think, the tension of doing nothing, just sitting there, listening to the Doors, and never coming out of your room.

In this sense, and no other, was I a sixties activist. Anyway, the story is how I became an activist in the seventies, just when the temptation for doing anything at all had stopped.

It all began in November 1972, when I was brooding about S. and sitting in my room, and some of my roommates were getting worried.

One of them, Bob Metzger, asked if I wanted to take a drive with him that weekend up to Pennsylvania.

"No," I said.

"You can't stay here and sulk."

"Why not?"

"Because that's not how you get over these things. Look, why don't you come up with me and be an observer in this Mine-workers election?"

"It doesn't interest me."

"Come on . . ."

He had talked about this before. While few people may recall it now, the Mineworkers election was a mildly prominent national story in 1972, partly because it arose out of a murder. Tony Boyle, then the Union president, was widely supposed to have murdered his rival, "Jock" Yablonski, and Yablonski's wife and daughter, while they slept in their home. (Boyle was convicted of the murders years later.) The murders came just after the 1969 election, in which Boyle beat Yablonski. But Yablonski was still a threat to Boyle because he was going to protest the vote. Anyway, the pallbearers swore vengeance, and they and other rank-and-file miners formed a group, Miners for Democracy, which was to carry on the fight. After a long legal battle, the MFD convinced the Labor Department to file suit to overturn the 1969 vote and to hold a rerun. This time, the Labor Department would supervise the balloting. And now, in November 1972, the new election was here.

Bob had a friend, Ed James, who until the Yablonski murders had been a grad student at Columbia; then he left school, bought a gun, and joined the miners. Ed was now the campaign manager, and even though the Labor Department was counting the ballots, the MFD group still wanted observers, people who could pass, and run, and observe on the day of the vote. Ed talked Bob into going up to Sheridan, Pennsylvania, and Bob was trying to drag me along.

I desperately wanted not to go.

So we left late Friday afternoon. We drove out of Washington, D.C., radiant with the autumn light, and headed north up into the hills. The hills turned into mountains, and as the light faded and we climbed higher and higher, the idea of all this was beginning to appeal to me.

I thought, "She'll be sorry if I'm murdered by miners."

It became darker and colder, and the mountains were like dark, cardboard cones, higher than the Alps, and yet we were only a few hours from Washington, D.C. When we passed Scranton, Pennsylvania, and I looked back and saw it twinkling like Manhattan, I began to wonder if I would ever see a city again.

Suddenly, I had a change of mood: I wanted to go back, I wanted to *live*.

But Bob kept talking away, saying over and over, "Yeah, my old friend Ed James . . . he carries a gun with him all the time now."

I thought, "Well, we don't," and I just wished he would stop talking.

Up here, it was dark and freezing and lunar, and there were craters everywhere. The land had been gutted and strip-mined, and looked like the moon, except that the moon was overhead, high and bright, shining down on us like planet Earth. It was as if we had a rover and were driving up the sides of the mountains of the moon, to join up with a lot of murdered miners.

The next morning Bob dropped me off at a union hall and he left me there, alone. I stood confused for a moment or two in front of the hall. Was I supposed to go in? I was the "MFD observer," but I had never been an observer, and didn't know what to do. And at that moment, I was thinking, for some reason, of the state motto of West Virginia, which I had heard once before. *Montani semper liberi.*

It means, I think, roughly translated: Mountaineers always have guns.

Then I saw the Boyle goons, in front of the hall, blocking the door.

One of them said, "Look, here's one of the Nader boys."

He came over to me and said, "You work for Nader, don't you?"

I said I didn't work for Nader.

"Yeah," they said, "come on, you work for Nader?"

Later I was warming myself by a stove or fire. Others came over and smirked and said, "You work for Nader, don't you?"

I think I denied it three times.

They probably weren't going to kill me. They just wanted to know: Hey, what are you doing up here?

And what could I say? I could hardly say I was up here grieving over a junior at Radcliffe.

Suddenly there was a hand on my shoulder, and I froze. An old, old man stood there, and told me not to be afraid. He would be with me, and help me observe.

I didn't know where he came from, or even if he was in the MFD. But he stayed with me all day. After the voting, we both went outside. He was short and Magyar, and he was crippled, too.

He told me that years ago he was in an accident in a mine.

It was dark, and I could barely see his face.

Where? I said.

Oh, he said softly, it was in Russia, in 1912 . . .

Oh, I said.

This was how I learned about "the Anthracite." The Anthracite was the home of the Molly Maguires, who were the Irish terrorists of their day; and then the home of the Magyars and Ukrainians and Poles. And now it had been in a deep economic depression for years. The pension fund was broke, the mines were closed, and it looked like the moon. Many years ago, utilities and factories had stopped using "anthracite" or "hard coal," which is found here, and now they used "bituminous" or "soft coal," which is found everywhere else.

So now most of the miners were pensioners or retirees. Because there were so few of them, and they had so few votes,

Boyle ignored them, wrote them off, and things were even worse here than they should have been.

The old people up here now hated Boyle, hated him fiercely. They were drawing pensions, in 1972, of $30 per month: that was all, for thirty years in a mine, for black lung, for emphysema, for living in a place that looked like the moon. They had $30 a month to live on.

Not that they would live long. This was Boyle's big advantage here. Because he was stronger in the "soft coal" states, and up here, in the bitter cold, with their black lung and emphysema, these old people couldn't go outside. They couldn't breathe the air.

Some were so ill they couldn't lie down at night. They had to sleep standing up, just to fight for a bit of air. I was staying in a miner's house, and I remember looking at a wall and wondering if someone would sleep here tonight. I wondered what kind of dreams you would have if you were standing against a wall.

Anyway, that Saturday, all of us knew, standing there, outside the hall, that if these old men could get down here, if they could get up the stairs and into the hall, every one of them would vote against Boyle.

But it seemed impossible. It was just too cold.

And then, all day, the old women drove up and stopped and would drag their husbands up the steps, poor old men, eyes shut, stiff as corpses, maybe still dreaming that they were upright against a wall.

I wasn't sure that some of them were alive, but they sure looked like our votes.

The Boyle goons tried to block the door or stuff cards into their hands. And the women, these tiny women, would grab the cards, and spit, and fling them to the ground. Then they pushed the goons out of the way. Then they dragged the husbands into the hall and across the floor and over to the voting booth, and closed the curtain.

For just a minute, husband and wife would be in there, just the two of them, and nobody knew what was going on, and nobody had the nerve to go over and stop them.

Then the women came out, leading the men, and we let them pass.

I was affected by the women (the men were just inert). I was affected by the way they wanted revenge, a terrible Ukrainian blood revenge on everyone, revenge on the companies, revenge on Boyle, even revenge on the Union, for having left them there to die, on $30 a month.

From that moment on, I think I wanted to join the Union somehow, and even to help them take this terrible revenge. And I didn't realize that if we won, if we took over the Union, then I would be part of the Union and would have to defend it. And then I would be implicated in the evil, too.

Arnold Miller, Michael Trbovich, and Harry Patrick, the MFD slate, swept into office. It had never happened before, not in modern times. Rank-and-file miners, with rank-and-file candidates like Miller and Patrick, who had never held any office, even any *local*-union office (except maybe mine safety committeemen), but were pure untainted "workers," had thrown out the rascals.

The UMW was like a Stalinist regime, thrown over, like East Germany, by its own people. This was a shocking thing. In some ways, it was even more shocking than the Yablonski murders (people are always being murdered, after all). No one in labor had ever seen anything like it. Because this was not a palace coup, as sometimes happens in the AFL-CIO, but a revolution from below, with the miners voting in their own.

The AFL-CIO was in shock. Put Boyle in jail for murder? Well, O.K. But throw him out of office in a rank-and-file election? That kind of thing wasn't done. In fact, in most unions it literally could not be done. At the time, only two of the major American unions, the Mineworkers and the Steelworkers, even permitted such elections, in which members could vote directly for their top officers. Other unions had scrapped such "rank-and-file" elections many years ago, and instead they used indirect voting, delegate conventions, etc. This is the basic system, like Whig England in the 1700s before the Reform Acts. As a result, while there are changeovers in the local unions, there are never changeovers at the top. Or nothing like the Mineworkers. There are no national campaigns, no national candidacies to mobilize voters. There are just palace coups, poisonings, and back-room deals. Even the UMW had rank-and-file elections only by accident. John L. Lewis, president for almost forty years, had been something of a Caesarist and liked being proclaimed by a mob. He stole the elections anyway. And after his death, it never occurred to anyone that maybe one day the government would count the ballots. Why should it?

So Boyle never bothered to scrap them. He forgot he was going to murder Yablonski. And this is the only reason he lost. And the election was just the start. Then came the convention. Then a new constitution. Just like in Crane Brinton's book *The Anatomy of Revolution*, which in my day every history major in college had to read, and which I should have been reading, to find out what would happen next.

The defeat of Boyle was just the start. It was like the first stage of the revolution, i.e., taking the king captive.

Next was the convention. In 1973 the miners elected delegates. They swarmed out of the hills, met in Pittsburgh, and rewrote the constitution, so that now it read like the Declaration of the Rights of Man.

From now on, everything would come from the rank and file. Even the bargaining proposals in negotiations would come from the rank and file. Everything that came from headquarters—i.e., from Washington, D.C., where everything had always come from—was impure. It was corrupt.

The new constitution was true to Rousseau. It was like nothing else in labor. It was Union Democracy, the New Politics, the whole Sixties Enlightenment. It was the whole sixties experience come at last to organized labor. Of course, it had come after the sixties were over, but in America everything gets down to the working class after it's over.

Still, it's odd that the Mineworkers, of all unions, brought the sixties to the labor movement. A union of Baptists, church deacons, people in Appalachia, who had never heard a Bob Dylan song in their lives, the most tsarist, autocratic and backward union in America: *this* is where it started. But then, Marx never thought that Marxism would start in Russia.

But there is a logical explanation. The UMW is the only union where it *could* happen. Nobody else in labor had the right to vote.

To the rest of Big Labor, with its nobility, its crowned heads, its landed estates in Dupont Circle, it must have seemed like the French Revolution. It was their worst nightmare come true: the "members" crossing over the Beltway, running wild through the buildings, swinging from the chandeliers. I think that's what they hated most about the UMW: we let them roam through the *building*.

By "we," I mean the staff, which I had joined. They hated the staff, i.e., the "kids," the people like me, the VISTA volunteers, the grad students. To them, we were the real Jacobins.

To this day, they still talk about it in Washington, and they point us out and say, "See? See him? He was one of them. The ones who ruined the Mineworkers."

You think I'm kidding, but they've never forgiven. To hear them talk, you would think we had set up guillotines in the streets.

Yet, despite all the reform, the "old" UMW was always there, like a shadow government, ready to return at any minute.

Every day as I walked into the building, I would look up to the landing and see the huge head of John L. Lewis, in its own little shrine, with lighting that cast a huge shadow on the wall. It was a dark, glowering head, black as a lump of coal, scowling down on us like Stalin as we came in the door.

It was his building, Lewis's. It was like his tomb or mausoleum, almost airless. Some days I felt like a miner going into a mine. The air in the building was dark and brown, like the air the rank and file breathed down under the ground. I used to think that just from working here, in this building, I would get black lung.

Lewis was our Peter the Great, and perhaps just as mad and cruel. For forty years he had run the UMW, and even as a statue, he was still president of the UMW. With his huge head, huge eyebrows, he watched our every move in the building.

After it was over, after it had all gone wrong, I realized it was that statue we should have destroyed.

John L. Lewis, born in Illinois, was the son of a Welsh miner. In 1920, at the age of forty, he became president of the UMW and held the office for forty years. Lewis was one of the geniuses of his age. He created, out of his Zeus-like head, not only the modern UMW but organized labor as well. He was vice president of the AFL, then founder of the CIO, and finally, to a very large extent, the man who created the modern American economy.

He was a great man for three reasons:

First, as founder of the CIO, he led the great organizing drives of the 1930s in auto, rubber, and steel and established industrial unions in this country.

Second, as president of the UMW for forty years (when being that was like being the Sun King of OPEC), he modernized coal mining and shaped America's energy policy around coal.

Third, he reshaped American capitalism. He created the pension funds and welfare funds and an economy in which wages were continually being raised. In 1990 when we talk about the collapse of Communism and the triumph of "capitalism," we mean not Adam Smith's idea of it, or William Buckley's, but the mixed economy of pensions, health insurance, cost-of-living allowances, that we owe, at least arguably, to some extent, to our leader, John L. Lewis.

He was also a tyrant and a bully. But we, the staff, and everyone else at the UMW, would bow down before him, or before his graven image, and worship him. Because our union had given Lewis to the world, and because he was great, we were great, too.

Yet time had passed, and the Union was much smaller now. The UMW building, which was a block or so away from the White House, had seemed to be once, under Lewis, an equal to the White House itself. Now it was just a dumpy little building. It was still full of old men and cleaning ladies who remembered "Mr. Lewis" and spoke about him as if he were still alive. It was still *his* building, not ours.

A few weeks ago, I had dinner with a labor reporter, and I mentioned something about the UMW, and he said, surprised, "Were you part of that group?"

"What do you mean?"

"The staff . . ."

"Yes," I said. "Well, barely. I was very young. I wasn't anyone important on it."

"I've always wanted to write about those guys. None of them sold out, did they?"

Well, not too many.

It was a staff, I think, such as no one had seen in a labor union since the 1930s, or ever.

We had two former Supreme Court law clerks in our legal department. There were two grad students from Columbia. There were two or three VISTA volunteers, who then joined the UMW. And Bernie, who's now Assistant Secretary of State in the Bush administration.

Most of them were older than I was, and I was like a kid brother, always hanging around. We would all go drinking together after work, and charge it to the "rank and file." This impressed me a great deal.

Suddenly, overnight, I was a "union man." I didn't know any workers, of course, but that didn't matter. None of my friends outside the Union knew that. To them, and to many others I met in town, I spoke for the workers, heard their voices. And who in Washington, D.C., could really call you on it?

I began to seem dangerous, even to myself.

Yet it didn't seem like too much of a career risk either. I still wore suits from Brooks Brothers, like other lawyers, and it was still a "Washington lawyer's job," with big, complex, federal court type of litigation. I told myself not to panic, this would turn out fine, and it would be a kick to represent the "workers" (I was coming to like the sound of it) for a year or two, and then go on to something else.

This must be what people tell themselves when they start experimenting with drugs.

A staff member once told me, "There's nothing, nothing, you'll ever do in this life that's more fun than collective bargaining." Not that they would let *me* do it. But when I came to the UMW, the national negotiations were about to start.

Well, you find out fast what John L. Lewis must have liked

about the job. Walk in a room, look the operators in the eye, and know that you, yes, *you*, could, if you liked, pound the table, storm out of the room, and plunge the whole country into nuclear winter.

We, the younger staff, used to have a song, "Negotiations," sung to the tune of "Oklahoma." I remember the first line:

"Negooooooooooooootiations . . ."

And what could they do? Call out the National Guard? There is an old saying at the UMW: "You can't mine coal with bayonets."

The UMW was always on strike, too. In the legal department, we had poster-size blowups of old newspapers with headlines like:

"Truman Calls Out National Guard, Army."

"Lewis Held in Contempt."

The headlines reminded me how lucky I was. I thought, "I have the only job in America where it's legal to incite a riot."

O.K., sometimes legal.

O.K., never legal. But so what? How could they stop us?

I could see myself ripping up injunctions.

I could see myself standing before a federal judge and saying, "Judge, the men will never obey this." I could see myself swirling my London Fog around me, like Lawrence of Arabia in his desert robes, and disappearing into the fastnesses of Appalachia.

It may have been the very last time at the UMW anyone could still have thought this way. In 1974, the nation still depended on "union coal." The White House, *The New York Times, The Wall Street Journal*, still paid attention to what we did.

But the coal industry was moving West, and in the West it was hard to organize the new strip mines, or surface mines. Not because of the "culture" out West (Utah, in labor history, is at least as radical as West Virginia), but because the mines out there were surface mines, not the deep underground mines where solidarity was automatic and the Union was a matter of life and death.

I think we already knew then that aboveground, in the air, the UMW couldn't breathe. Aboveground, it was like any other union. It had to rely on the law, i.e., the Wagner Act—and the Wagner Act was useless.

Before I came to the UMW, I had never heard the term "rank and file." In other unions, it is only another word for the "client population." But at the UMW, it meant a real army, or more like a host, and we, the staff, believed in the rank and file, almost ontologically, as a real thing, not a concept but something that really existed, two or three hours away in West Virginia.

There were some of us who began to think and talk in military terms. It was hard not to. I started to think of "injunctions" and "strikes" as military subjects, like "cavalry" and "munitions."

I began to think, "This is the military I had missed sitting in my dorm room." I was being given a second chance.

I read *The Labor Injunction* (1930) by Felix Frankfurter. I read about Napoleon's campaigns. And if I wasn't in the Army, and if I was cheating to think I could make up for Vietnam in this way, still it was something to know that out there in West Virginia there was a real rank and file ready to strike.

Yet except for Tony, the security guard, I didn't yet know a single miner. I would be upstairs in the law library, like the poet in the tower, and reading and reading with the light on late at night.

I would try to imagine them, out there in West Virginia:

First of all, they seemed very young. It was no union for old men. For the first time in years, there was hiring in the mines. So all through the seventies young men who were my age drifted into the mines, back from Vietnam. They, unlike me, had been in a real war. A strange homecoming, too. Back from Agent Orange to black lung. There was a faint menace to their coming back, as if the sixties they had missed were about to start now.

Second, they all seemed very old. This was no union for young men. No, the old men were the real radicals, the ones who corrupted us all. They were sleepless and dying, and slipping into their golden years of emphysema (the government, in 1969, had just discovered black lung as a disease). Black lung. It was like a fog. It put everyone in a mood for murder.

This is not the union you would have picked as the very first to try out something like . . . Union Democracy.

The general counsel for whom I worked was Chip Yablonski. He was Jock's son. His family was the one they had murdered. So I could never forget, even in the legal department, that one thing a union (or at least this union) was about: it was about revenge.

I suppose he was in his thirties then and still a fairly young lawyer, but to me he already seemed like an old soldier, General Counsel Yablonski.

As I read more and more law, I came to notice that the big, famous labor cases often involved the UMW.

"This is a litigating union," Chip said to me.

In a way, this is surprising. The UMW is very small, only 200,000 or so members.

But in a way it's not so surprising. The UMW, at least in the old days, before I got there, had a fondness for sometimes blowing things up with dynamite.

In the first case Chip gave me, *Kinty Coal* v. *UMW*, you could almost smell the gunpowder. Well, both sides probably used it. In the early 1950s, a Union organizer had come into a valley, and someone, at some point, had started using dynamite, blowing up railroads, tipples, entrances to mines. A suit had been filed against the Union in 1955, when I was in the first grade at Cardinal Pacelli School, and now, twenty years later, it was finally coming to trial. My first case. Waiting for me until I finished school. And now almost everyone was dead. Nine of the thirteen employer-plaintiffs were dead. The organizers were dead. The lawyers who first handled the case were dead. Two judges who were sitting on the case were dead. Only the widows were around to testify, and they could remember nothing except that once, twenty years ago, their husbands were very upset. So most of the claims had to be thrown out.

Chip was very pleased. He told me, "This is a case that was properly handled."

Our job up in the legal department was to keep all the cases going like this for twenty years, until everyone was dead. As I read through our files, fifteen or twenty years old, I came to know the history of the UMW, and indeed the history of American labor, too. I would dust off an old file, full of soot and coal dust and gunpowder, and then after work go out to the dim hotel bars. And I would never meet a single miner.

But I did work on one case from the 1970s: Harlan County, the strike to organize the Brookside mine.

I had almost forgotten about this, until one day a few years ago I went to see a movie (a documentary, actually), *Harlan County, U.S.A.* I was in Greenwich Village, with nothing to do, and I went past a theater, some little art-film house, and walked in. And suddenly I was sitting there in shock. All around me, there were young men, in earrings, eating popcorn and yawning. And there, up on the screen, were the miners, the strikers, begging for help, like ghosts from my past.

And an old woman's voice, thin, scraping, whining, singing the same lines over and over,

> Which side are you on?
> Which side are you on?

It was the closest I have ever come to an out-of-body experience.

I thought, "My God, what am I doing here? How could I have left those people?"

I could have been twenty again, in Cambridge, at the Brattle Theater, watching *Children of Paradise*. Except this was *real*. Yes, I knew these people up on the screen. There was Chip, and there was Bernie . . .

I had worked on this strike. Well, I had written a memo, actually, but all the time I would try to imagine what it was like in Harlan County, and now at last, years later, I could see it.

The state police on one side, cocking their pistols (you could hear the clicks), ready to fire.

The miners on the other side, ready to die.

A miner did die.

I saw the miners' wives locked in jail. "Oh my God," I thought. "Oh my God."

Someone next to me kept crunching his popcorn.

Harlan County was in Kentucky, and had such a violent history that it was known as "Bloody Harlan." In the 1920s, employers with private armies would open fire on striking miners. In the 1930s, a commission of writers led by Theodore Dreiser even went down to Harlan to write a report, much as Amnesty International might go into El Salvador today.

The UMW organized the Brookside mine, then lost it, then took it back again, and then lost it again. It was like World War I, with the armies going back and forth over the same ground. Now, in the 1970s, we wanted it back again. And we wanted to show, by the way, that the UMW was back, and that we were just as tough now, with our "new democracy," as we had been in the John L. Lewis days.

Now, as I watched the movie, I thought, "Where's the staff?" Yes, yes, I wanted to see the miners, the wives locked up in jail, but then I noticed that *we the staff* were missing. Yes, I know, we couldn't have done it without them, but . . .

It was really annoying.

We, the staff, had won that strike. *We* had organized the boycotts, the rate challenges, even a brief nationwide strike (which, for legal purposes, we had to call a "memorial period for the union dead"). *We* had gone to the White House and the Labor Department to demand that they intervene, and to tell them, "If you don't want a national strike later this fall, you better fix things in Harlan County."

Now I could almost resent the rank and file, up there hogging every scene.

I remember, some mornings, Chip and others, looking awful, sleeping an hour or two after being up all night in negotiations. These people, working night after night . . . this is what was real.

The movies never tell you the truth. Sometimes only a bureaucracy can win a strike. Sure, we did it for the rank and file, but we also did it for ourselves, to prove ourselves to everyone else, to the other bureaucracies, to all the other people in labor, the other professionals, who didn't think we had it in us.

So we won the strike in Harlan County, and they only killed one miner, and John L. Lewis himself couldn't top that.

/ 23

It was always tempting to drive down to Harlan County while it was happening, but I wasn't a fool. My father told me, "Don't go there, for God's sakes, with out-of-state license plates," and I finally decided not to go there at all.

In fact, I never went into a mine. I just read about going into mines. I read George Orwell's *The Road to Wigan Pier*, and I read James Agee's *Let Us Now Praise Famous Men*.

Then one day I decided it was not enough to read the Orwell and the Agee books, and that I had to go out there and go down into a mine.

I knew I had to do it when one day the woman I was dating then, who was from New York and who wrote poetry and read Rilke and worked in a bookstore, said to me after three months of dating, "What is this group, the United *Mind* Workers?"

"No, it's the United Mine Workers. They work in coal mines."

"Oh."

At first, I didn't think much of the mistake, and then a friend of mine at the Mineworkers took me aside.

He said, "What's the matter with you? You date a woman three months and she thinks you work for the United *Mind* Workers? Do you think that could happen to anyone else here? We're obsessed, *obsessed*, we can't stop talking about it. What's the matter with *you?*"

What was the matter with me? It was as if I was standing against a wall at night and dreaming, as if nothing beyond the Beltway was really real.

So I told Chip I wanted to go out there and see a mine.

I was sent out to Kentucky, not to Harlan, thank God, but somewhere else, where it was fairly safe. I was sent to do a hearing on a mine safety issue, which was not my expertise. Back then, my specialty was supposed to be the little aridities of federal courts: how many angels can dance on the head of a federal judge?

Not mine safety. Not drag lines, machines, and diggers like the "Jim of Egypt."

I was flown to a remote mining hamlet in Eastern Kentucky, and it was worse than I'd supposed. There was a small hotel, or lodging house. I was told there were more millionaires here, per capita, than anywhere else in America. And the land was so ravaged, that it had to be true.

Three miners took me out to dinner, and they told me what to say and do at the hearing the next day.

I said, "I've never been in a mine."

"Well," one of them said, "want to go now?"

"Now? It's a little late, isn't it?"

It was after eleven and we were in a bar. The men looked at each other. "No, it's not too late."

"Well, is it far?"

"No, it's not too far."

We went out to the car, and as I got in the back seat, it suddenly occurred to me, for the first time:

We were all drunk.

The night air helped my wits. I said, "Hey, how far is this?"

"Fifty miles."

"*Fifty* miles? It's almost midnight . . ."

"Good dirt roads all the way."

"We've got a hearing tomorrow, at nine *a.m.*"

"Won't be any traffic," another man said.

I could see us speeding along, doing fifty or sixty, and then dropping dead drunk down a mine shaft at two in the morning. I couldn't believe that Orwell or Agee had ever done this.

This is as close as I ever came to going into a mine.

I rarely left town. West Virginia to me was just another version of the UMW building anyway. The same sense of gloom and oppression. It's still a state I want to drive through and out of as soon as I can, leaving behind the strange and mysterious lights and bonfires and abandoned mines.

In the daylight, it was a horrible place. Claustrophobic, like midtown Manhattan. Nowhere to live. In the seventies everyone seemed to live in a trailer camp or in the crevice of a mountain. There were no "company towns," but the timber and coal companies owned so much of the state that maybe it would have been better to have had them. There's more space in a company town than there is in a trailer camp. It seems cruel to lock people up when there is so much open space. Even in New York City they don't lock the homeless up in camps.

There is something about coal mining that seems to brutalize a place. It was amazing that in the mid-seventies, in the new silicon-chip economy, we were mining coal at all. It's the most primitive of industries. Even old industries, like steel and the railroads, which started in the nineteenth century, seem modern or high-tech compared with coal. But while these industries are now in decline, we still have a coal industry. We still have to get people down under the ground, where there is no air or light, and make them stay there until they sicken and have to sleep standing up against a wall. And we will go on forcing people underground, I suppose, when there are Apple Macintoshes in every miner's home.

All of us at the Union headquarters much preferred Washington, D.C. Even the rank-and-file staff, who came out of the mines, didn't want to go back. When I first came to the UMW, there was still talk of moving the Union headquarters "back to the coalfields," but that kind of talk soon faded fast. It's silly to leave, anyway, when everyone else in organized labor is here, too. I would enjoy running into the other union people, the other union staffers, at dinner parties, bookstores, and gallery openings. I would nod to them, and they would nod to me, because we were all there fighting for the rank and file.

Move the headquarters back to the coalfields? It would be as strange as moving it to France.

I had a friend on the staff who came from West Virginia. He hated Washington, hated the principle of it, but as time passed, he couldn't leave. He said that one day, when he was back in West Virginia, he went into an Arby's or McDonald's.

He said, "And I looked around, and I had been in Washington so long . . . and now, I saw these people, and I was a little scared."

It was then he knew he had the Dupont Circle disease.

But sometimes I would see the rank and file here, in Washington. Sometimes they even roamed through the legal department, and I would be in the law library and look up and see a miner, like an apparition, standing in front of me.

For a moment or two, we would both be embarrassed. Then he might say, very softly and gently, "Hey, buddy, how's it going?"

I never knew what to say. Should I say, "Hi, buddy"?

I was a bit jealous of the staff who could say, "Hi, buddy," and be cool about it. Especially the rank-and-file staff, who came out of the mines. Of course, I wondered how rank-and-file they really were.

There was Rich Trumka, my office mate. He was a young lawyer, just out of law school. We had the same secretary. He was no different from me, really, but he was the son of a miner and he had been in the mines. Rich Trumka was just as much a Washingtonian as I was, but he was a *miner*. The miners could pour out their hearts to him and call him "buddy," and he could call them "buddy" back.

And I couldn't, and that's what annoyed the hell out of me. I was also jealous that he could chew tobacco. I thought that if I could chew tobacco, it would be a start, and without radically changing my personality, it would be . . . well, mind-altering, like other kinds of tobacco back then.

So one night, Rich and another miner taught me how to chew tobacco. They leaned their chairs against the wall, and they chewed and spit in long arcing free throws into a basket (a wastebasket) across the room.

I had to get up, walk across, lean over the basket, and drool.

This is as close as I ever came to being rank-and-file, and I didn't even get a high.

I looked down on the miners who had supported Boyle, and assumed they must be hacks, or murderers, or the friends of murderers. Then I met Sam Littlefield.

Sam Littlefield was from Alabama and was president of District 20, which took in the rich coalfields around Birmingham. At first, he seemed like any other union hack, a holdover from the Boyle era.

In one of my first cases, though, I was thrown in with Sam Littlefield. I was suspicious of him, because he didn't have the true faith, as I did, and someone had told me, "Watch out for him," but didn't tell me why, exactly.

The UMW had a complaint before the Commissioner of Customs to block the importation of coal from South Africa into the United States. This was my case, partly because no one else had time for it. We were relying on an obscure provision of the Tariff Act of 1930 which prohibited the importation of any product or mineral that was manufactured or mined by "indentured labor under penal sanction." We thought we could show that all miners in South Africa (all black miners, anyway) were "indentured laborers under penal sanction," because they could be fined or even imprisoned if they walked out of the mines and left their employment.

I would tell my friends how shocking things were in South Africa, where miners could be fined or jailed simply for quitting and walking out of the mines. They would be shocked.

To me, this was "our" case, the International Union's. But Sam seemed to think that it was his case. He didn't want any South African coal coming into Alabama, and he began to court me and take me out to lunch.

I found myself starting to like Sam. I knew it was wrong, and that he had been a Boyle supporter, but he was so charming. I was touched.

Sam said to me, "Now, Tom, we can't let that coal land, can we?"

"No," I said. I wasn't sure what he was saying.

Meanwhile, a ship with the coal was steaming across the Atlantic. Sam was not one to wait for litigation. Already, he had been running ads in Alabama papers saying, "Slavery was abolished 100 years ago in Alabama, and now the Southern Utility Company is trying to bring it back."

He began to call me two or three times a day. "Tom, do you think you can find out where that ship is now?"

"Sure, Sam, I'll try."

Soon I had a contact with a South African journalist, and I could almost plot that ship, as in the movie *Sink the Bismarck!*

Sam would call. "Where's it now?"

"Day and a half out."

I knew the ethical canons. I knew Canon 9: "A lawyer should avoid even the appearance of impropriety." I knew, deep in my heart, that somewhere in Alabama a terrible impropriety was going to occur, but I kept telling myself, "He's a Boyle supporter, he's one of the regulars, he's one of them . . ." I kept thinking, "He's only a bureaucrat . . ."

Well, the second the boat landed in Mobile, it was surrounded by miners. Every mine in the state went on strike. Hundreds of miners ringed the Port of Mobile and shut down the whole port. Nothing could go in or out. Food was rotting on the wharves. That wasn't all. Sam sent miners to the headquarters of the utility importing the coal, and they broke into a meeting of the stockholders and chased them out of the room.

I have never seen so many injunctions all at once. The NLRB, the Justice Department, the state of Alabama, the port, the employers—there were a million TROs. Millions of dollars in damages. And it wasn't funny. It took three or four years to dispose of all the litigation.

I was aghast. Chip called me down to his office, and he said very slowly, "WHAT IS GOING ON?"

Sam was delighted, of course, and kept telling me what a great piece of work this had been. By then, I realized he was mad. Off his rocker.

A few months later, ironically, Sam was up in Washington for a Union meeting and later, back at his hotel, he was robbed and killed. I keep talking about murder and danger in the coalfields, but they weren't half as dangerous as Washington, D.C., or at least the few blocks around the Union building.

Everyone said, "He's been assassinated," and this is surely the way that Sam would have wanted to go, but I don't think he was.

By the time he was murdered, I had already lost touch with him. I didn't want to talk to him or see him ever again after all the trouble he got me into, and I never again trusted any of these old union hacks.

The rest of this story is darker.

For two years, 1975 and 1976, the "wildcats," or illegal strikes, would rage all over Appalachia. These small, local, mine-by-mine strikes started breaking out in 1972, and by 1975, when I was there, the miners would walk out all the time. This was completely illegal, because a contract was in effect. The federal courts would issue injunctions, impose contempt, etc., but the miners kept walking out. A grievance man would be fired, somebody's pension would be denied, and there would be a little strike, maybe twenty-four hours or so, and then they'd come back.

It was as if the men, unwittingly, had stumbled upon a crude form of worker control.

The companies, hysterical, were filing hundreds of lawsuits. Against us, the International Union. For a while, there was a federal lawsuit being filed *every* day . . . no kidding, one a day. I know because my secretary, Georgia Thompson, used to log them. It was frightening. Sometimes a single coal company, like Peabody Coal, would have over 150 cases pending against the International at the same time.

Yet we didn't call the strikes, or approve of them. They were simply happening.

The scary part was that every August, in 1975 and 1976, a big, nationwide "wildcat" would start. It would start at a single mine, and then go like a forest fire from state to state. Soon it would be a national strike, burning wild and out of control.

Whole districts, dry as tinderboxes, would go up in smoke. I can't remember exactly how it would spread: District 17 (Kanawha), then to District 31 (Fairmount), then to District 20 (Birmingham). Wildcat strikers, in their cars, driving from mine to mine.

The entire Union was like a roaming mob . . . and back in Washington, we had nothing to do with it. *Nothing.* I would sit there, stunned, and every August I would wonder if this was the big, final wildcat that was predicted in the Book of Revelation.

The first one (1975) was almost "normal." At least, it was against the companies. But the second one (1976) was a strike against the federal courts. The picket signs even said, "Strike Against the Federal Courts."

Here I should explain why over a hundred thousand miners were striking against the federal courts.

It all starts with the Supreme Court. In fact, with the "liberal" Warren Court of the 1960s. For years, the federal courts had left the unions alone or at least not issued injunctions against ordinary, run-of-the-mill contract strikes. In the 1930s, Congress had passed a law, the Norris–La Guardia Act, which took away the very jurisdiction of the courts to hear such labor cases or issue injunctions at all. Then, in the late 1960s, although Norris–La Guardia was still the law, the Supreme Court—i.e., the liberal Warren Court—decided that we don't oppress workers anymore and that we don't need Norris–La Guardia to protect them.

In 1969, in the *Boys Markets* case, the Supreme Court held that it would now issue injunctions to enforce no-strike clauses in contracts. Then the Court went even further. It said it would "imply" no-strike clauses even if they weren't there, and it would enjoin all strikes over issues that were "arbitrable"—i.e., that could be raised before a neutral arbitrator. The Court reasoned that we don't need strikes anymore and everything could be decided by a neutral arbitrator.

So all strikes were illegal now, all over the United States, for three- or four-year periods, or the "life of the contract." Put another way, the right to strike was now banned in the U.S. 99 percent of the time or more, except for certain "window" periods when the contract would end. So if miners were worried about a safety problem, they couldn't go on strike, at least during the contract. They had to arbitrate like civilized people.

The problem is, it's not so civilized down there. The *Boys Markets* case changed the balance of power between the UMW and the companies. Previously, the companies could only bring damage suits (which for the quickie "twenty-four-hour strikes" were pointless), but now they could get TROs, with immediate fines. Now they could sit on grievances for years. They could change the safety rules, or fire militants, and know that the union couldn't strike, or do anything except wait and wait and wait.

The rule is: "Management acts, the union grieves." And grieves and grieves. Like Rachel for her children. So after *Boys Markets* the grievance system in the coalfields simply broke down, because the companies had no incentive anymore to deal with the grievances when it could get injunctions, contempt, and punitive fines.

Then, in *Gateway Coal* v. *UMW*, this new body of law was applied even to safety disputes. In *Gateway*, the miners had walked out because the company wouldn't fix some faulty wiring. The Supreme Court held that the men would have to keep working, safety lapses or not. The men could leave the mine only in a true emergency, i.e., when the roof was literally collapsing. This really angered the miners. *Gateway*, for us, was like a prison gate slamming shut.

Even the Baptists and the church deacons were fed up. Did the Supreme Court want a war? O.K., they would get a war.

More miners walked out.

The judges fired back. They issued an injunction a day. By August 1976, there was probably an injunction in effect against every local at every mine east of the Missouri River. That is, the men here were subject to contempt fines, even jail, if they dared to go on strike again.

With so many injunctions, the miners were beginning to seem like "indentured laborers under penal sanction." In theory, they could go to jail for refusing to work. Secretly, I'd always wondered, "How do you force people underground, except by a court order?"

For a while, in the mid-seventies, that's exactly how it was done.

By the way, it was Earl Warren and William Brennan, the "liberal" judges, who did all this. The judges who had been my heroes back in law school because they were the activists. And another irony was that Felix Frankfurter, one of the conservatives, had drafted the Norris–La Guardia Act back in his youth. Then later, when he was old and crotchety, he warned us about the Warrens and the Brennans. He told us that all this judicial activism would come to no good.

And now, to my horror, I was quoting him all the time. I was a liberal, the federal courts were our "friends," and I was an activist, too. Except now, in my first job, all I did was represent defendants and write briefs pleading with the judges, liberals as well as conservatives, to please, please, just leave things alone.

So a war had started in the coalfields . . . not between the miners and the companies now, but between the miners and the judges. And we, the staff, were caught in the middle. And for me, being a new lawyer, an "officer of the court," well, it was pretty delicate.

We, the union lawyers, would tell the men, "Gee, this injunction looks pretty serious."

They would shrug. One miner told me, "Boy, your job as the union lawyer is not to keep us out of jail. Your job as the union lawyer is to get us *out* of jail."

He laughed and laughed. And he was one of the moderates.

I remember once trying to explain to a group of miners the difference between "criminal contempt" and "civil contempt," and not being too sure myself. Much of this stuff I had never even heard of in law school. Once I asked my colleague Lew Sargentich, "Lew, what is 'mass action criminal contempt'?"

"Drumhead justice," Lew said. One of those writs last used in peasant rebellions in the 1400s. Even then, only on the field of battle.

Well, the judges were furious. They wanted our heads on pikes . . . I mean, the staff's. Wasn't this our fault? With all our talk of "Union Democracy"? The judges thought that we, the Peace Corps volunteers, had turned these guys on.

Turn them on? My God, how could you turn them off?

In a way, the wildcats were beginning to work. At first the companies hadn't minded too much. They would get lots of injunctions and huge contempt fines, and anyway, the strikes were making money. Companies could draw down their stockpiles and drive up coal prices, without paying anyone's wages, and still get contempt fines and "damages."

But as the strikes kept going, the companies became frightened, because their authority had collapsed. They must have felt like wardens in a prison riot.

So they told the judges that we, the staff, had to stop the strikes. If the companies couldn't, then *we* had to impose the discipline: find the ringleaders, fine them, kick them out of the Union.

Yeah, and start running from the mob that would come to lynch us.

All that August, the strike got worse.

It was like a hundred little Protestant sects, the Gnostics, the millenarians, the anabaptists, marching up and down the back roads, tossing away helmets, lanterns, etc., as in some war for the end of the world.

I would go to work in the morning, and think, "It's over, the Union's gone . . ."

How many miners were on strike that day? Would there be 80,000? Or 100,000?

We knew there were roving pickets, with CBs, going from mine to mine. Who were they? Our enemies? Should we call the FBI?

Maybe it *was* the FBI. Maybe the government was behind this. Somebody had to be organizing it.

At times I would feel like a student moderate again, back in the sixties. I wanted to go up to my dorm room and shut the door.

Meanwhile, I was writing brief after brief. Upstairs, in the legal department, we had developed a careful legal strategy:

It was to throw ourselves, groveling, on the mercy of the courts.

The courts, after all, could destroy the International Union: they could put us in receivership. So we whispered to the men, politely: *Please*, go back to work. But out there in the coalfields, people didn't seem to care.

I used to think, "My God, don't they know how serious this is? Don't they want to save the Union?"

Now, by "Union" I meant . . . well, the building, the legal department, my office. To me, this was the "UMW." But out there, they had their own "UMW." And they figured: Wipe out the UMW, their "UMW," and they could raise it up again in three days.

But it was a simple, childlike view that *our* UMW and *their* UMW could just go their separate, merry ways.

We just wanted them to behave . . . Be the rank and file, but behave.

Now I think that maybe, after all, the judges were right. Maybe we did turn these guys on. We had wanted Union Democracy, and the New Politics, and the whole Sixties Enlightenment.

And these are good things.

But toss them down, down in the underground, and better step back for the explosion.

In the end, to "save" the Union from the courts, we had to

destroy it ourselves. The locals, the districts, the International, we all had to denounce each other, and then we all had to denounce the men. It was the only way to save the Union, to save it from contempt fines and then from bankruptcy. The "Union" broke into a hundred factions, each one denouncing the other.

Which side are you on?
Which side are you on?

Well, I was on . . . I don't know, it was very murky to me.

At first I had liked it when they went on strike. Well, of course I would. I liked Yeats, and medieval history, and anything strange or apocalyptic, and in law school I had even written a paper explaining how the wildcats were good: how such occasional conflict could lead, in the end, to a longer-lasting "industrial peace."

I should say, though, that no one up in the legal department took me seriously. Up there, it was like trying to defend cholera to a bunch of doctors.

Then I changed my mind, and I began to hate the wildcats. I could see how I was wrong, how they were like a disease, and how the Union as a "union" was such a delicate, fragile thing.

But that was the history of the UMW. To die, and to die, and to die. I remember how an old Union lawyer, Harrison Combs from Eastern Kentucky, had told me when I first started work, "In the UMW, it's always five minutes to midnight."

He meant that the UMW was always about to be destroyed. But I really thought, in August 1976, that it was destroyed.

The Union was split now, right and left and right down the middle. Arnold Miller, our leader, was a weak man. It was as if our real leader, Jock Yablonski, had been murdered in the first scene of Act I, and there was no one in the lead from then on. Miller *looked* like a union president, the way Warren Harding looked like a President, but he was a simple, foolish man, frightened of sitting in Lewis's chair. In this vacuum of power, the "executive board" took control. This meant that the Boyle crowd was back (it was never really gone), and with all our

Union Democracy, etc., we just made it easier for them to skewer us.

Soon we, the staff, were being purged. My friends were being fired one by one: even Bernie, the future Assistant Secretary of State. Every morning I would come in the lobby, and the head of John L. Lewis would be looking at me with more and more contempt. Some days I could look at that terrible head, at the scowl, and I would know that upstairs there was fresh blood on the floor and that another staff member had been fired.

There were many, many farewell parties, at all the bars we used to go to after work, and I still remember the songs. Not "Which Side Are You On?" I can't stand that damn song. No, something more modern, like Eric Clapton, and I remember in the bars that people sang:

> I shot the sheriff,
> but I did not kill the deputy . . .

I still love to hear those old Mineworkers songs.

I was not important enough to be purged, but it was time for me to go, too. I left in the middle of the big wildcat of 1976, and I suppose it was a cowardly thing to do. It was much easier than I expected. More or less, I just walked out the door, and kept walking. I found out that no one even noticed. By then, the whole Union was burning down anyway, and when the flames got up to the fifth floor, where I was in the law library, it was only sensible to go. Everyone else was going, so why not me?

Still, it was awkward saying goodbye to the few who were left. Rich Trumka told me then that he was going back into the mines. Eddie Burke said that he was going back into the mines, too.

I didn't know what to say to Rich. He was young enough to go into the mines, I suppose, but my God . . . I knew he had vague political ambitions, which seemed quite strange and farfetched to me, but there was something else, too. He seemed angry or embarrassed, I don't know which: angry with people like me, angry with the rank and file . . . angry and embarrassed the way someone can be who doesn't really know which side he's on and both sides are trying to embarrass him.

I thought all this was melodramatic, and I tried to make a joke. I said, "If you ever run for mine safety committeeman, I'll come back and work on your campaign."

It wasn't very funny. As it turned out, I didn't see him again for many years, and it was the last time we were friends . . . or perhaps I should say "buddies." I wrote to him once or twice, but he didn't answer, and then I realized he was never going to answer.

But I did see Eddie Burke about three years ago in Atlanta. I had walked into a hotel and saw Eddie in a coat and tie across the lobby registering at the desk. And the thought came to me instantly, "He's out of the mines," and when I went over to him, I almost said as my very first words, "Thank God you're out of there." Thank God I didn't, though, and we just chatted for a few minutes about the UMW.

Eddie is now back on the staff. And Rich is now president of the Union.

After the purges, there were long years, very dark years for the UMW. A Boyle ally, Sam Church, became president of the UMW, but the rank and file destroyed him, too. Church couldn't get them to ratify the contracts he negotiated, or get them back in the mines by snapping his fingers. It seems that now they were too corrupted with Union Democracy to ever get the Boyle crowd back for good. This is how we, the staff, had our revenge.

Trumka became president in 1981. And today the UMW is probably the stablest, most adult, most democratic union in all of labor. Yes, the rank and file went a little wild when they had their first taste of real self-government . . . what did anyone expect? But they sobered up, became responsible, democratic adults. And now the UMW officers don't have to sit around trembling, like the rest of them in labor, wondering what would happen if they, the "membership," ever got the right to vote.

Or at least this is how I feel about it on some days. Other days I think how close they came to destroying the Union and leaving it in a pile of ashes. And I think how Rich Trumka will never admit, even now, that he had anything to do with the rest of us, the VISTA volunteers, the grad students, etc., people like me, as if he had obliterated forever that part of his life by going back down under the earth and coming out again as someone else. Sometimes I think they just used us—Union Democracy, the New Politics, the whole Sixties Enlightenment— just used these things as a means to an end.

I perfectly understand the way it all had to turn out, but I'm a little bitter about it.

Anyway, I live in Chicago and don't think about the UMW now. Except sometimes, driving in my car on Sunday nights, I'll listen to the bluegrass-music hour on public radio, and suddenly, listening to that music, I'll have a strange, uncontrollable desire to go out on a strike. What is it about that twangy, whining music? Is there something primitive and Dionysian in it, with dithyrambs and cymbals, that is more maddening and strike-inducing than Eric Clapton and rock and roll?

I turn off the music, and realize that I'm a labor lawyer out here now and shouldn't let myself think about the UMW. It's distracting. It has too much claim on the imagination, and it's unfair, really, for other unions to have to compete with it.

My friends used to wonder, "What are these strikes about?" And it makes me furious today to see the way American papers glom on to the Soviet coal miners and explain in some detail the issues of their strikes. Yet in the 1970s, when I was at the UMW and American miners were in much longer, bigger, and more bitter strikes, you might find out that the strikes were occurring but you wouldn't know the reasons why.

I said this recently to a friend of mine who's a journalist.

He said, "It's because the news is managed."

"I don't believe *that*," I said.

He said, "Don't be naïve. All countries everywhere in the world manage the news."

I don't quite believe him, but when I look back, even I'm not too sure what happened now, as if it might have been a dream and I was living in a foreign country. If I were to say, for example, that for two years in the middle of the 1970s almost all the coal miners in America were engaged in a strike against the U.S. government, would you believe me? If someone else wrote it and I read it, would I believe it, even though I was in it and even lost my job as a result of it?

I can see how in a different country, under a different government, I could be talked out of believing it as the years went by and I didn't write it down as I'm doing now, before it gets too late.

As to the miners, before I saw them in the flesh, I would see them in photographs. Back in the 1930s, Walker Evans took a famous set of photographs that were published in Agee's book *Let Us Now Praise Famous Men*, and when I came to the UMW almost forty years later, and had those photographs in my head, I found out that the miners would still sit, striking the same poses, looking oppressed . . . and then later they would go off for tennis or a round of golf. And I used to think to myself, "Is this real? Or are these people just a figment of our PR machine?" The hardest thing to accept about the UMW was that every part of it might be real, that the Walker Evans photographs were just as real as the golf games, and that in America in the 1970s, for this small group of people, there were two kinds of culture moving in parallel lines with each other, the Appalachian UMW culture and American mass culture, and yet nimbly, incredibly, most of them seemed to know, at just the right times, which side they were on.

Now I have ended up where I started, simply looking at them in photographs, in books, before they rose from the pages and scattered into bodies and by accident we were chained together down in the caves.

CHAPTER 3

Before the Lean Years

Once, in secret, to learn American history, I would read old back issues of the *UMW Journal*.

I would stay up late at night, when the building was quiet and dark, and sit in the law library on the fifth floor, just under Lewis's old private suites, where he liked to have his brandy and cigars, and go through the crumbling pages. And one night I made a shocking discovery:

That "labor history," which I had never studied, was the secret history of the Democratic Party.

Nobody had told me. Fascinated, I kept reading the back numbers from the 1930s, and I realized, "My God, this is how it happened." All alone in this dark building, I felt like one of the two kids in *Absalom, Absalom!* who stay up all night in their freshman dorm room at Harvard, to spin out, like a ghost story, the secret part of American history, the part that is Greek tragedy and that, outside of Faulkner, isn't written down in any book. Or there is no single book where it's all written down.

Yet once, years ago, there were many "labor" books. In almost every bookstore, there would be a whole section for "Labor," the way there is today for "Self-Help" or "Sex." And if you go down to the old used-book stores around the University of Chicago, and climb down the creaky wooden stairs to the basement, and keep from fainting from the smell of the mold and the mildew, you can still see some of these "labor" books.

Hundreds, I'd say, that were published in the 1930s and 1940s, during labor's golden age, and it's amazing what would be published then: biographies of local-union presidents, histories of the district councils of carpenters, and with the same titles over and over, *Union Man, Rank and File, My Life in Labor*, all the proud autobiographies, and biographies, too, books by assistant professors at Gouverneur State, shy young academics who thought, with these books, to win a small measure of fame, and now the books are rotting away in this mass grave, down in the basement.

The history I want to tell starts with the 1930s. But there was much labor history before then, too: the Knights of Labor, the Molly Maguires, the IWW. But by the 1920s they had all had their rise and fall. It seems like that history took place in a hundred years of solitude, the Latin American kind, with dynamiting, murders, troops in the streets, and the heroes all going to jail.

The greatest hero of that time is Eugene Debs. Debs should have been the father of American labor. Debs is the closest thing we have, outside of Lincoln and Darrow, to an American saint. Debs led the greatest strike of all, against the Pullman Railroad Car Company in 1893. The strike was smashed, and Debs was thrown in jail. Well, he was really captured by the U.S. Army like a rebel general. But Debs himself was a pacifist. A pacifist, a socialist, and many other wonderful, otherworldly things. And perhaps, for these reasons, he was not the man to be the father of American labor.

Even now, one can still see in Chicago the "topography" of this old class war. There is still a Fort Sheridan, which was built originally so that the Army could quickly march on a strike. There is still a Great Lakes Naval Station, north of the city, so that the gunboats could be sent down to South Chicago. Sheridan Road, which winds so prettily through the North Shore, used to be a military road for moving troops.

Which is hard to believe at rush hour.

The Haymarket martyrs, men and women who were hanged because they supported some of the strikes, lie buried, unnoticed, near a suburban mall.

Well, to sum up all this old history:

Labor boomed in the 1880s,
went bust in the 1890s,
then boomed in the 1900s,
and went bust in the 1920s.
Or something like that.

Then it *really* went bust, flat, dead bust, in the 1920s. I mean, even deader than now. Which is, of course, what gives people like me so much hope.

By the 1920s, there was nothing left but the American Federation of Labor, or AFL, which came out of the wreckage of the old Knights of Labor. The AFL was mostly the old skilled-craft unions, with a few oddball unions like the Mineworkers. It had no social vision, no social agenda, and it was just for people with "skills." Sam Gompers, who started it, and who rolled cigars (this was a skill), didn't even want to organize the steelworkers, or other industrial workers of the time, because to him they weren't "union material." He wanted men who would meet in lodges, like the Elks, and hold tag days for needy kids.

That was the 1920s: a fairly depressing sort of minimalism.

A fine labor historian, Irving Bernstein, wrote about this period in his book *The Lean Years*, and there is an uncanny similarity between labor in the 1920s and labor in the 1980s. Whole passages of the book, which he wrote in the 1950s, by the way, could be lifted verbatim to describe American labor today.

For example:

Union members vote for Hoover then, and Reagan now.

Employers start "work teams" then, or "quality work circles" now, which are supposed to replace unions.

Union membership drops and drops.

There is the same cult worship of the businessman, of Andrew Mellon then, of Donald Trump today.

And Bernstein quotes one journalist after another saying that unionism is not only "dead" but "obsolete" in the new, post-industrial, service-sector economy of . . . yes, the 1920s. Every thoughtful observer, in *The New Republic*, etc., seems to agree, by 1928, that organized labor is through and that history has passed it by.

I can read *The Lean Years* and laugh on every page, and say, "This is great."

Yes . . . but this doesn't prove the Depression will save our necks again.

One night in Cambridge a few years ago, I drank scotch with my college teacher, Samuel Beer, and I asked him what he thought.

He said, "Well, look what people used to say about Reagan and Thatcher, that history had passed them by, and now they're the dominant . . . well, not the dominant, but a major influence."

I said, "Do you think there could be another depression?"

"Could there be? I don't know. Some people think so. This fellow Rohatyn does, for example. . . . But one thing we do know, from experience. If there ever is another depression, people will turn on these business leaders and say, 'You sons of bitches.' "

At least this much has to happen if labor is ever to have a big comeback. As Sam said, when the Depression came, people turned on these business leaders, Ford, Mellon, Jay Gatsby, and said, "You sons of bitches." But this did not lead, directly, to people joining unions, because they were saying, "You sons of bitches," for six or seven years before labor started to organize, in the late 1930s. The laws had to change, and the changes had to stick, before workers realized what they were now free to do.

It is not a matter of "culture" or "law" being more important. Each had to influence the other: the culture had to change so the law could change, then the law began to change the culture, and so on.

Then, all at once, there's the Big Bang. As if under the new "culture" and the new "law," certain chemical reactions can occur for the first time, and people who have been atomized for years can suddenly bond together. And later it may look like an act of God. But you could jiggle with the labor laws now and perhaps get something like the same Big Bang.

Anyway, for a few years, starting in 1930 or so, Congress could pass just about any labor law it liked without having to clear it with the "sons of bitches." For one brief moment, business didn't have its normal privileged hold on public policy.

So, in 1932, Congress passed the Norris–La Guardia Act, which may be the greatest labor law ever passed. In a way, it's not a labor law at all. It does not grant the right to organize. Yet this is the law that created American labor.

Before this, progressives in Congress had sometimes passed mild, ineffective laws that favored unions. But the federal courts ignored them and would enjoin just about every strike. Then the militia, or the U.S. Army, in extreme cases, would enforce the injunction. So this time, the progressives didn't try to pass another "labor law" that the courts could ignore: instead, they stripped the judges of their very power, or jurisdiction, to hear cases involving strikes.

This was a tricky idea, thought up by the young Felix Frankfurter at Harvard, and you really have to take an esoteric course called Federal Courts to understand it. But anyway, it worked. The judges couldn't even hear labor cases after that, and they couldn't issue injunctions.

After the Norris–La Guardia law, there was no "law" at all. No injunctions. No U.S. Army to enforce the injunctions. Nothing. It was a total vacuum. It was in this total vacuum that the Big Bang occurred.

Because now the workers could run wild. Sit-ins, sit-downs, mass picketing. They could have "secondary" strikes against "neutral" employers. They could run naked in the streets, and no law, no federal judge, could stop them.

The states still could, but the federal government had left the field: the forty-eight governors stood there alone.

Then, in 1935, Congress passed the Wagner Act, which said that workers had an actual, affirmative right to organize. The Wagner Act created the National Labor Relations Board, or NLRB. This was the agency that would "certify" officially when a union should be recognized.

But the Wagner Act did not create the Big Bang. When the autoworkers and steelworkers rose up in the late 1930s, they didn't file petitions with the Board, or hire lawyers, or say politely to government officials, "Are we an 'appropriate bargaining unit'?"

They just ran all over the plants. Lawyers like me were the "superfluous men." We really weren't necessary until the 1950s.

But still, the Wagner Act was important symbolically, because it did declare a "right" to organize. It was like a speech from *Henry V*. Except it was from Roosevelt, the new President, and the message he was sending out was:

"Come join the New Deal."

But even with the new culture (the "sons of bitches") and the new laws ("come join the New Deal"), there would have been no Big Bang, without another equally important event:

Organized labor broke apart. The AFL, when the Depression came, split up on the rocks, like a ship in a storm. And John L. Lewis stepped out and walked on the waves.

And it's amazing that kids today have never even heard of him. The other day, I interviewed a law student, from Harvard, who wants to be a *union* lawyer . . . labor side, O.K.?

Just curious, I asked her, "Have you ever heard of John L. Lewis?"

She smiled. "No. Who is he?"

So about a week later, at the country club, in the buffet line, I asked my brother John, who's about thirty, and a salesman, if he knew who John L. Lewis was.

He took a guess. "Didn't he start the AFL?"

That was pretty good, I thought. Except, of course, it's totally wrong.

John L. Lewis, in 1930, was a dissident vice president of the AFL. Since 1924, he'd been president of the Mineworkers. Probably, he lied and stole his way to the top, and he was not a nice man, no Eugene Debs, but in a more complicated way, Lewis was also on the side of Good.

When the Depression came, Lewis saw his chance. Unlike Gompers, he wanted to "organize the unorganized." So he picked a fight with the AFL leaders (he despised labor leaders, called them the worst purple-prose names), and then he stormed out of the AFL. In 1935, with a few other malcontents, like Dubinsky of the Ladies' Garment Workers and Hillman of the Clothing Workers, Lewis set up a new federation, the Congress of Industrial Organizations, or CIO. And now, as president of the CIO, Lewis was about to begin his life's great work.

It is odd about a labor leader, or a really great one, like a Lewis or a Lech Walesa: most of your life is "downtime," and you don't do anything but sit around for twenty years and watch your position crumble. Then, for five minutes in history, you get your chance. And into those few minutes you have to squeeze the work of twenty years.

First, Lewis had to reorganize his own UMW. In the 1920s (as in the 1980s), the UMW had almost disappeared. There had been gunfire, real bullets, employers with private armies of goons.

But now Lewis had the Wagner Act. Not that the Wagner Act had any serious sanctions: it didn't. But Lewis could now send out his organizers to say, "The President of the United States wants *you* to join the UMW."

Now there were too many people to shoot. Because this was the "new American patriotism," as people might call it today. Roosevelt's signature on the Wagner Act was like a bonfire, a signal on a hill (much as later, in the 1980s, Reagan's firing of the air traffic controllers would be a signal to other employers).

Now Lewis organized new unions. And in doing so, he showed what a genius he was, because Lewis would go to workers and attack not only the Boss, Big Business, etc., but Big Labor, too. This was right up America's alley. What could be more American, really? He could tap into people's resentment twice, by railing not only at the Mellons, the Fords, etc., but even at these pathetic old guys like William Green of the AFL, who didn't think any of them were "union material."

Maybe this is the secret if American labor is to come back in the 1990s: A dissident like Lewis will have to emerge. Attack not only corporate America but the AFL-CIO. Denounce Big Labor and start a new labor federation like Lewis did.

And by the way, why should the AFL-CIO care? Because one day, this new federation will run out of gas, and it'll be folded back in with the old "Fed," and Lane Kirkland and his pals will collect their dues. In the meantime, it's funny that Big Labor today thinks of itself as being the "product" of the 1930s . . .

when, really, it wasn't the "product" so much as the "target" of everything Lewis did.

And so came the great mythical rising up of the CIO. It was like a single flash of lightning, from 1935 to 1937:

First, the autoworkers rose up, in violent strikes, like the sit-down strike in Flint in 1936, with Lewis himself going into the plant, sticking his head out of a window and roaring at Governor Murphy, daring Murphy to dishonor his own father, who had been a workingman, too, and send in the militia. Murphy didn't. Then the steelworkers rose up, under the gentle Philip Murray, who was Lewis's lieutenant and his vice president at the UMW. Steel was not as violent as auto was, but there was violence here as well: the so-called Memorial Day Massacre, when Chicago police opened fire on a crowd at Republic Steel, and twelve workers were shot and killed. When I lived down near the mills, I would meet men who had been there as little children and seen the men die.

Then came the rubber workers, then the others.

Then it was over. Contracts were signed in a single day; there were new constitutions everywhere (Ford, U.S. Steel, etc.). Sometimes history goes very fast, as in Poland, East Germany, and Czechoslovakia recently, after nothing seems to happen for a hundred years. This was the "Big Bang," and many labor structures today came out of that first two or three minutes of blazing-hot time, although now the labor universe has cooled, and maybe it's contracting back into that tiny original ball.

Why did they rise up all at once? Well, the Depression and the laws. It was not that the Depression made workers "poor," or at least the ones who still had jobs. In fact, because of deflation, the wages of those working actually went *up*, in effect. They were better off, not worse. And by the way, there was a Depression going on in France and England, too, and workers there were fairly listless. They didn't go nuts like here.

Yet it wasn't just the "culture" and the "law." Someone like Lewis had to stand up there and be the general . . . the "organizer of victory." And Lewis was such a tremendous stage prop. This was another part of his great genius: he actually looked like John L. Lewis. The wild, curly hair, the huge eyebrows: he was the greatest Welsh actor of his generation, or just the greatest actor. Next to Lewis, an actor like Charles Laughton, maybe his only serious rival, would seem like a face in the crowd: a guy who would be an "extra" if Lewis was on the set. Maybe the peak of Lewis's career, or at least his stage career, was the winter of 1936, when he toured the cities of the Midwest plains. That winter, in places like Detroit and Akron, he would speak with his own thunder, at huge open-air rallies of workers, roaring like Lear into the wind and rain, and denouncing Wall Street and the AFL, both of them, with Bible-type blasts, in the cadence of King James, and bringing to it all the grandeur and majesty of the English stage.

You couldn't read a Lewis speech now. The bombast, the alliteration, the pseudo-erudition that some people back then would take for the real thing. They would cuff their kids, drag them to the radio, and whisper in awe (more to themselves):

"John L. Lewis, you are a *deep* man."

Well, it would sound hokey to us, honed as we are on Bush, Reagan, postmodern phrasings, the "vision thing," etc.

But a friend of mine, a labor reporter, would say I'm wrong. He thinks the Lewis speeches are the most powerful he's ever read.

He says, "You know, I've read a lot about the thirties, and you sense the effect of Lewis, and others . . . There's something different about workers then. It's the way they write and talk. There's not that inferiority complex, which you sense all the time now . . . Back then, it just didn't exist."

I think I know what he means.

In Chicago a few years ago, a black, Harold Washington, ran for the office of mayor, an office that no black had ever held. Although the city was 40 percent black, no one expected Washington to win, because blacks just didn't vote for a black.

Then there was a debate on TV, with Washington and his two rivals, Daley and Byrne, who were leading in the polls.

Washington creamed them. He started with a stunning cross-of-gold speech and never let up. And all over the city, you could hear the sounds of black people's jaws dropping.

Our guy, the black guy, was smarter than the white guys.

Not as smart. Smarter.

And Lewis had a similar effect:

Our guy, the labor guy, was smarter than the other guys. Ford, Mellon, and all the rest. Not as smart. Smarter.

It was as if, through Lewis, all the workers were parents of a child they had sent to Harvard.

Actually Lewis didn't write these speeches. A man named Jett Lauck did.

By 1938, the CIO was huge, and Lewis was like a Mussolini. As Lewis's biographers (Melvyn Dubofsky and Warren Van Tyne) write, crowds would even follow Lewis into the bathroom when he went to football games. In 1940, Lewis could give a speech and all three national networks would carry it live.

Try to imagine any labor leader today even getting on cable.

Up in the law library, late at night, I used to wonder, "What if I'd been here at the UMW back in the thirties?" Surely, nothing could have been better in the whole New Deal.

I would see myself being dispatched on delicate missions to Steel and Rubber. I would come back late at night to Washington by train. Then take a cab to the Hotel Carlton, and dance on the rooftop with girls from Vassar, and probably, back then, they'd all be Communists. I'd be surrounded, being a Lewis man, by girls in the "Party."

I'd be in danger every night, back in the New Deal.

I know I shouldn't be joking about the Communists. They were in the CIO, all right, and there were even "Communist unions," like the United Electrical Workers, or UE. But there are so many books on "American labor and Communism" that it's almost like a kind of vanity press, i.e., academics writing about themselves, or their thesis advisers. And what about the big "purges" that came later? Supposedly, when the Communists were purged, the labor movement lost its "soul." Well, maybe so, but there are a lot of radicals, sixties activists, people my age, who got into labor, and have never been purged. And how much "soul" does the labor movement have now?

That's my only point.

Sometimes Lewis would ally with the Communist unions, like the UE. Still, he was not only an anti-Communist but a red baiter. In fact, he was a Republican. Now it's confusing, because he's also the founder of the modern Democratic Party. Yet it's simple to explain: John L. Lewis was very strange. I mean, *very* strange.

Although he was a miner's son, he seemed to think that he was, or ought to be, part of the WASP Ascendancy. He liked to have tea in the afternoon with Alice Roosevelt Longworth, the grande dame of Washington, and the two of them, these two bitchy old ladies, while the whole nation was burning, would sit there gossiping about everyone in town.

Perhaps to get a sense of the 1930s, the workers, etc., you have to read a writer like John Steinbeck. But to get a sense of Lewis, their leader, you have to read someone like Edith Wharton.

Lewis hated FDR, and they were rivals. As Dubofsky and Van Tyne say, Lewis and Roosevelt each wanted the other's job (without giving up the one he had). But for a brief period in the late 1930s, Lewis threw in with the New Deal, and perhaps in a single, accidental, unwilling emission, John L. Lewis became the father of the modern Democratic Party (with Franklin Roosevelt being, well, sort of the mother). Lewis came to regret it, almost bitterly, but there's no denying the paternity.

That is to say, it's no accident that the years in which Lewis organized the unorganized, 1935–37, were also the time in which the great "realignment election" of 1936 occurred. It was this second election, most historians say, and not Roosevelt's first, that saw the birth of a new Democratic Party. In this new party, the CIO took the place of the old ethnic, big-city machines, which were passing away. It wasn't Tammany Hall but the CIO that held the torchlight parades and drove voters to the polls. The CIO "turned out the vote." Maybe the Democratic Party wasn't a "labor party," in the European sense, and maybe the Wagner Act by itself didn't create the new party. But it is a fact that as the CIO organized more workers, the stronger the new Democratic Party became. Even in the 1940s and 1950s, labor would go on organizing an *additional* 1 percent of the work force every year. An additional 1 percent being organized to vote Democratic and being turned out at the polls. This went on for years, as if both organized labor and the Democratic

Party would go on expanding forever, simply from the force of the first Big Bang.

We have lost our sense of what this old CIO culture was like. We listen to old radio shows like *Fibber McGee and Molly*, and think, "How simple and sweet people used to be." But then read the back issues of the *UMW Journal* . . . it's pretty strong stuff. Crude, vulgar cartoons about Wall Street, the bosses, etc. It's the crudest, most vulgar propaganda you could ever see in the free world, and it was coming into people's houses, with their favorite radio shows, and apparently this was quite routine. My God, no wonder they were voting for the Democrats. If you read the old *Journals*, you'll be surprised that's all they did.

The Republicans, by the 1940s, were becoming frightened. With the CIO growing every year, America was threatening to become a one-party state. So if Republicans couldn't stop the CIO, and stop it soon, they could end up extinct, like the Federalists or the Whigs.

Then, in 1946, the Republicans had a break. World War II was just over, and the voters were sick of the Democrats. There was inflation, rationing, etc., and red meat was in short supply. Also, after five years of official no-strike pledges (although there were many wildcats), the CIO unions all seemed to go on strike at once. As Michael Goldfield writes in his book *The Decline of Organized Labor in the United States*, it seemed like one big general strike.

So after fourteen years of solid, wall-to-wall Democrats, the Republicans won both houses of Congress. Knowing it might be their last chance, the Republicans came to Washington to stop the CIO. Not roll back the welfare state (it barely existed). Not repeal Social Security. But stop Labor. Stop Lewis. Before it was too late.

Because they didn't have much time. The CIO, in 1946, was planning a big organizing drive in the South. As Goldfield points out, this drive, Operation Dixie, was pulled back at the last minute, to avoid alienating Southern Democrats. And the Republicans, meanwhile, went on to pass Taft-Hartley, to stop just this kind of mass organizing. If the CIO *had* organized the South, American history would have been different, because labor would have been a truly national force, and not a regional one, trapped in the Northeast and Midwest.

In 1947, over the veto of Harry Truman, Taft-Hartley was passed into law, by Republicans and Southern Democrats. And Truman screamed about it, too, long after it was passed, as no "moderate" Democrat would do today: but back then, even the moderate Democrats like Truman knew what was at stake.

Taft-Hartley had three effects:

First, it ended organizing on the grand, 1930s scale. It outlawed mass picketing, secondary strikes of neutral employers, sit-downs: in short, everything that Lewis did in the 1930s.

When people ask me, "Why can't labor organize the way it did in the thirties?" the answer is simple: everything we did then is now illegal.

And Taft-Hartley doesn't kid around. When the Union violates this law, the NLRB must seek immediate injunctions from the courts.

Other penalties quickly follow, like treble damages and jail.

The federal courts were back. The Norris–La Guardia days were over.

The second effect of Taft-Hartley was subtler and slower-working. It was to hold up *any* new organizing at all, even on a quiet, low-key scale.

For example, Taft-Hartley ended "card checks," which the NLRB had begun using to certify unions. The workers could just sign cards, saying, "Hey, I'd like to join." And this is the system still used in Canada. But this would have been too easy, so Taft-Hartley required hearings, campaign periods, secret-ballot elections, and sometimes more hearings, before a union could be officially recognized.

It also allowed and even encouraged employers to threaten workers who want to organize. Employers could hold "captive meetings," bring workers into the office and chew them out for thinking about the Union.

And Taft-Hartley led to the "union busting" that started in the late 1960s and continues today. It started when a new "profession" of labor consultants began to convince employers that they could violate the Wagner Act, fire workers at will, fire them deliberately for exercising their legal rights, and *nothing would happen.* The Wagner Act had never had any real sanctions. Maybe, after three years of litigation, the employer might lose, and have to pay a few thousand bucks, if that much: a cheap price, though, for keeping out the union.

So why hadn't employers been violating the Wagner Act all along? Well, at first, in the 1930s and 1940s, they tried, and they got riots in the streets: mass picketing, secondary strikes, etc. But after Taft-Hartley, unions couldn't retaliate like this, or they would end up with penalty fines and jail sentences. In a sense, Taft-Hartley gave employers a license to break the Wagner Act, but it took employers twenty years to realize, at last, how far they could go.

Finally, Taft-Hartley had a third and even subtler effect. The beating heart of labor was enchanted to a stone. Or to a rock. Or to a piece of marble, maybe, that the builders would put into one of the big marble palaces in Washington, D.C.

No doubt, even without Taft-Hartley, the CIO would have become a big, lumbering bureaucracy. Eventually, they would have built the big marble palaces anyway. But Taft-Hartley put all of this on "fast forward."

For example, Taft-Hartley made collective bargaining agreements enforceable as "contracts," and made unions "responsible," to make sure members complied. Before then, unions could not be sued for breach of these agreements. Taft-Hartley envisioned that unions would never need to strike. If disputes arose, there was arbitration. The unions would hire lawyers to file the briefs.

And I'm grateful now to Taft-Hartley for creating my career. I was born nine months after the law took effect, as if Taft-Hartley, astrologically, had called me into being. Me, and all the other lawyers, economists, and staffers who would work in the marble palaces.

But something in American labor started to go dead. When the AFL and CIO merged in 1955, it was like the merger of two football leagues, which merged because they were both playing the same game. George Meany was the first president, the first commissioner of the two leagues. As a child, I remember seeing his picture, a big fat man who went to Florida every winter, sat in a cabana, played cards, smoked cigars.

And now organized labor began to lumber. It stopped being loose, catlike, fast on its feet . . .

And now people sniff at us and say, "Oh, you're such an ugly bureaucracy . . ."

I want to say, "O.K., we are an ugly bureaucracy, but who made us that way?"

For a while, in the fifties, labor kept getting bigger. Bigger at the bottom, bigger at the top.

But as the new federation, the AFL-CIO, became bigger at the top, power seemed to leak out of it, at every crack. As David Greenstone suggests in his book *Labor and American Politics*, the stronger labor became as an "organization" in the 1950s, the weaker it became politically, at the polls. It was stronger politically in the 1940s, when it was just a sprawl, very decentralized, and workers had to go to the meetings.

Slowly, as power leaked out, the Democrats began paying less attention. Technically, Big Labor was bigger now. But in the late thirties, the CIO was new, raw, and no one knew which way it would go. Roosevelt was obsessed with Lewis. He probably paid him as much attention as he did Hitler or Stalin. But later, when Lewis was gone, the Democrats didn't have to pay as much attention. And curiously, Big Labor didn't expect so much attention. Most of the time, it was like a big dog, loyal, doglike, wagging its tail.

And the "working-class culture," or whatever it was, that came out of the CIO, back when John L. Lewis was on all three networks, seemed to lose its juice, or most of it. The "inferiority complex" was back. And once again, workers didn't speak. They didn't speak, and no one wrote novels about them either.

They were still voting for the Democrats. But no one talked. It was like they were married to the Democrats, husband and wife, and nobody argues, but nobody talks.

So what happened to Lewis after 1947? At first, he tried to ignore Taft-Hartley (he and the Communists). But then he was dragged into court, slapped with huge fines. Even *Truman* began using it against him. Oh, he was still a power. He was no longer the head of the CIO, but he was still president of the United Mine Workers, when the nation still depended on coal. But by the mid-1950s, Lewis seemed to burn out. History had turned on him. He became more petulant than ever. He took the UMW out of the CIO: just walked out of it, just as he had walked out of the AFL, just as he walked out of everything sooner or later. He became remote, sulking, even senile possibly.

In the 1950s, he even decided to liquidate his own UMW, when almost overnight he forced the automation of the mines. I agree, this was good in principle, but Lewis did it brutally, very fast, putting hundreds of thousands of miners out of work. Maybe in the end he *was* mad, mad like Lear, alone and left to die with a dwindling little UMW, not much of a patrimony, really.

The "new" man of labor now was not Lewis, Lewis the tragedian, Lewis the great actor, but George Meany, a plumber from Brooklyn. Meany, who used to brag he had never been in a strike. But after Taft-Hartley, that was all we could afford: a plumber who would charge you a fortune and never really fix your sink. We couldn't afford a Lewis, and all his strikes, or anyone else who, too theatrically, would try to organize the unorganized.

By the 1960s, the end was near for American labor. The decline in organizing rights, the bureaucratization of labor (spurred on by Taft-Hartley), and changes in the economy were starting to have an effect. Yet, for a while, American labor seemed fat and happy, and a little, moderate organizing continued. But it was dying now, without knowing it. It began to have, in the sixties and seventies, a nice, rosy, tubercular glow.

By the time I came along, in the mid-seventies, even I could tell something was wrong. Labor was getting weaker, more brittle, more bureaucratic. I could see that "union busting" was on the rise, that employers were firing workers at will, that unions couldn't organize. But I thought, "Well, it's the culture, or the economy . . . ," and it was, too. But I didn't think it was really the *law*. To me, Taft-Hartley was part of the natural order. And I remember how I used to laugh, reading the old *UMW Journals*, at how Lewis was so hysterical about Taft-Hartley, how it would be the end of labor, and I smiled and thought, "How silly people were then."

I mean, look at all the marble palaces around D.C. It looked to me like labor had survived pretty well.

And it took me years to realize, looking around, the slow-working poison of *something*, and then to know, one day, that all along, it had been that damned law.

All along, it had been like an Ibsen play, and people like me, who were born after Taft-Hartley, and grew up, and got jobs with labor . . . we would find out, in the end, that labor had been doomed all along, cursed before our birth, and that Mr. Taft, Mr. Hartley, were laughing from the grave.

And in 1969, when we were in college, knowing none of this, John L. Lewis finally died. By now, a darkness seemed to cover the UMW. Just a day or so before Lewis died, his successor, Tony Boyle, was ordering the murder of Jock Yablonski and his family. And Lewis, as he lay there dying, knew that the UMW, his own UMW, had turned, in his own words, into a "cesspool."

And how it must have galled Lewis to die like that, with the bitter knowledge that, even though he had turned American history upside down, he was already being forgotten, and that he would be shunted off to the side in history books because there was no simple or conventional way to fit Lewis in: because to fit Lewis into American history, you'd have to throw out the normal version, and go back to Lincoln, and start writing it all from scratch.

Why tell this long ghost story? To explain why I became obsessed . . . why I read old union magazines, why I'm obsessed with the thirties, with Lewis, and with the New Deal.

And by the way, to me the New Deal isn't old or passé, but new and futuristic . . . and I want to go *back* to the New Deal, back to the old one, which is still yet to come.

Sam Beer told me that night in his home in Cambridge, "We don't know what the New Deal really was. We think of it in terms of the welfare state, that it was a redistribution of income. But there wasn't much of that. The New Deal wasn't so much a redistribution of income as a redistribution of power. Look at the Wagner Act, look at labor . . ."

When people now say "New Deal," they mean "government

regulation," etc. But the early New Deal was much like the New Left in the late sixties, except in a far more extreme, radical version: it was about democracy, the right to vote, going to union meetings, standing up and *talking* . . .

And if it was such a golden time back then, why didn't it last? Can I really blame it all on Taft-Hartley? On this one little government *law?*

I don't know what went wrong, but I remember something Sam said that night:

"The thing that was different about American labor . . . well, there was a fatal moment, back in the thirties, when American labor embraced the state, and it really threw in with the New Deal . . . Now, you look at labor in England . . . they never embraced the state, they never threw in with it, the way labor did here."

So when the state turned on labor, as it did later on, labor didn't know how to fight back. It had no "anti-statist" tradition to fall back on, as Lech Walesa or Solidarity would have now, if their "New Deal" in Poland ever fell apart.

This is what Lewis knew, too, and what he was trying his damnedest, even in the thirties, to say:

We should never, ever, embrace the state.

We should never completely join the New Deal.

Lewis did realize, too late, that he had made a mistake. In 1940, he broke with Roosevelt, and to the shock of everyone, he endorsed Wendell Willkie, the Republican candidate for President. Perhaps by then Lewis was already half mad. Or maybe it was not madness at all. Maybe Lewis knew this was his last chance to break away, to get out of the "fatal embrace" before it was too late. But it was too late.

CIO members were stunned. Willkie? Had Lewis lost his mind? They hanged him in effigy, they called him a Judas. He had to resign as president of the CIO.

It was as if Lewis had wanted to murder his own child, the new Democratic Party he had created. Perhaps he looked at the child and sensed treachery ahead. Yet it does seem like an act of madness.

The story goes that just before the break, Lewis went to

Roosevelt, and hinted, or demanded, that Roosevelt name him as his running mate. That would have been a ticket: Roosevelt and Lewis. But didn't Lewis know how impossible this was, even back then—to put the head of the CIO in the Oval Office?

Roosevelt must have smiled. He probably laughed about it later with aides after Lewis left. The very thought of it, Roosevelt laughing at him, must have haunted Lewis in the years ahead and followed him to the grave.

A few months later, Roosevelt won the election.

CHAPTER 4

In the Heart of Basic Steel

One night, on a train, while I was still at the Mineworkers, I began to read a novel, *Bread and Wine*, by Ignazio Silone. The hero, Pietro Spina, is an anti-Fascist running from the police in the Italy of the 1930s. Spina (an agnostic) takes the disguise of a priest. He goes back to his homeland, the Abruzzi. He meets the working people, the *cafoni*, who take him into their homes because they think he's a real priest. And without meaning to, he starts to become a sort of priest, a confessor, and people come to him . . .

That night, I thought, "Isn't that what I should do?"

Not become a priest, of course. But wasn't being a labor lawyer a kind of disguise? One I had stumbled upon by accident. I hadn't meant to go on with it after a year or two at the UMW. But now, having come this far, why not go all the way? If I could go out somewhere, get out of Washington . . .

I thought, "Maybe people will invite me into their homes."

I went back to my book and kept on reading.

From the first time I heard about Sadlowski, I think I wanted to join his campaign. But I wonder now how many people still know who Sadlowski was.

In 1976, Ed Sadlowski was running for president of the United Steel Workers of America. He was thirty-seven years old, a militant, a rebel in the backlands of American steel (what is called "basic steel"). He had just been elected head of the Union's biggest district, out in Chicago, and the whole Union leadership was terrified of him.

Sadlowski even had his own Miners for Democracy, a group called Steelworkers Fight Back. That was the message of his campaign in two words: "Fight Back." There was a deep anger in those words, such as no one had heard in the Union in a long time. The Union was now torpid, old, bureaucratic, and the anger was over the Union's quiet decision to castrate itself in the early seventies by giving up the right to strike, *even* when the contract had expired. This was the so-called Experimental Negotiating Agreement. The members had not been consulted. There was no discussion, no vote. I. W. Abel, the Union president, had just done it. It was as if this union, this once tough old macho union, had simply unmanned itself, and even the older men, who could remember what a strike was like, felt castrated, helpless, hesitant to revolt, but sick at what had happened and ready to listen to a younger man who said to them over and over, "It's time to fight back."

What made Sadlowski so exciting?

I have heard many good speakers in my life, but no one any better than Ed Sadlowski on a good day. He could say the word "Boss" with fifty-five different nuances of contempt, and use just the right one for each occasion. He could pack a union hall, as no one in the seventies was supposed to be able to do. If he was a radical, he was a radical in labor's mainstream. He could talk in the language of the founding fathers . . . of Lewis, of Debs, of men he seemed to know like members of his own family. In his home, he had more labor history books than the Library of Congress. He could tell the stories that by then, in the seventies, were halfway down the road to the collective unconscious, that even the old men had begun to forget. Sadlowski was the younger son who reminded them of their own fathers.

Yet he wasn't from the Stone Age. He was in *Rolling Stone*. He was sixties, and hip. He was smart. And he wasn't a brontosaurus, some old beer-hall union politician. He was also good, uncannily good, on TV. When the Union tried to red-bait him, or paint him a screamer, he could present himself as a man of almost angelic moderation. He could be "red hot" or "medium cool." This is what drove the other side nuts.

It didn't hurt to be handsome either. I remember a woman telling me, "He looks like a movie star."

He was also at a funny age, being thirty-seven and born in 1939; too young for John L. Lewis and the Old Left and a bit too old for the sixties and the New Left. And yet Sadlowski, a big man physically, seemed like he could inhabit several worlds: Old Left and New Left. That's what made him seem ambiguous and dangerous.

I recall the first time I saw his photograph, on a campaign poster: it's a black-and-white shot of a young man, Sadlowski, wearing a work shirt, open at the collar, and a T-shirt underneath. There's a long row of black mills smoking in the background. And the poster says, "Fight Back."

If that poster had been around in the late sixties, it might have outsold Huey Newton's. Yet in 1976 young steelworkers were grabbing it, and sticking it up, not in Cambridge or Berkeley, but in Youngstown, Pittsburgh, and South Chicago.

And soon the press began to come around, as they had not come around a labor leader in years. *The New York Times, Meet the Press, The Wall Street Journal* (which had a college friend of mine covering him, almost full-time). It's hard to believe now, but in 1976 this was a big story. America was sleepwalking through the election of Jimmy Carter and Gerald Ford, and at least to some people, the Sadlowski campaign seemed more important.

The leaders of the Steelworkers were regarded as "mature," "responsible," "statesmanlike." Men like I. W. Abel, the Union president, and Lloyd McBride, his heir apparent, were then the darlings of the editorial pages. Men so "mature," so "responsible," they had given up the right to strike.

Now came Sadlowski. The old gods of labor seemed to be on his side. His rise seemed to be their act of vengeance, and so far it had been dramatic. At age twenty-four, president of his local. At thirty-three, candidate for district director in Chicago. The Union leadership, which called itself "the Official Family" (I'm not kidding), tried to stop him. It tried red baiting, intimidation. It then tried stealing. But the ballot stuffing was so blatant that even the Labor Department was roused to do something. In the rerun, which was government-supervised, Sadlowski smashed the "Official Family" candidate.

Now he was coming for them. It seemed like a "second Mineworkers," the same militancy, democracy, rank-and-file control.

The AFL-CIO was hysterical. It was one thing for the New Left, etc., to go out and "ruin" the Mineworkers. That was a hillbilly union, off in a hollow. But the Steelworkers? These were people who lived in *cities*. And this was the flagship of organized labor. If this ship went down, the whole fleet could be lost.

This was not true, because there were only two unions, the Steelworkers and Mineworkers, that let the rank and file vote. So there were only two unions that people like me could "ruin." But no one in Big Labor was calm enough to realize this at the time.

Indeed, the future of the Democratic Party seemed to hinge on the Steelworkers election. Back then, hard hats were beating up college kids, future Dukakis voters, and there was a terrible split in the party between the Old Left and the New Left. In 1972, organized labor had even refused to endorse George McGovern, the New Left candidate. But what if the New Left were to take over the Steelworkers? What if it were to take over the whole AFL-CIO? Couldn't Sadlowski, who must have felt the split of the American left in his own person, be the one to transcend it? Wasn't he the next stage of history, in the Hegelian sense?

So "outsiders" came to the aid of both sides in the Steelworkers election. It was like Spain in the 1930s. I was one of the "outsiders," a liberal from the East, with gold-rimmed glasses. But there were many "outsiders" working for McBride. On the New Right, Sadlowski's election was viewed as being much worse than Carter's. It was part of their religion, as it were, that God created the "workers" to kick the shit out of "liberals." And they didn't want "kids" going out to help Sadlowski. They didn't want us doing drugs with their precious workers.

Commentary even sent one of its editors, Paul Feldman, to work full-time for McBride. The CIO, the CIA, *Commentary* magazine, all thought as much as I did that the Steelworkers election could change the world.

You would think that after the UMW, I would have sobered up a little. But really, my condition was worse than ever. I wanted even more romance, more contact with the rank and file. I was sick of hearing the same stories from the older staff at the UMW . . . how *they* had gone out to West Virginia once.

I, too, wanted to go outside the city gates, to join the barbarians, the way some labor bureaucrats crack and do.

Besides, if Sadlowski won out in Chicago . . . well, I thought a victory in Chicago would help lift the siege in D.C.

And I wasn't being an "outsider." Hadn't the Mineworkers created the Steelworkers? Didn't it have the same constitution as ours? And wasn't it in our genes, as UMW men, to teach them our ways?

And this time, it *wouldn't* be a "second Mineworkers," with people swinging from the chandeliers. This time, we would have a strong leader, Sadlowski.

This time, everything would come together.

So I helped talk a friend at the UMW into going out to Chicago, and then he did the same to me.

I begged Joseph Rauh, who was Sadlowski's lawyer in Washington, to send me out to Chicago to help him. Rauh intended to bring several suits; e.g., to stop partisan attacks on Sadlowski in the union press, to find out where the polls were, and to place observers at as many of the polls as possible.

The legal work was staggering. But this didn't worry me. I was going to Chicago, that secret city.

I drove across Indiana, and the city came up on me, almost too fast.

I passed a sign that said,
"Welcome to Chicago,
Richard J. Daley, Mayor."
Then I passed another, bigger sign that said,
"Welcome to the Tenth Ward,
Edward R. Vrdolyak, Alderman."
I was in the country of the rank and file.

Down by the mills, some friends of mine had rented a house.

It was on a block like every other block. Ten bungalows and a bar. And every bungalow had a sign that said,
    "Howlett for Governor."
Every house but ours, which I noted uneasily as I pulled up the car.

I walked into the house, and just as I put down my bags, there was a knock at the door. At first, I thought it would be Ed or Bob, one of my roommates, but it turned out to be . . . the "assistant" precinct captain.

I let him in, and as he walked around, I said in a friendly way, "Hey, I'm a good Democrat . . ."

He picked up a book on the floor . . . something highbrow. Maybe it was Kafka. He looked at the book, looked at me, and then he said, "So . . . uh, you working for Sadlowski?"

I gasped.

Then he smiled and walked out.

Probably he went straight to Vrdolyak, to say that a kid with a copy of Kafka had moved into the Tenth Ward.

Later my roommate Ed came by, and I said, "Ed, we've got to get a Howlett poster in our window, and fast."

"Who?" he said. "That hack?"

"My God," I said, "not so loud."

We were in Chicago, that secret city.

That night, we drove to the Golden Shell, a Croatian restaurant. Now I saw, for the first time, Lake Michigan and the mills. I saw the ocean ships parked like station wagons, and the flags of Norway, Denmark, and Japan whipping in the breeze on top of hulls that rose from the parking lot of the restaurant and up into the sky.

Yet the Indiana line was a few feet away. I felt that here I was on the wilder shores of American labor.

It looked to me like Europe after World War II: bombed out, beaten up, the gravel, the drawbridges, the coal barges moving up and down the little rivers.

Everything was gray. The sky was gray, the mills were gray, Lake Michigan was gray. Only the French dressing in the coffee shops had another color: it was orange, oily and bright, and in fact, it kind of blinded you.

Everything was a machine, too. The mill was a machine. The Union was a machine. Even the Catholic Church was a machine, with a cardinal, named Cody, who was straight out of *The Untouchables*.

On every block there was a bar.

Same bar.

With the same sign.

And on this sign, the same mug of beer, yellow and foaming.

Sometimes the sign said "Old Style," and sometimes it said "Schlitz." Chicago was pluralistic in that sort of way.

Old Style. The whole city was Old Style. Gray, bleak, full of Old Style and steel.

Yet it gave me a sense of peace to be here. Shouldn't some place in America be like this? I had grown up in suburbia, gone to school in the East . . . but until now, I had never seen any of the factories. I used to wonder: Weren't we America, this great industrial power? So where were the factories and the mills?

Now at last I had seen a mill. South Works, for example, which went on for blocks. There were still 10,000 Union members working there in 1976. You could go over and see it, like a big whale washed up on the shore. And all around it, like little birds, were the bars and shops and beauty salons with names like "Curl Up and Dye."

See South Works and Dye. Well, now I could.

Once a friend of mine from Harvard Business School came to visit, and I took him to South Works, just to see it.

"Wow," he said. "I've never seen so much capital just *lying* on the ground. At B School, we used to laugh at how conservative these big steel companies are, but then you could come out and see all this capital, just lying on the ground . . ."

He chuckled. "Can you imagine *replacing* it?"

I was quiet: by now, I had the feeling the Machine had me under surveillance.

At the UMW, I had never gone into a mine, and when I came out here, I thought, "Well, at least I'll go into a mill." I used to ask some of the steelworkers, "Can you get me into a mill?"

They would say, "Sure, sure, kid. We'll set that up."

But no one ever set it up.

Maybe I was living with the rank and file, but every day, it seemed, they went to work on another planet. I just stood outside the gates and watched.

My first day, I went out to jog, in my running shorts. I realized, in such a place, I must seem naked. I could feel the neighbors looking at me, peeking out from behind their Howlett posters.

Then I looked up and saw it, really *saw* it, for the first time: "The Skyway."

It was an interstate highway, up on stilts, that flew over the houses and through the burning air. But the Skyway wasn't for us, the mill people, who lived down below. It was for the upper middle class in their station wagons that rumbled over our heads at night. Sometimes, you could go out and see the headlights like shooting stars.

That is, if it was a clear night and there was a hole in the sulfur.

Sulfur.

A yellow mist, out of South Works, Wisconsin Steel.

It was in my skin, in my eyes . . . it was in my hair, like traces of cocaine. It was on the glasses, the plates, and the forks.

The waitress would pour you a cup of coffee. The bartender would pour you a glass of beer.

"Here, drink this . . ." A big, foaming glass of . . . sulfur.

Here, drink this, and be like us. I would raise the glass to my lips and hold it there for a horrified second and then gulp it down.

There. Old Style. Now I was one of "them."

To me, coming from the UMW in 1976, the Steelworkers seemed almost inert. In basic steel, there had not been a major strike in seventeen years. Seventeen *years*. I had just come from a union that had a major strike every *week*. O.K., maybe the UMW had gone too far, but how could you have a union that never went on strike?

And now in ENA, the Union had given up the right to strike altogether.

Yet the Steelworkers was the big success story of American labor. The Union didn't go on strike, and still the money came in. It was like a money machine: the hourly wage, $8.20, $8.37, $8.63, clicking off, like a taxi meter. And Big Steel was such an oligopoly, it could pass on to the consumer each little click in the wage meter, provided, of course, the men didn't want too much.

And there was no chance, ever, not one, in seventeen years, to blow off steam, to face off with the Boss as an equal, like two Americans, both in their cars, out on the Skyway. Because a strike has that same feeling. It gets you back, for a moment, your equal citizenship with the Boss. It's healthy. It's good for you, good for the Boss, good for America.

That's not how the last strike in 1959 is usually described. It was a long, bitter strike, 119 days, and at the end of it the men had gotten nothing. It was like a family scandal. Something the older men didn't talk about, as if they had once tried to strike and had flopped at it. Or at least that is what I read in the books. Sadlowski said that the strike had been a good one, a healthy one. After that, there were no strikes, and something dark and secret entered the Union. You could smell it, like the sulfur coming out of the mills.

After that the men said, "More," and they got More. And they didn't strike, and got even More. It was like a dark, Faustian deal. And then one day, even the *right* to strike was gone. And maybe now, as in *Faust*, it was too late to get it back.

It was all like a machine. People wanted to kick the machine. But they didn't want the machine to stop.

To know how many of them felt, I think you had to go to Pittsburgh and stand in front of the Union headquarters at Five Gateway Center. You had to see it, this office building full of office workers, bureaucrats, rising in the air. And looking like a big tin can, about to be crumpled up.

All right, you say, so the Steelworkers had a bureaucracy. Big deal, right? Are we supposed to be shocked? Mosca and Michels wrote about unions turning into bureaucracies a hundred years ago.

Yet the Steelworkers bureaucracy was unique. It was the pride of American labor. There were 600 or so "staff representatives" who, like the proconsuls, would go out to the provinces and govern. This was called "servicing the locals." It meant that the staff reps did all the arbitrations, the bargaining, the organizing for the locals, and the elected officers did nothing. The members could still elect local officers, but it was like electing your classmates to student council. You could just sit back, relax, and let yourself be . . . "serviced."

So this big tin can, Five Gateway Center, remote, impersonal, far away, took over the whole Union. And you had to wonder if this big tin can could ever lead a *strike*: too many staff meetings, too many memos, too much paper.

And when Sadlowski said, "You go in there, and after a while you start relating to the mahogany more than you do to the guy out in the mill," people stood up and cheered.

Tear it down, they felt. Except that's where I wanted to work, if Sadlowski won.

Meanwhile, back in Chicago, I hadn't met the workers. I was still an "outsider," and it was beginning to bother me.

One night (this was October), one of my friends said, "People out here aren't very friendly, are they?"

I said, shocked, "I think they're friendly."

"No." He shook his head. "They should be inviting us into their homes."

I said, "Well, I think they're friendly."

But secretly I thought he was right.

I had met the Sadlowskis, who were very nice, but I hadn't met anyone else. And Sadlowski himself, back then, was always on the road.

Some of us who came from the UMW were expecting something more . . . maybe some good old rank-and-file folkness. Some, unlike me, had lived in West Virginia, and for them it had been a place where the kissing never stopped. But this was South Chicago. These people were Slavs. Some of them didn't talk to each other. Why should they talk to us?

Besides, it was too cold to meet people.

There would be nothing to do on a Saturday night except to go to the Golden Shell. We, the "outsiders," would sit together and argue over who would get *The New York Times* the next day. There would always be a wedding and dancing going on all around us. One night, the dancing seemed to roll up like a wave and crash into our table. A woman, who was sixty or so, and a little drunk, pulled me out of my chair as we were arguing over who would get *The New York Times*.

And Jim said, as I went flying past him, "I knew she'd pick you."

For a moment, I was dancing. And I thought, "I'm making it in South Chicago."

Then the music stopped, and she walked away. This was the only time I ever danced anywhere around the mills.

I was lonely most of the time. I would read in the little coffee shops around the mills. Sometimes South Chicago seemed a lot like Cambridge.

I began to read Dante, *The Inferno*. And all that winter, I could feel that I was descending, canto to canto, circle to circle, deeper into this book. At night I could smell the sulfur literally coming off the page.

I knew I needed help.

And slowly, I got to know John Askins. John had worked in a can plant on the West Side of Chicago, and he was always, mysteriously, on layoff. He lived in our campaign office, above the Roma restaurant, though I couldn't figure out where he slept at night.

I had heard about John even before I met him. My friends said, "He's a prince among men," or "I'd give my right arm for John Askins."

But the first time I met him, I was shocked. Prince? He was short, beer belly, cigarette ashes all over him, and a Tennessee whiskey voice so gravelly I couldn't make out a single word. This was a prince?

Yet he could put his hand on your shoulder, mumble some words you couldn't make out, and you'd follow him anywhere. He used to teach kids how to stand at a plant gate and pass a handbill and say, "Hyee . . ." Or "Mmmmbb . . ." So that the whole plant would go for Eddie.

I was in awe of him. He was a kind of artist.

But he was a troubled man, too, and I don't say this lightly. Every seven weeks, he'd be gone, for two or three days, on a wild, life-threatening drunk. And we, who all loved John, would fan out across the city to find him and carry him back.

He'd be embarrassed. "Boys," he'd say, "a gang of wild Puerto Ricans took me prisoner and held me down spread-eagled and poured Jim Beam down my throat."

Then we'd carry him back like the Ark of the Covenant.

Sometimes, in Washington, when friends of mine would ask, "What's this guy Sadlowski want?" I would talk about democracy, the right to vote, etc., as if he was a good-government liberal (which, by the way, he was). And to some other friends, I would go further and talk about the right to strike. But I never went all the way and said the one *big* thing Sadlowski wanted.

Sadlowski wanted "More." Of course, all union leaders say that, but Sadlowski wanted a whole lot "More."

He said, "The American worker should get a larger share than he's getting now. That's simple—a simple solution to a simple problem. All I'm advocating is that the worker get his just due."

Now, at just this time, in the mid-seventies, although no one may remember it now, unions like the Steelworkers were already threatening, in a big way, to break into the middle class. There were no headlines back then: "U.S. Becoming Like Sweden." But by the end of the Great Society (it's odd how people used to talk, isn't it?), steelworkers were sending their kids to law school, and some of them had second homes. Unions were bargaining for dental insurance, as if scraping the barrel to come up with new benefits.

And young professionals, people like me, were not vastly far ahead of them. The high salaries of today just didn't exist. In 1976, my first year at the UMW, I made about $19,000, and that was respectable for the first year out of Harvard Law. Now, in New York, it would be more like $90,000.

So back then, among my friends, even some liberals, everyone was getting a little touchy about unions. I remember a friend of mine coming back from England and saying, bitterly, that union members were making almost as much as she and her husband did.

I could talk about the right to vote, union democracy, and so on, but I think some people were suspicious.

And it used to worry me, too. How much more "equality" could unions get?

In the mid-seventies, in England and the United States, there was a big debate about the future of labor. Inflation was growing. Harold Wilson, the British Prime Minister, had offered the unions a historic deal: a "social contract," it was called. The government would limit wages, and in return the British unions would have more power on the shop floor.

The unions rejected the deal, and I thought they were stupid to do so. The governments of the West weren't going to put up with inflation forever. Why not cut a deal, before it was too late?

It may seem odd that someone supporting Sadlowski would have wanted to limit the power of unions to raise wages. Well . . . it was odd. I didn't mention it to anyone.

But I was in love with the idea of a social contract. I thought we should take this equality, this secret equality that people barely sensed yet, and put it in a contract before it was too late.

Maybe if Carter was elected he would offer a social contract. And maybe I would be in Pittsburgh, and maybe I would be next to Sadlowski, and would whisper in his ear, "Take it, take the deal . . ."

Well, it all seems so fantastic now. As it turns out, there was never going to be a social contract. There would just be the bankers, like Volcker, slamming the country into recession.

And then we didn't have an inflation problem. We also didn't have a manufacturing sector, or not the one we had.

I should have known it would turn out this way. I once read Rousseau's *The Origin of Inequality*, that bitter book. He said we accept inequality, even prefer it, so we can all look down on each other.

Sadlowski said, "There are some ninety million people in the work force. Do they all look down on each other?"

It's the genius of the Skyway: everyone can look down.

Meanwhile, what did I do every day, as a lawyer? I was trying to figure out where they were holding the election. You think I'm kidding, but we didn't know.

There were over 5,500 local unions, and 15,000 polling places, and the Union wouldn't tell us where they were.

We had no list of members either. Somewhere out there, in North America, there were 1.5 million eligible voters. But it was like looking for 1.5 million needles in a haystack (the haystack being the size of . . . well, Mars).

The big shock to me was that basic steel, where we were strong, was only a *third* of the vote. By the seventies the Steelworkers was no longer a union, truly, of "steelworkers." Outside basic steel, the members could be anything . . . copper miners, or cops. The Steelworkers even had picked up the waitresses at Chock Full O' Nuts in New York.

This was Sadlowski's nightmare. How did a waitress in New York even hear about Ed Sadlowski in Chicago? Multiply her a million times, and you get some idea of the problems he faced.

It was bad. He had no list of members. And no money. And without a membership list, he couldn't raise money, at least from the members.

Then, when he took money from "outsiders," i.e., liberals, he was savagely attacked by the Union.

McBride had the money, the staff, the entire infrastructure of the Union behind him. With the staff, he had his own Tammany Hall, an army of men controlling the locals, the balloting, the distribution of campaign literature. The Official Family was like the phone company. Sadlowski had to set up his own private communications system, just to let the members know he *existed*.

But the biggest problem was the stealing. Even when we got the lists of the polls, as we finally did, we still needed 15,000 observers. No, double that, *30,000*, two per poll, people with "iron butts" who could sit there all day.

David McDonald, the former Steelworkers president, told the press at the beginning of the campaign, "Sadlowski will have to win the U.S. by a large margin. Because they'll steal it from him up in Canada. I know, I stole four elections up there myself."

This was the ex-president of the Union talking!

And yet, incredibly, despite everything, we still thought we had a chance to win. If we could win every vote in basic steel, *every* vote, then they couldn't steal enough in Saskatchewan or whatever to make up the difference.

Although, really, there was no reason they couldn't.

There was no heat in our campaign office that winter. I used to sit there and shiver.

Sometimes I would see a map in front of me, a map of the U.S. and Canada. And I could see the pins where we had our observers.

Then I would see other places, where the map was blank, white . . . the terror of the blank page.

I would say the names of the mills.

Sparrow's Point, it sounds like a bird sanctuary.

Homestead, it sounds like home.

South Works, so nice and warm.

The big forts, where we had our votes. Then I'd feel better.

This was my new land, "the United States of Basic Steel." How could I have been living here all my life and never really known it before?

Sometimes I would travel in it, mostly to Pittsburgh, which I didn't like. The first day I was there, I knew it was a bad place . . . It was the air: I could breathe it.

There was no smoke, no sulfur. It wasn't dark and tragic like Chicago. A lot of steelworkers in Pittsburgh were kids, in their twenties, who were on layoff and going to grad schools, or just getting up at noon every day to listen to the Who.

It was like Seattle. I thought, "What is this?"

Here, even Sadlowski's campaign was different. Once I went to a bar to meet some of our "workers," and they were sitting around drinking with businessmen.

Not socializing with them, just in the same bar with them.

I turned to my friend Betsy and said, "Betsy, it's not like this back in Chicago."

But she was just watching as Pat Coyne over at the bar was picking up people by the hair.

But Pittsburgh could be sobering. Once I had to go to Five Gateway Center to attend a meeting on election rules, since Joe Rauh for some reason couldn't go.

Before I went, Joe said to me,

"Are you up to this?"

I said, "I think so."

"Have you ever walked into a room with twenty or thirty people and known that everyone in the room *hates* you?"

I gulped. "No."

Joe said, "Oh well, you'll get used to it."

So I walked into Five Gateway Center and walked into that room, and thirty faces, full of hatred, turned as I walked in.

I was "the Outsider."

I only spoke once, and only to say, softly, that this election would be a fraud.

Six or seven staff reps leaped up, beet red, screaming:

"WHO IS THIS PERSON?"

"IS HE A MEMBER OF THIS UNION OR WHAT?"

"MR. CHAIRMAN, DO WE HAVE TO PUT UP WITH THIS?"

But later, back at my hotel, one of the staff reps saw me and came over, smiling, holding out his hand.

"Hey," he said, "you were great at that meeting."

"Really?" I said. "I thought they hated me."

"Ohhh . . ." He waved his hand. "No . . . in fact, everyone was saying, 'Who's that Irishman they sent from Chicago?' "

I thought, "I don't know. Who?"

He was saying, "Of course, I've always liked Eddie myself . . ."

Back in Chicago, we were trying frantically to get observers. In the South, we had nothing. We were going to get creamed.

At the beginning, Ben Corum, one of our best men, had gone down to Texas. One day, he was shot down in front of a plant gate. Shot right through the throat.

The Labor Department did nothing.

Then John Askins was assaulted in Florida. There were other incidents. It was the end of our campaigning in the South.

When I called to get observers, sometimes the wife would answer, and her voice would quiver, in that Southern way, "He's . . . not here . . ."

"Will you ask Jack to give me a call?"

All our supporters in the South had the same name, Jack.

"I don't know . . ."

We both knew her husband was next to the phone.

I would hang up, disgusted. But then, I was feeling pretty brave after Five Gateway Center.

Now it was January. The election was coming faster and faster.

Every morning, we'd get up to leaflet at plant gates . . . well, some of us got up.

I wanted to. But every morning, at four-thirty, when my roommates got up, I'd look out the window . . .

The wind would howl. There'd be ice: black around the edges where the beer bottles stick out.

Mayor Daley was dead, my car had broken down . . . I don't know.

"Jim," I'd groan, "go on without me."

Then Jim and the others would leave. Then around eight or so, they'd come back to the Roma and have eggs and toast and maybe a shot. Then they'd all go upstairs, and someone would say, "Hey, Tom, coming with us tomorrow?"

"Oh, no," someone would say, "he can't. He's reading Dante." (But it was drawn out like this: "Daaaante . . .")

I'd say, "Hey, leave me alone."

I was a lawyer. I had work to do. I couldn't go around having shots at 8 a.m. and come back up here and write a brief.

But Jim was a lawyer, and he went out there. Years later, he said to me, "You know, I came out to be a lawyer like you, but I hated the lawyering part. Then I started going to the plant gates, and going out every day with these tremendous people . . . There was one Jewish guy, I can't remember his name . . ."

Jim has his picture, a bony little man holding up a fist . . .

"And the others, too . . . Some of them were giving up their *vacations* to do this, to stand there at the plant gates for Sadlowski . . . It was amazing. Once I came back and called up this girl back in Boston, and it was eight o'clock in the morning, but I'd been up for hours. And she said, 'What's the matter with you? Have you been drinking?' And actually, I hadn't. I just had to call and to tell her what was happening out here."

And I thought, "I never went out there."

But Ben Corum would be out there. It was spooky to see him after he'd been shot. Like having Lazarus around the house after he'd been brought back from the dead.

But I did go out for the mostiociolli. This is a form of pasta. Not the kind I eat now as an adult in Lincoln Park. More like pasta back when we knew it as macaroni and cheese.

We were hungry, we had no money. Most of us on the staff made $100 a week or less.

All we had to eat was the mostiociolli, and we were supposed to be saving that for the little fund-raisers around the neighborhood. But by January it had gotten as hard as the rock salt out in the parking lot behind the Roma, and nobody would eat it but Jim and me.

We'd go to the fund-raisers, and stand in the back, and eat mostiociolli . . . mmmm, it was good. The steelworkers would step back and watch.

I'd look at them and think, "Well, who are the outsiders now?"

But this is how I got to know the rank and file. Jim Balanoff, Alice Puerala, Millie, Marlene Sadlowski . . . many others, who took pity on us, took care of us. People really did take us into their homes.

Sometimes, after the mostiociolli, we would go over to the Import Tap. Jim and I and a few others. Maybe a steelworker would join us.

He might say, "Now tell me, if I work for Inland twenty years, shouldn't I get to own a piece of that company?"

"Well, I agree with you."

Then his wife would roll her eyes and say, "Come on, George, let's go home."

At first, I thought the name of the bar "Import Tap" meant you could get a Heineken. But it was a sailors' bar back when the ore boats first came to South Chicago. A bartender, in 1976, still didn't know what a Heineken was.

Sometimes we'd be joined by Gary, who was a radical. He was a young cub reporter with a local paper (Jimmy Olsen we used to call him), and he had a wonderful laugh.

Now, there were a lot of radicals in South Chicago, and some of them were real pests, the Spartacist League, etc. Sadlowski would go to a union hall, and be moderate, and reasonable, and then, as everyone walked out . . . some kid in a windbreaker, "Sadlowski for President," would be handing out copies of *The Daily World*.

Some of them had jobs in the mills. On "assignment" from "the Party." Mostly, these were just harmless kids, down in South Chicago roaming around like Moonies. People in the neighborhood were used to them.

But Jim and I really liked Gary, and besides, he was a Trotskyite, which, to the extent I understood any of it, made a bit more sense.

We used to kid him.

"Come on," we'd say, "come over to our side."

"Yeah, Gary, be a liberal."

He'd laugh. "No, no . . . you guys . . ."

Actually, I was afraid he'd get assigned to some mill.

I'll tell you what was scary about some of these kids: they would come down here to play at being "workers," and sometimes, without meaning to, they really did become "workers."

But at least they were in the mills and getting steelworkers' wages. What about me, $100 or so a week? How crazy were *they*?

But then, I was a liberal.

Now, in Chicago, I often tell people how I lived in "Milltown" my first year. They're amazed.

But in fact, I sneaked out after a few months. I had found out about Hyde Park and the University of Chicago, a few miles to the north.

When I first saw Hyde Park, I felt like a sailor seeing land
. . . the brick town houses, the bookstores, the BMWs on the
street. This looked like the kind of place where a Saul Bellow
would find a plot.

It was Jim, though, who went up first. He found a place for
us to house-sit, and then slowly, one by one, we moved into it
and out of Milltown, like men crawling through a tunnel back
to freedom.

The owner of the town house was a doctor traveling in India.
I remember gasping when I first walked in: the artwork, the
oriental rugs, the wood-burning fireplace. And he had even
left his BMW, with the keys, in the garage.

And I thought, "I'm home."

Then another friend came up, and we couldn't get him to
go back. He slept that night on a rug in front of the fireplace,
and the red ashes of the fire warmed him as he slept. And the
next day, he was so happy. He said, "I know now I'll always be
middle-class."

Yes, we thought, the CPs, the Trots, the Spartacist League,
they could all live down by the mills if they liked. To them, it
was like Williamsburg, a "colonial village" from the 1930s,
something to be preserved. But I knew, from then on, that a
"real" radical wouldn't want to save South Chicago. A real
radical would want to get rid of it.

And in that respect, more than any of us, Ed Sadlowski might
have been the most radical of all.

By now, I'd come to see he was a pretty skilled politician. The
Official Family must have thought it would be easy to red-bait
him, paint him as a radical. But Sadlowski didn't offer much of
a target.

For example, he could have called for the right to strike. He
could have attacked ENA. But he didn't: he wanted to bring
along everyone, even the older men, who didn't know whether
they wanted to strike or not. So Sadlowski simply called for the
right of members to *ratify* ENA. Who could be against the right
to vote on it?

I remember seeing Sadlowski and McBride on *Meet the Press*,
and as a debate it wasn't even close. McBride spluttered, yelled,

got red in the face. Sadlowski spoke quietly, moderately, as if he was the statesman and not McBride.

The next day, a judge I know, a man who didn't like Sadlowski, said, "Now I know why they're so afraid of this guy."

He kept hammering away at one simple question: Do you, Lloyd McBride, favor the right to ratify ENA?

McBride was in a real spot. If he said yes, his patron, Abel, would be furious. If he said no, then he was telling the members, in effect, they were children who couldn't be trusted with the right to vote. By the way, many unions *do* let members ratify their contracts, but don't have rank-and-file elections of officers. The Steelworkers, by a quirk of history, had it the other way around. So McBride had to crawl to the members and beg for their votes, while saying that, normally, they shouldn't be allowed to vote at all.

If we could have only kept the issue that simple, the right to vote, like the right to vote in Selma, Alabama, maybe we would have had the election . . . or maybe not. I think Sadlowski by himself could have kept it that simple. But it was hard for the rest, his troops, the ones who stood at the plant gates, to hold everything inside them, hold it to that one goo-goo little point. I mean, for example, the little bony man with his fist in the air, with that strange, startled look on his face, as if maybe he's surprised to find himself, at last, with his fist in the air. Or maybe it's a look of peace, such as you might find on the face of St. John of the Cross. Some had been in the mills their whole lives on the chance that, maybe, someday, something like this would happen, an Ed Sadlowski would come along and change their lives. So how could they all just sit around and talk about the right to ratify? All of this going on now wasn't about the right to ratify. It was about the whole damn wreck of their lives.

Then one day, Sadlowski said that. I think that after a million politic quotes, he just gave up and figured, what the hell, he'd say it. He said it in *Penthouse*, of all places, in a long interview that came out just before the election that February.

He said: We should live in a country where people don't have to work in coke ovens.

Everyone knew what he meant (in fact, he *said* it): We should also live in a country where they don't have to work at McDonald's either.

But a terrible howl went up from the Official Family and from some of the older workers. "This guy," they said, "won't stop these plant closings . . . this guy will try to speed them up. Read this . . ."

And I thought, "Well, they don't know what he means," and some of them didn't, I guess. But there were others who just didn't want to hear it. They knew Sadlowski was right. They knew all about the mills, about the cancer. Some of them try to speed it up: they work there, *and* smoke three packs of cigarettes a day.

Why throw away your life like this? But for them, it was too late.

What I'm quoting now, the part of the interview I'm breaking into, had to be heard in Sadlowski's voice, which is low and softly rumbling:

". . . Working forty hours a week in a steel mill drains the lifeblood of a man. Nothing is to be gotten from that. Society has nothing to show for it but waste."

He said how much he hated working at South Works as a young man. So what, he said, if the Mineworkers dropped from 400,000 men down to 100,000 or 60,000? That should be the *goal* of American labor, that no one should have to go into a mine or a coke oven ever again and just throw away their lives. When would we end all this waste?

"How many guys in that mill could be whatever they wanted to be? Whatever the need is—carpet layers, doctors, plumbers—whatever society needs. Let's have the steel industry, by virtue of what it is capable of producing, subsidize education. Do that!"

But do workers themselves believe that? he is asked.

One can almost hear Sadlowski groan. "If you had asked that question six or seven years ago, I would have answered yes . . ."

But now, he said, it's 1976, and there's a recession. (Here I must interrupt and say that, incredible as it sounds, we thought 1976 was a recession.) So, Sadlowski said, "a recession is made

in order to throw people back into their earlier positions . . .
That's how the industrialist operates . . ."

So we go around begging to get the steel mills back, when
the important thing is, he said, we shouldn't be putting kids
into these mills at all.

He said, "Look, I've been snow-jobbed, too, like everyone
else has been snow-jobbed . . . but it's time to bring that era to
an end."

I have often wondered, in later years: Should Sadlowski have
said all that he did in that interview? For he knew, even at the
time, that maybe the moment for saying it had passed. Once,
in the sixties, one could have said it. But now a dark age was
about to begin. Men were scared now. It's like when you come
across the Book of Kells and see the new way that the men are
drawn, eyes closed, books shut tight in their hands, and you
realize that it's late in history, 600 or 700 A.D., and the spirit of
the age has changed.

It's disturbing for me to reread this interview. Because I went
on to do just what Sadlowski warned against. In the eighties,
people like me would glorify the mills, and go around begging
to bring them back, just as he predicted. And I wish there was
some way, somehow, that we could fight to bring back the mills,
with all the high-wage jobs, and then start fighting with our
very next breath to knock them down. But I don't have the
agility to do this yet.

And now I think that Ed Sadlowski was about a million light-
years ahead of "incomes policy" and all the other futuristic
ideas I had back then. And no, I don't think he ran too soon,
as some people say, but just the opposite, that he ran too late
. . . The sixties were over, people's eyes were shut, the books
closed in their hands . . .

That February, we lost the election. Only, I don't quite believe
it.

We expected to lose the South and Canada, where we had
no observers. McDonald had told us they would steal. Yet I
don't think we expected they would be quite so brazen.

The locals in the South had vote counts like these:

49–0
62–0
38–0

And Canada? As Paul Johnson said later, "There were fifty-nine locals in Quebec that didn't give us a single vote, not one, not even by accident."

I thought in some of these locals where we had no observers (we aren't even sure they had an election), the Union was dumb not to spot us a single vote. It would have looked less suspicious.

As it was, it was amazing that Sadlowski won as much as he did . . . 44 percent of the vote. He won basic steel. He won where he had observers. And in the local elections, the Sadlowski slates won over and over.

But in the end, we didn't win.

It was quiet that night above the Roma. Hundreds of people jammed into a room, all the phones ringing, and yet everything was dead quiet.

After the election, John Askins disappeared.

I lost my house in Hyde Park and ended up sleeping in somebody's basement.

My roommates went back East.

I had to stay on to write up the protest, which no one in the Labor Department would ever read.

And then the years went by, and one day a friend of mine, J.M., a labor lawyer, said to me, "What do you think historians will say when they try to figure out why, in the seventies, these guys in the Mineworkers and Steelworkers rose up the way they did?"

I looked at him in disbelief.

He said, "Why those two unions?"

I could have said, "Those were the only two where people could vote." But that's not why I looked at him as if he were nuts.

What historians? It's as if the whole thing never happened now.

And I think no college kid should sit on a train late at night and read any of this.

I'll just say that eventually I went to Paris, and that's what I advise all young people to do. And it was perfectly O.K. . . . It wasn't any moveable feast, but it fit my mood.

And sitting on the St. Germain des Prés, I would sometimes think about South Chicago, and how it was really a much more romantic place than I'd thought, and how much the South Side was like the Left Bank, and how, most of all, it was such a secret city . . . and how everything that changes the world, or breaks our hearts, must always start out from a secret city.

Chapter 5

Always Bring a Crowd

I am still in Chicago, fourteen years after Sadlowski, and I still practice labor law. This is not "Washington type" labor law: it has no "policy" component, it is not at the cutting edge of anything. It is just a local practice and not, I suppose, what I dreamed of doing in law school. It is quite unsettling how one step in life leads to another and I could be out here, in the Midwest and not the East, living out my life.

Yet in a way, in the eighties, I could see everything in Chicago. Or at least I could see them wreck the mills. In the Greater Chicago area alone, 70,000 steelworkers lost their jobs in the Reagan years. And I saw some of them, too. Like refugees, streaming out of South Chicago. Streaming out of the shuttered pension funds. Some of them would pass through our office, on their way to nowhere. Abandoned by their employers, abandoned by the Union. Some of them, scared, would grab me and whisper, "Give me a pension."

Some of them were short of a pension by just one year. One year. But what could I say? The rules are the rules. I am sorry, I am sorry, I am sorry: that was all I could say.

There were the drowned and the saved. Some of them stumbling, exhausted. Others walked out of it, and seemed O.K.

People in South Chicago thought the mills would last forever. They thought of them as public utilities. It was as if, once, the whole industry was part of the village commons. Then came the barbed wire, the security guards. Then the mills, which had been there for seventy-five years, which were half as old as the city of Chicago, were suddenly gone. I think of it like the enclosure movement in England, in the 1400s, when the nobles started to enclose the village commons. But the enclosure movement in England took centuries. There was a humane royal government, Tudor or Stuart, to slow the thing down. Here the dislocation seemed to happen overnight. Our government, perversely, even tried to speed it up.

In the East, my friends would say to me, "Look, we were going to start losing our steel industry anyway."

Well, O.K. . . . But overnight? The whole thing?

It all seemed to happen in a single night. Out of principle, Free Trade, Reaganomics, etc., the whole industry was knocked down with a loud whoosh. People heard a noise, looked out their windows, and said, "My God, it's gone." All the mills I lived near in the Sadlowski campaign: South Works, Republic, Wisconsin Steel, gone, or mostly gone, in just one night, in '81, '82, '83, one long night, when the dollar got jacked up artificially and it was all so quickly and casually done.

And it was so maddening because everyone knew, even then, that the dollar would come back down. Only, when it did come back down, the mills would be gone, and nothing, nothing, would ever bring them back. Oh, we would still have a steel industry, and some of it would be new: small, low-wage "mini-mills," mostly nonunion, mostly in the South. But there would be no more South Works, Wisconsin Steel, all of that. That way of life would be gone forever.

I know, of course, it wasn't just the dollar . . . There was also greed, plastics, stupidity, the loss of markets in the Third World. The switch to aluminum beer cans. And worse than the dollar, I suppose, was the run-up in the interest rates that went along with it. But it was the dollar as a precipitant of it all, or as a symbol of everyone's indifference that still makes me mad. Some of us back then, a few lawyers, economists, union types, we ran around saying, "Wait, wait, it'll come back down." But nobody could wait, there was such a big rush.

People had seen the mills close before, temporarily, but they had never seen them *wrecked*. It is hard to imagine wrecking one. It is like wrecking a city, a science-fiction city, made of ice and smoke, somewhere on the planet Venus, with the smoke swirling everywhere, and at night, with the lights hanging from the ladders, up and down for hundreds of feet, like the white lights on the trees on Michigan Avenue. The strangest, most unearthly city people have ever seen. And they just wrecked it.

And nobody planned it, it just happened. Or so it seemed to me at the time.

To me, it was a miracle there was never a riot. In Pittsburgh, there were a few sit-ins, invasions of churches, minor civil disobedience. But it did not get much press. And in Chicago and other places, nothing much happened at all.

In the end, I think, they did not know how to riot. Even the older steelworkers hadn't been on a strike in twenty years. It was mostly quiet in the 1960s and 1970s, when they were putting in their time. Also, typically, they had gone from the Army or Navy straight into the mill, and now, somehow, it was all mixed up in their minds: World War II, Korea, Vietnam, then the job in the mill. Some of them thought it was America's way of saying "Thanks." They thought America had guaranteed the whole thing.

In my desk somewhere, I have a letter, a crude, handwritten letter signed by "the Big Boy." It was written sometime in 1983. Another labor lawyer, a friend of mine, sent me a copy. The Big Boy was a local-union president in Ironton, Ohio. And in his letter, an open letter to Lane Kirkland, the Big Boy is saying, "Anarchy is not a pretty word, but that's what's going to happen." The Big Boy admits he does not know what can be done. But then, in the rank and file, people like the Big Boy never presume to tell us what should be done. In fact, the letter is almost obsequious. The Big Boy, when he hints at anarchy, is still respectful, apologetic, as if talking to a superior.

There was no anarchy, of course. No one would have dared, not in the Reagan years. The high-wage, high-pension "union middle class" (an upper middle class) was a tiny minority, like French Huguenots. There were not enough of them to start a riot. Besides, there was the specter of the Professional Air

Traffic Controllers (PATCO), and the rest of the country was probably glad to see them busted. A single steelworker might make $40,000 or more, with Sweden-type benefits, and in the rest of the country, the median income for a family of four, the entire household, would be $24,000 or below.

So these steelworkers were not going to riot. How dare they? They were just coming down to everyone else's level. My friend Ann Feeny in Pittsburgh said, "Most people around here were glad when the mills closed. I heard women say to me, 'See? See what happens? They got too greedy.' " They were glad to see their neighbors lose their former imperial glory: my God, some of them were buying *second* homes. Since no one else had a chance to be in labor, why should they? Anyway, there should just be one class in America, one big middle class, like in *Les Misérables*.

Yet there could have been riots, I think, if the pensions had not been paid. Then there could have been Hoovervilles, bonus armies ambling off in a daze, just like in the 1930s, when Douglas MacArthur had to disperse them. This time the country was saved, not by MacArthur, but by the PBGC. The Pension Benefit Guaranty Corporation is really the unsung hero of Reaganomics, and it was set up, accidentally, just in time for "deindustrialization." The PBGC insures the benefits of the workers when their companies go bankrupt or the pension plans go bust. So the PBGC took over the shuttered pension funds, paid most of the benefits, and kept everyone quiet. But the PBGC did *not* insure all the pension benefits, and it did not insure health or other nonpension benefits. And there were horror stories, like Wisconsin Steel. But there were no riots, no marches, no "veterans" roaming around Lincoln Park, like bogeymen out to bother the joggers.

There was a strange, uneasy peace in the city. Like the peace of the postindustrial grave.

Recently, I stood on 63rd Street with Ed Sadlowski (yes, he is still here). We had just come out of Frank's Pizzeria, a great, great find, to which, Sadlowski said, he had been led one night, mysteriously, by the hand of God.

We looked up and down the street. "The whole can industry,"

he said, "used to be on this street. There must have been 15,000
. . . oh, 18,000 can workers on this one street. Now I bet there
aren't 1,000 can workers left in the whole city."

He pointed out a little boarded-up union hall, about the size
of a bar. "That was Jerry Emert's local."

I was shocked. Once I had been in a lawsuit about that local,
and now . . . that was it?

Just a few years ago, 18,000 can workers on one street. Now
where were they? Nobody really knows. Even social scientists
get spooky, heebie-jeebie feelings when they have to think about
it.

There are no great studies. Despite all our universities,
research grants, etc., we don't know ultimately where these
people went. It is a mystery, a problem one day for paleontol-
ogists. Tonight, standing on 63rd Street, looking at the rubble,
the boarded-up union halls, I think how divided the city is. On
the North Side, there are parks, beaches, giggly girls at Wrigley
Field. And down here it is so quiet you can hear the glaciers
scraping up and down the street.

What if the can industry—all those jobs—were still here? Not
for the whites, who are gone now, but for the blacks, a few
blocks away. What if there were blacks in the American Legion
halls on Friday night? The black wards of the city, flowing with
milk and honey, instead of coke and AIDS . . .

Anyway, where did they go, the people who left?

I asked my friend Deborah, a city official in the mayor's Office
of Employment and Training. Deborah runs a job-training
program at Republic Steel, to place steelworkers in new jobs.
She is the last to see them before they disappear.

She does not know either. She admits there are no jobs and
wonders what the hell she is doing. She talked to me about it
in despair. She said, "I've tried so hard to build something. It's
so frustrating."

Then she smiled. "The one nice part is graduation."

I said, "What?"

She said, "Oh, we have a real graduation. It's like a com-
mencement. We have a dinner, give out awards. People get
dressed up in caps and gowns."

I said, "Deb, do any of these people have jobs?"

She looked away. "No." She was quiet.

Some people, she said, have graduated twice. Two commencements. Sometimes I try to imagine these graduation nights all over the city: old steelworkers, in caps and gowns, graduating a second time. In my mind, I can see them on an open boat, sailing away, and they seem to be waving, waving goodbye.

Once, in real life, I was on a boat full of steelworkers, and we sailed through South Chicago. It was part of a Union outing, on a chartered boat. We sailed through the city, down the Sanitary District Canal, down the Cal-Sag Channel, and down past the mills. The old mills just stood there, quiet, closed, rusting away.

Everyone on the boat fell silent. The old mills, which had employed thousands, seemed to stretch on for miles. It was cold and raining, and we seemed to be sailing through the Underworld, on that ferry, with Charon the Boatman taking us past the shores of the union dead.

Some of the men who had worked in the mills talked softly, pointing things out. Was that the bar mill? Was that the melt shop? It was odd, but they had never seen their own mills from the water.

The mills look so much colder and wetter from here: I watched with horror as Katy, my date, started turning blue.

The men on the boat, who stood around me, had been hard-liners when the mills began to close. They had said, "No concessions." Let it die. There was something noble, almost Roman about it all: Let the steel industry be my funeral pyre.

But most of these men had been for Sadlowski. This was my party in labor, and the hard-line rank-and-file party. But even in labor we were on the outs. Now, as we sailed past the mills, I thought, "Thank God we weren't in power; nobody can blame us." Thank God I was not in Pittsburgh when all this happened. Thank God we did not have to preside over the dissolution of the Steelworkers Union.

It hurts me even to look at the Union. Once, when I came to Chicago, the entire International was 1.6 million members. Now it is down to 600,000 or so, and that is probably optimistic. Millie, a secretary who works at the Union, says, "Whatever number we say it is, subtract 200,000, and that's the real number."

But I cannot believe it: it cannot be 400,000.

The famous Steelworkers bureaucracy is now a wreck. All the staff reps I know are retiring, or thinking about it, or going to the Union "retreat," up in the mountains somewhere outside Pittsburgh, where they watch the trees and the birds and the sun rising: and up there, they can try to forget about the steelworkers, the one million steelworkers, old people, some of them in caps and gowns, whom they have packed into boats and sent out to sea. It is a terrible thing to have on your conscience. No wonder they take early retirement. Or go to the Union retreat and wash their hands over and over and say, "I'm not guilty. I'm not guilty . . ."

In some cases, the Union went out whipped. There was no dignity to it. At South Works, for example, U.S. Steel (now USX) made them crawl. It said it would build a rail mill but wanted concessions. The Union made the concessions. Then it wanted more concessions. The Union made those concessions, too. Then it canceled the mill anyway and issued a press release blaming the workers.

In other cases, the Union did not budge. There were no concessions. The Union said, "You're going to kill it anyway. Just do it. Get it over with."

Maybe they should have made concessions. I looked around at the men on the boat and wondered if any of them had second thoughts. They seemed emotionless as we passed the mills, as if, like Orpheus in the Underworld, they could not look back. Better to go forward. Better to starve, if necessary, in a plastic suburban mall than go back to South Chicago in chains.

Actually, the Union tried everything. It was like a cancer patient, trying chemotherapy, then surgery, then Laetrile, and nothing worked. It just continued dying.

The industry, under Reagan, had little chance to save itself. For some time, since the 1920s, it had been a conservative, uncompetitive oligopoly. It restricted output, raised prices, lost market share year after year, and it was just too late to turn things around when the Reagan policies, the high dollar, etc., mindlessly began to take effect.

Labor costs, by the way, were not the big problem. I know, no one believes me. But in heavy industry, the capital costs are so large that labor costs are only 10 percent or so of the cost of the product going out the door: raise wages 10 percent, and you raise the entire product cost by just one little penny on the dollar.

As one union rep used to say to me, "Hey, $15 an hour, $10 an hour, $5 an hour, what difference does it make?" Not too damn much.

If that is true, why did the companies want concessions? Discipline the Union. Break it, even. Get a free hand to change work rules. There were many reasons. Mostly, it was a PR battle: the whole point of concessions bargaining was to decide who would take the fall. Management wanted the Union to get up there on the stage, pull out the knife, and stand there, Hamlet-like, in front of the whole world, with the choice of killing itself or killing the mill.

The hard part about being in labor is to keep telling yourself, "It's not my fault." Labor just does not have that much power. But labor always loses the PR battle, and often I, a labor lawyer, even lose it within myself. I too believe we are guilty, and it somehow is all our fault. Labor is too *dumb*, in more than one sense of the word, to get its story across, even to itself. We cannot even tell the story the New Left would like to tell for us, because even if it is true (and it might not be), it would overwhelm us. So I'm tempted to say nothing, but there is one story I have to tell. It's not as noble or stirring as some of the stories about Pittsburgh . . . but this just happens to be the one I know.

For seven years (1981–88), I represented 2,500 former employees of Wisconsin Steel. We sued International Harvester Company, their former employer, for the benefits they lost when Harvester sold the mill to a tiny, undercapitalized company that quickly went bankrupt.

Wisconsin Steel was the first of the big Chicago mills to crash, and the crash was the most dramatic, because here, unlike most mills, the workers were cheated of their shutdown benefits. Even with the payments from the PBGC, the workers still lost nearly $45 million. By 1988, if the interest on this money was added up, they had lost nearly $90 million. The benefits they lost, among others, include severance pay, supplemental unemployment benefits pay, extended vacation pay, "special payment," health insurance (for retirees). They even lost two weeks of wages because the paychecks bounced without warning when the mill suddenly closed in March 1980.

But worst of all, 500 or so of them lost their pension benefits, often up to 60 percent, especially the "Rule of 65" pensions, which were the special shutdown benefits that went in effect only if the mill closed.

So not only did the workers lose their jobs; that would have been bad enough. But they also lost the $45 million, which was their "deindustrialization" money. The closing of Wisconsin Steel was, in many ways, like an earthquake. The first shock was that the mill closed. The second shock, like an aftershock, was that they would not get this money either. The money that would have cushioned the blow, that would have given them time to think, figure out what to do next, hold on to the car or the home a little longer: it was not much money, really, but it was enough, just enough, to make people lose their balance. Some of them could never get their balance back.

I spent all the Reagan years on this one case. It was endless. I felt like I was in prison. I used to think of that line from *Richard II*: "I wasted time, and now doth time waste me." I came to hate "deindustrialization." The mill had closed, but it seemed as if the litigation would never end, and I might have to clean up after this mill forever. I felt as the men must have felt: I was always living in the year 1980. I could not seem to leave 1980.

I wanted to move, go to New York, do anything else, but people told me, "You can't, you're stuck here," and they were right. I was stuck here. I was trapped in a way, just as the people in the neighborhood were trapped, trapped in homes they could not sell, like victims of an earthquake. Nobody was moving, nobody was going away. I was a labor lawyer, like it or not, until this damn case was done.

Here is how the case started:

In 1977, Harvester had owned Wisconsin Steel for seventy-five years, and the mill made the specially hardened steel for the trucks and machinery that Harvester manufactured. Gradually, Harvester had let the mill run down, and sometime in the mid-seventies, it began looking for a buyer. But no one in the business wanted to buy Wisconsin Steel. Not only was it run down, but there was an even bigger problem: the pension fund was short $65 million.

Wisconsin Steel, in short, was unsalable. Yet Harvester did not want to close it either. If it did so, it would owe the whole $65 million in pensions, plus another $20 million in special shutdown benefits, like severance pay. It almost seemed as if Harvester was trapped into keeping the mill open. Nor was Harvester the only steel company in the 1980s to have this problem. A union lawyer once told me, "The only reason half the steel mills in this country are still going is that they can't afford to pay the pensions." It was the revenge of the weak on the strong. "Shut us down, Mr. Employer, and you die, too."

So Harvester tried to close the mill indirectly. It transferred title to a dummy corporation. Then, when this corporate shell went bankrupt, Harvester could say, "Too bad, they're not our pensions now." But Harvester had to have an accomplice. It found one in a small engineering company, Envirodyne, Inc., which knew nothing about steel. Envirodyne was not much of a company, just two yuppies in a garage. But Envirodyne did not want to have to pay the pensions either. So Envirodyne transferred title to a subsidiary it created, EDC Holding Company. Then EDC transferred title to a subsidiary it created, WSC Corporation. One corporate shell came after another. It was like a game of Chinese boxes, and when you got to the last box, nothing was in it. Nobody would be paying the pensions.

Under our law, a subsidiary can go bankrupt and normally the parent company will not be liable for its debts. So when EDC or WSC went bankrupt, Harvester and even Envirodyne could say they owed nothing. Indeed, Harvester was not even the parent. But Harvester was the biggest creditor and held on through mortgages to everything of value. That was the malign beauty of it all, which I spent seven grudging years admiring. Harvester had dumped all the pension liabilities but kept control of all the assets. It could keep running the mill as if it still owned it. Envirodyne could conduct its little engineering experiments. And the workers, who may have been there twenty or thirty years, would lose their pensions, health insurance, severance pay, etc. Dumb, stupid organized labor would take the fall.

The deal was so mean, so vile, that even the investment bankers gagged. Lehman Brothers, the investment banking firm handling the sale, went to Harvester and objected on simple moral grounds. Peter Peterson, the president of Lehman, came out to a Harvester board meeting to express his distaste. He talked about the "appearance" and the "reality" of the transaction. He was ignored, but he made a record, at least, and it does show a certain honor: sometimes, even on Wall Street, someone *may* write a memo to the file.

Harvester kept the mill going for a decent interval (two years). Then, on March 28, 1980, with no warning to the workers, Harvester pulled the plug. It foreclosed on the mortgages, and the mill went down the drain. In minutes, WSC was in bankruptcy.

Everybody was stunned. They thought, "How could anything be wrong?"

Right before the mill closed, production almost cruelly began to go up. People were getting more overtime than ever. They were like old ladies, on their deathbeds, rougeing up their cheeks.

But no, it was something else: they never knew they were about to die, it was a total shock. They say people who die sudden, violent deaths are most likely to become ghosts and haunt the earth. On March 28, 1980, all the workers died a sudden, violent death, no time to say goodbye.

Men were obsessed with "the last day." Even seven years later, as we prepared for trial, they could not talk about anything else. Dozens of times, I asked potential witnesses, "Now what did you lose as a result of the closing of the mill?" And they answered with non sequiturs, their little stories about "the last day."

Mr. J. said, for example, "I'm walking off the shift, and my foreman comes over and says, 'Don't come back.'

"I said, 'What?'

"He said, 'Don't come back. It's over.'

"I said, 'What? What?' "

Another man said he was asleep, and someone phoned and woke him from a dream and said, "Don't come in, it's gone."

These stories might go on for fifteen, twenty minutes, just pointless stories. As witnesses, they worried me. They did not seem to care about the loss of pensions, etc. It was that phone call saying, "Don't come back." I was afraid that, as witnesses, they would talk about nothing else, and the jury would think, "What's the big deal about the last day?"

But maybe it was the day he died. The last day a man could remember himself as middle-class. The rest of his life began happening to someone else.

Over the years, I drove down to South Chicago to talk to the workers. I saw the neighborhood around Wisconsin Steel change. At first, in '81, '82, it was simply dead. By '85, it was beyond dead, and much more skeletal-looking: old tires, hubcaps, rusted human bones. Once, in the seventies, I used to dine in Slavic splendor at places like the Golden Shell. But nothing was that good now. Now I went hungry. Or I would drive twenty blocks north to the U of C and eat tunaburgers with biologists.

In the old days, driving down here, I used to see a sign: "Welcome to the Tenth Ward, Edward R. Vrdolyak, Alderman." Now I see a sign about a clinic for male impotence. This is how you know now you have entered the Tenth Ward.

Even the geography has begun to change. Now there is a whole mountain range of chemical waste rising to the south along I-80. What was once the Midwest has begun to look like the Adirondacks. There is even talk of ski lodges. Steelworkers from sex clinics could run the lifts.

When the mill crashed, so did the Union. Same week. Nobody ever saw it again.

It had never been much of a union anyway, just a small independent, not affiliated with the Steelworkers or the AFL-CIO. It did not even have a real labor lawyer: just Edward R. Vrdolyak (or ERV), the alderman, who wanted the worker-comp cases. ERV had a little office, and Tony Roque, the Union president, was an employee. Roque was an investigator or "runner," who brought in the injured men. Under Vrdolyak, the Union became a big, grinding worker-comp. machine, spitting out missing fingers, broken bones, all of it money in Eddie's pocket.

When the mill went down, ERV closed down the Union and walked away. He's got nothing against labor law. But there is no money in it, see? The money is in worker comp.

Poor Roque, the president, was in over his head. He was just a working guy, no genius, trying to figure out a Wall Street deal, with no one to help him, not even his boss, Vrdolyak. Even a good labor lawyer might not have been much help.

When Roque complained, Harvester handed him a sheet of paper. It said this document was a guarantee of the pensions. Roque signed it. Didn't really grasp it. In fact, the paper guaranteed just a tiny sliver of the pensions. By signing it, Roque unwittingly released Harvester from *everything* else: $65 million in pensions, $20 million in shutdown benefits.

Despite the shell, some lawyers at Harvester had thought the company could still be liable for the pensions. But now there was Roque's waiver. Harvester was delighted, amazed, that the Union could be so dumb.

When the mill went down, Tony Roque fled. Nobody saw him. He unlisted his phone number. People said he was in the hospital. Or he was dead. He was like a pilot who crashes a plane and 600 people die, the bodies lying all over South Chicago.

It was a mess.

Frank Lumpkin survived the crash. He was an old steelworker, about sixty-five, a black man from rural Georgia, an ex-boxer, a quiet, mild-mannered man. He had never held union office. He was just rank and file. But the day the mill closed, and the Union disintegrated, he seemed to come out of nowhere. He was not an officer, but there was no one else. He said to me, "I read somewhere, 'If you can't find a leader, be a leader.' "

So Frank and a few friends met in someone's house, and they started a committee, the Save Our Jobs Committee. It was a great name, Save Our Jobs. It never saved a single job, I think. But it filed suit, it picketed, it gave food to the hungry. It was like nothing I had ever seen. I used to think I had died and gone to rank-and-file heaven.

Save Our Jobs became the union, not officially, but spiritually. It was "the Union" as it was in the beginning: no buildings, no bureaucracy, just a crowd of people, desperate, broke, their backs against the wall. The day the mill closed, the paychecks were bouncing in the bar. No one knew if the mill would reopen or not. A mill had never crashed like this before, not in Chicago.

People used to meet in a room over the Roma restaurant, the same room where I worked in the Sadlowski campaign. It was a terrible room. Low ceiling, small, just an attic. Save Our Jobs could barely pay the rent. Sometimes, in the middle of the meetings, the lights would go out. I would be talking to 150 or 200 men (they were always men, maybe one or two women), inches from my face, in total dark, jammed into the room. I could hear them, smell them, but I could not see anyone. And no one would move. The meeting kept going. In the dark, they would ask about their pensions.

It was an old work force. Out of 2,600 workers when the mill closed, at least 800 or so were eligible for pensions. That means they must have worked twenty years or more and been at least forty-five years of age or older. They all wore T-shirts and looked grim and Polish. Even the blacks and Mexicans looked like Slavs. It is just a big melting pot down there of long-suffering looks, and a few years near a blast furnace and every guy ends up with the same face. I call it Slavic just because the Slavs were there first.

At all the meetings, I never saw young men. They did not care about Save Our Jobs, they cared about getting a job. They had options. They could go off to Texas and California. Then they could come back.

I saw old men who were blazing mad. And others who were passive, sitting in folding chairs, and leaning to one side. They'd start to lean over as I spoke, and one or two very old men would be almost horizontal, and I'd think, "They're going to fall," but somehow they never did.

And they all somehow became a union again, or became a union for the first time. It seemed to re-form around Frank. Everything seemed to come to him, without his even trying. It was odd to me that Wisconsin Steel finally had a real union, just as the place technically ceased to exist. Frank, like an old sergeant, had to start them all from scratch.

First, he had to teach them how to picket. It may sound strange, but none of them knew how. I remember the first time he brought a group downtown to City Hall, to picket outside for the pensions. Frank went to my colleague Leon Despres for advice. Frank said, "I went to Leon, and he said, 'Now, when you hold this press conference, just tell them to come. Don't tell them what it's about.' "

Frank did it just right. When it came to PR, he was a natural. Someone in Manhattan they would bow down and adore.

Frank laid out the picket signs on the sidewalk, but nobody wanted to pick them up. Everyone was nervous. Then some reporters came. The TV crews showed up. The cameras began rolling. The media were expecting something, but the men just stood there, frozen. Frank realized he would have to pick up a sign and just march, even if he was the only one. So he did. He walked a few steps, looked over his shoulder, and . . . everyone was picking up a sign. Old men, for the first time, walking a picket.

After that, they picketed like crazy, all over town, in front of banks, businesses, federal buildings. Chicago was not big enough, so they went to Springfield, too, then to Washington. I said, "O.K., picket wherever you like, but don't picket the court." So, of course, they picketed there, too. I heard about it in my office. "Your clients are out there picketing in front of the court." My God, I thought, it would look like we were threatening the judge. I had to run screaming through the Loop to wave them away.

Frank apologized, but he still laughs about it: he had never seen a lawyer run like that screaming through the Loop.

For years, I never saw Frank except in a crowd. He said, "That's the one thing I learned from the Union early on . . . they're not afraid of one man. If you want to see someone, always bring a crowd with you." Somehow, in a quiet, understated way, Frank could always bring a crowd. I have many pictures of Frank in a crowd. Twenty or so grim men in every picture, and they all carry signs saying, "Save Our Jobs."

Except for one guy, with a beer and sunglasses, grinning and waving. I see him at every meeting. I keep asking Frank, "Who is this guy?"

Every picture has blacks, whites, Mexicans. Save Our Jobs had to be that way, and it was just Frank's style, nothing forced about it. Everything he touched came out that way.

Sometimes, when I looked for witnesses and I was with whites, alone, one of them might say, "What do you think about these niggers, like Harold Washington, running the city?"

The man would grin at me, to see what I would do.

"Of course," he said, "I don't mean Frank. You understand that, don't you?"

Frank in this sense (and only in this sense) was like Prince or Eddie Murphy. White people would go to his concerts.

They went because he gave out food. Because he helped them with evictions and cutoffs. And because, most of all, he had hope. This was so stunning in South Chicago that people came just to gape at him in awe. He was like a freak show at the carnival. The man had hope. It was just so weird.

For that reason, too, the nuts would go to scream at him. I said, "My God, Frank, don't you ever want to knock one of these guys down?"

He spoke with the serenity of an ex-boxer. "When I was young, I wanted to knock a lot of guys down. Now, some people burn you up, but you have to tell yourself, 'The next guy who comes in the office, just treat him brand new, like the first person you ever met . . .'"

I only saw him mad once. Some of the old union officers, Tony Roque's crowd, came and told Frank to drop the case. They said, "You're raising false hopes." He used to sit in my office and repeat the words, "false hopes, false hopes," and shake his head.

"Right when this thing got started," he said, "I get a call from Sam Howe. He invites me over for breakfast, and I didn't know him, but you know, he was one of our leaders. I'm sitting there at the man's house and his wife gives me breakfast, and finally he says to me, 'Now look, Frank, I think you better just drop this thing.' When he says that, I slam the table. Coffee spills. I . . . I say, 'That what you call me over, to tell me that? You call me over and tell me to drop this thing?' I get madder than anything. I tell him, 'You should be . . .' I can't tell you what I said. I just hit the table again. I had to get out of there."

It was interesting, I thought: Howe was a black, so they had picked out a black, not a white, to tell Frank to back off.

Frank said softly, "Well, I cooled down, and I called him to apologize, and I had no right to get mad like that. Not in the man's house, not in front of his wife."

And that is the only time I heard of Frank getting mad.

So for seven years, Frank picketed, held rallies, handed out surplus government cheese: with the cheese as the bait, he kept the group together. No, it was the suit, not the cheese. It was the suit that created, and kept alive, Save Our Jobs.

The years went by. Frank would call up once a week:

"Any news?"

"No news."

"Man oh man."

We waited for rulings on the motions to dismiss, which Harvester kept filing. The men could not fathom the motions, the procedural issues, etc. Why could we not just go to the jury?

Actually, it was a good question.

Frank kept asking me to come down and talk to the men. I never wanted to go down there.

Frank would say, "Can you come down and give us a report?"

"Frank, there's nothing to report."

"Well, just come down."

"And say what?"

"Whatever you want."

"They'll throw bricks at me."

"No, no . . ."

If we could get before a jury, we could win. The problem was to find a claim we could bring under federal law. Could we invalidate Roque's waiver waiving all the pension earned up to the time of the sale? Could we prove that the sale was not a true sale at all and that Harvester remained liable for the pensions earned after that?

I began to think that maybe we should never have started this. We had filed suit to pass judgment on Harvester. Now the suit was becoming a judgment on us. Or, I should say, me. After all, Frank was not a lawyer, and I was the one who had filed the damn thing.

The suit had always been a long shot: first, because of Roque's waiver, and second, because of the corporate veils. But I thought at the time, "So what? Give it a try." But now we had raised people's hopes. I had never thought about it before, this dark side of legal activism. It was one thing, back in law school, to trace out cute legal theories, like circles in the air, while I sat in the stacks eating oatmeal cookies. Back then, it was a game. And often, in the big firms, it is still a game. It is all a bluff between two big, rich companies, and the suit can go on and on.

But steelworkers, desperate, unemployed, do not know any of this: they think it is all for real. And they cannot afford, like big companies, to be in suits that last ten or fifteen years.

Some people began to doubt Frank. He had led them into the desert. Old men used to mutter about him, rail at him, as the Israelites did to Moses.

The rallies, however, always went well. Loud rock music blasting away at these old guys. Then, with everybody dazed, a minister would speak. Then Congressman Savage. Then Frank would give a great speech. Then he would introduce me, say, "Here's the lawyer," clap me on the back, and I would feel like a hero even though I was not. I would look out at the men, on the metal folding chairs, and they were not heroes either. Frank used to call them the "peoples." As in "the peoples want to do this" and "the peoples wants to do that." This was not bad grammar, I think, but his way of seeing us all, in the plural, every one of us with a name and face. It was what made Frank give out the food or loan some money to a man out of his own pocket. And we all had to live up to Frank's vision of us.

Frank was going to lead us out of the desert. We all knew that, even if we had to wait forty years or so.

In the early years, I think, Frank did not care as much about the suit as he did about the mill. It was the mill, the mill, the mill . . . people were haunted by the loss of the mill, the fire in the sky, the smoke, the white lights running up and down the ladders. They wanted the mill back.

It began to dawn on people only slowly, very slowly, that they were never coming back to work. Save Our Jobs turned out to be an ironic *nom de guerre*. For years, people sighed and sat around, as in *The Cherry Orchard*, and waited for the axes to start chopping down Wisconsin Steel.

Once or twice I went to see the mill. It was impossible to get in, so I just stood there, wondering how much stripping of wires, etc., had been done. There was a small engineer's shack, and inside the shack, a man sat at a desk, all day, year after year . . . he was a *lawyer*. Cuyahoga Wrecking would hire lawyers, not engineers, to wreck the big mills, and put them in little shacks, because there were so many permits and government agencies to be dealt with. I liked our lawyer when I met him. He was laid back and came from California and was always working on a tan.

The mill had quickly turned into a junkyard. Even Frank knew he could not save it all. But he still hoped to save one piece of it, the bar mill, or No. 6 Mill, which had just been built. Why tear it down? It could be a mini-mill that took scrap steel and rolled it into bars and other finished products. As a mini-mill, it could employ maybe 600, 700 workers. At that moment, 1984, the dollar was still too high, and there was no buyer.

Ann Markusen the economist came up with the idea: if the government just held on to No. 6 for a year or two, the mini-mill might become viable. When the dollar came down (and it *would* come down), there would be a lot of interest in No. 6.

We just had to convince the Reagan administration, which by a fluke had ended up owning Wisconsin Steel as part of the bankruptcy case. We struck out with them, of course. The very thought of the government owning a steel mill . . . well, it was just way too Mitterrand-ish.

So Frank, Ann, and I then went to the state and local government, to see if they would take over No. 6. We went to the mayor, to the governor, to anyone who would listen.

The city official was skeptical. "What are we supposed to do, just hold it?"

"Yes," we said.

"Oh, we'll have to hire a guard and everything."

"So what?"

"We can't do that. We've got to develop it."

"And do what? Round up the rats? Make it a wildlife refuge?"

I looked over at Frank. He sat there, talking to himself: "Dollars and cents, dollars and cents . . . you can't win no arguments with dollars and cents."

The official turned to Frank. "Look, Mr. Lumpkin, why don't you forget about steel and focus on something else?"

"Like what?" Frank said.

"Like our new Port of Chicago, like transportation . . ."

"But that's not *making* anything," Frank said. "That's just lifting and carrying things."

The official seemed to pause.

"Anyway," Frank said, "I talk to men working down at that port . . . They say, 'Everything's coming in, nothing's going out.' How can we keep going like that?"

The official just looked at Frank, and I thought, "Well, this meeting is over."

When they wrecked No. 6, there was no press release, no official statement, as if Frank Lumpkin would tell the men about it: that Wisconsin Steel was dead, that the last hope for it had died.

This was the second time I saw Frank furious.

He said, "Why *me*? We got a mayor, we got a governor. Why don't they come down here and tell them?"

I said, "Frank, they figure it's your job."

It occurred to me that Frank, who was once an innocent

rank-and-filer, had become kind of an official. We were all working for the Reagan administration, in a way.

He said, "Back in the thirties, FDR . . . he got jobs for people." He shook his head. "I don't understand this thing now."

I think at this point he almost did lose hope. Republic, South Works, Wisconsin Steel, all of them down, or going down. He sat in my office one day and said, "It can't go on . . . it can't go on."

I said, "Can't go on? Sure, it can go on."

He looked puzzled.

I wanted to tell him, "Frank, I don't know how to say this . . . I live on the North Side. I go to wine bars, I eat carrot cake. I date slender, elegant women. You think, living down here, the country is dying. You should live where I do. The rest of the country's doing great. It's like . . . well, it's like Hollywood."

In a way, I knew, despite everything, I had become a Reaganite. I wanted to confess my sin. But I had no intention to stop sinning.

After No. 6 was wrecked, we had just the pension case, which by now had gone through four judges, McCormick, Kocoras, Grady, and Moran. The suit kept surviving, barely, one motion to dismiss after another. "The judge is just keeping you alive out of kindness," the Harvester lawyers said. I tried one legal theory after another, RICO, ERISA, LMRA, and when one claim or theory was knocked out, I tried another one. I was wild with fear we would be disgraced.

I think the Harvester lawyers were shocked. One of them said, "Don't you have any intellectual honesty at all?"

I did not. And then something wonderful happened, in September 1987. The judge said he liked one piece of our suit and said he might strike down Roque's waiver, so we might have some but not all of the $45 million we were seeking. At least, he would be willing to let this piece of the suit go to trial.

At last I could prepare for trial. Suddenly, I needed witnesses, including hardship cases, those who had suffered. For seven years, caught up in the motions, I had paid no attention to the "peoples," and had not even seen them, except in the dark above the Roma restaurant. I had seen the billboard for male impotence, but I did not really know what had been going on down here.

I began driving down to South Chicago to talk to people, to look them over as witnesses. It was like an audition, really, as sick as that sounds. Their stories were numbing, all the same:

"I lost my pension."

"I lost my car."

"I lost my wife."

And I would think, silently, "Next."

I was not sure who I wanted. I wanted them to be unemployed, sure: but a man who had not worked could look like a malingerer. Anyway, after seven years, people get nasty. Some of them had become scroungers and had started to smell. As a lawyer, putting on a case, trying to impress a jury, I did not want any Brechtian epic drama: no *Threepenny Opera*, no Mack the Knife. That may be all right for the stage or literature. But for a trial, you want them pure, innocent, with no stain of sin.

I wanted a worker like Wayne, whose wife died of cancer. When the mill went down, Wayne, who had worked twenty-five years, lost his health insurance, with no warning. While his wife lingered on, in agony, he had no coverage at all. He had to sell the car, then the home, everything, and (here is the good part) he kept working. Wayne was never *unemployed*. So if he got on the stand, Harvester could not touch him. I could sit back and laugh. This is what I mean by "tragedy," when I can sit back and laugh at opposing counsel.

There were other "old" men, unemployed, who were tragedies, too. But these tragedies took a bit more explaining.

They were unemployed because they were "old." It sounds preposterous to call them old when they were just in their forties or fifties. Yet at that age, in manufacturing, everyone calls them "old."

A man who was in management at Wisconsin Steel told me once that he regretted even trying to keep the mill open. As he drove through the plant gate and passed the men going to work, he used to think, "Aren't I doing more harm than good?"

He said to me over lunch, "Now I think: Throw them all out

of work. Do it now, don't wait. Better they look for work now, when they're thirty, than later on, when they're fifty and fifty-five."

"Except," I wanted to say, "they *are* fifty and fifty-five."

But I was too impressed with this man, who was a yuppie like me but had the grace of acting like a German with war guilt.

Anyway, the "old" men could not find work when Wisconsin Steel closed, for several reasons:

At first, when everyone thought the mill would reopen, it made no sense to hire the old ones. With all their seniority, they would just quit and go back to Wisconsin Steel as soon as it started up.

Later, when it was clear that would not happen, the old men still were not hired, because, the employer said, they were "too used to the union."

The employer would say, "You wouldn't be happy with the wages we pay."

"Oh, I would be happy," the man would say.

"Nooo," the employer would say, "you really wouldn't."

"Oh yes, I really would."

The man would have to kneel and swear and say, "Look, I'd love to work for $5.50 an hour." But even a loyalty oath would not save them now.

Their biggest problem was having to drag around these old, puffy-looking, blue-collar bodies. These bodies were like booby traps. One crack or tear in them, and they would sag like an old bag of sand. These old bodies could cost a new employer thousands in worker comp.

It was a big shock to me how men in the mills got physically used up. Somehow I thought it no longer happened. But even now, down in the rank and file, even in "modern" industry . . . the minute they get lame, it is scary, they feel like animals. In my own life, I can have a bad elbow or bad leg, and so what? I go see a sports doctor maybe. But in manufacturing, I would be through. *Unless* I was already in the mill, in a job, with union seniority: then I would be O.K.

I was astonished at some of the men who were still working at Wisconsin Steel when it closed. I saw (no kidding) amputees, asthmatics, old men with pacemakers, men with arthritis, and many who were missing a finger or two. In some little knots of men at our rallies, it was hard to find a whole hand, I noticed. I used to think, "How had this mill been running at all?"

I understood, at last, why there is an organized labor when I saw the mills close and the men, like pack animals, wobbling out of them on shaky legs. Apparently, management left them alone because the Union and the Union contract made it a big nuisance to get rid of them. There would be step one, step two, step three, step four, and then the arbitration, and it was probably cheaper to work around the cripples anyway and not pay the disability.

The point is, no *new* employer would hire them and have these cripples walking around, lifting and bending and carrying things. Some of them, when the mill closed, were a year or so away from death.

The first witness I sought out, Pete Garcia, was dying when I found him. He was the kindest, most honest man on the Union's executive board. He could smell a rat, and he knew just how the men had been cheated. *He* had been cheated: he was two months short of a thirty-year pension when Harvester caused the shutdown, and he lost his health insurance, everything. After we filed suit, I almost ran to his house, because he was the best single witness I could have had.

But when I saw him, my heart sank. He had cancer and diabetes and could not move from the couch, and he was furious, because he knew, I think, he would never make it to trial. Poor Pete, he so desperately wanted revenge. "You get that company, you can count on me, you be our Abe Lincoln, right?"

His friend John Nuno, who sat next to him, said, "Yeah, maybe you can be like our young Abe Lincoln."

I gasped, and then I realized neither man was serious. They just knew they were stuck with me.

If I seem to exaggerate how used up these men were, remember I saw them *after* the mill closed. A steelworker can shut down just like a steel mill. When a mill shuts down and the furnace goes cold, it can take tens of millions of dollars to get it relit.

And you could look at some of these men and know: it would take tens of millions of dollars to get them relit.

I am looking at some notes I took one day when I was interviewing witnesses. By chance, this day I was talking to Mexicans. I used to see them in shifts: one day the whites, the next day the blacks, the next day the Mexicans. It makes no difference which set of notes I use.

The first man I saw, Al R., was in his fifties, still had two kids (he had married late), and no job. He had worked twenty-five years in the mill, and now he was on welfare. He presented himself as a liar, a cheat. He bragged about his "green card," being on public aid. He would not even look for a job, he said.

"Why?" he said. "I've got two kids. Where would I get a job that had health insurance for my kids? Hey, how can I take a job, with *kids*?"

"My God," I thought, "I can't put him on the stand."

As we talked, I realized this man was . . . well, nuts. He kept laughing, cackling, making wild, insane remarks.

His real problem, he said, was that he only had one arm. The other one was wracked with arthritis, from unloading the ore boats in too many Chicago winters. With two arms, he was middle-class. With just one arm, he was trapped in hell forever. He seemed to enjoy it, too. It struck him as funny.

I asked him if he was interested in settlement.

"No," he snapped. "No settlement."

"But what if you got, oh, $30,000?"

He almost spit. "What's your take?"

"Not enough." I was in no mood to be Lincoln.

"Look," he said, "I don't even know if I want to win. It's a lot of trouble for me if we win. I don't want to lose my welfare." Then he began laughing nastily.

Enough of this guy, I thought. But in fact, he was the best I saw. The other men were even worse, even less presentable. Al R. stayed on to translate for them, and he would laugh at their answers, unpleasantly, and then wink at me, as if he and I were on to these men. After a while, I began to wonder, "What is he translating?"

The next man, Mr. V., looked as if he bathed three times a

day. He wore a suit, and had a sombrero, and looked like the owner of a hacienda. He sat down, silver-haired, dignified, absolutely immobile.

Have you looked for any work? "I sent out applications." How many? Pause. "A thousand." Another pause. "That was a while ago." Send out any lately? Long pause. "No." Is your wife working? "No." He wanted to say something, so I waited. "We're divorced."

Well, how are you living? "My kids . . . they give me something." I could barely hear him.

I said, "Sir, if we use you as a witness, you've got to keep looking for work. It's very important, even if you don't find any. You understand?"

I did not care if he found a job. I just wanted him to keep looking.

He started to raise his hands, then let them fall. "Who would hire me?" He had been a steelworker for twenty years.

The next man was a pigpen, in gray filthy overalls, and the dirt on him seemed about seven years old. He was gray like a mouse and seemed to be a deaf-mute, unable to speak English or Spanish. This man had been a steelworker for *twenty-five* years. I could not understand how anyone, in just seven years, could have become so . . . unemployable. If I had seen him on welfare and known nothing more about him, I would have thought: Sure, O.K., "welfare," "culture of poverty," "unemployable." But this man's culture was Wisconsin Steel. Seven years ago, he was middle-class, and he would *still* be middle-class if Wisconsin Steel had not closed. And now look at him. I could not believe the guy.

Maybe we all have, within us, a "culture of poverty." It just needs a little luck to bring it out.

I gave up on the pigpen. He would have disgusted a jury.

Then, when I was about to go home, I saw the Santuccis, who had walked in by mistake. They were Italian, not Mexican, but somebody had mixed them up, and anyway, I thought I should see them.

The Santucci brothers, Delfino, Ugo, and Joseph, were no longer young: they were in their late forties or so. But they had the innocent, radiant strength of young men. And their smiles! They had the smile of that pope, John Paul I, the Italian one, who lasted only thirty days. When I saw the Santuccis, I wanted to embrace them, put them on the stand; a jury would have loved them.

But they had not suffered enough. They were not hardship cases. They had gone south when the mills closed, to the south suburbs, to places like Lansing, and they had been lucky. They had gotten jobs as janitors and garbagemen, working for a township or a school district. Each Santucci now makes $20,000 a year or so, which is a big drop from the pay in the mills, but still, it is real money. The Santuccis are no fools, they know how far they have fallen. But they also know they are lucky to be in Lansing, picking up the trash.

By now I wanted to settle, and so did many in the class suit. Even Harvester did not want a trial, with these poor old men out in the courtroom staring at a jury for three months. As a Harvester lawyer said, "Even *I* felt sorry for some of these guys." And there was only so much we could win now, since the judge had knocked out a big part of our case.

Some of the workers would have taken anything: ten cents on the dollar, five cents, anything. Just so they could get it *now*. Oh sure, they were very respectful, deferential to me. "Whatever you say, Mr. Tom G." "We'll have a victory party, we'll get you drunk." "I'll kiss you, and don't worry, I don't have AIDS." They would do anything for me, all right. And trample me down if I got in their way.

There was also a crazy lunatic fringe that did not want to settle. A class action can drive you crazy. It is like a Ship of Fools.

One man, Anthony M., said, "Even if we get everything, I still want a trial." I told this man that he was one of the few who would get "everything." He spit. "With interest?" Then he laughed like Al R.

Then there was Mr. M., who sent letters in crayon, one, two, three times a week. He scrawled them on pieces of newspaper, scraps of the *Congressional Record*, or junk mail that he picked up. Wild, scrawling notes like: "$$$ *Where* the Hell is our God DAMN CHECKS$?!"

More often he would just write: "STILL WAITING."

I have many letters from Mr. M. with just two words in crayon: "STILL WAITING."

Mr. M. was an artist, with a vision of God.

Lori, our paralegal, loved Mr. M. She was an art student, and she collected his letters, and said, "Oh, Tom, look at the beautiful handiwork on this one."

I used to see him at status hearings in the back of court. He always was the same: the Bears ski cap, the windbreaker, the pipe. He said he had been a union officer once, and with that pipe, he looked normal, solid, sane, with an air of reason to him, like the first mate of a ship.

Mr. M. was about sixty now, completely unemployable. A borderline case, and then deindustrialization had pushed him over the edge. He had a pension, however, of only $240 a month. Maybe if I had that pension, I would roam the streets like a bag lady, too, tearing out scraps of paper, stalking my lawyer. For people like him, we had to lock the office doors. They wanted to break in, tear through the files, look for the secret deals we had made to sell them out.

One day Lori said, "I think the letters are getting crazier."

We all were.

I had blown it. I should never have told the men they lost $90 million. After that, some people like Mr. M. could not sleep, or just now woke up, as if they had forgotten over the Reagan years how much they had been worth once, as steelworkers.

Half of the $90 million was prejudgment interest: it was not a real out-of-pocket loss. It was a shock for me to realize how high interest rates were in the Reagan era, how rich people got so much richer, while people like Mr. M. dived for pennies in the gutter. There was a nice irony in steelworkers asking for the same interest rates.

I should never have even calculated the interest. It was just a funny number that no one takes seriously, except the workers.

The true settlement range was always $10 to $20 million, which had been set more or less by the court's rulings. I was not happy about the range, but we were not likely to get any more. So for weeks, with the judge mediating, we talked about damages, what the workers had been earning in 1977 (the time of sale), 1980 (the bankruptcy), and so forth.

When we looked at the weekly pay that the workers had been getting in 1980, I was astounded. I had a glimpse, for a second, of paradise lost.

Our expert, Mr. Terrasina, said the median pay in 1980 was $30,000 or so a year. The *median* pay, so half of them were making more.

I said, "Mr. Terrasina, it can't be."

He said, "It shocked me, too."

"How am I going to tell Harvester's lawyers?"

Mr. Terrasina said, "Look, you throw in incentive pay, overtime, all that, and those mills were paying pretty well. Nobody worked straight time. Lot of them didn't even take vacations: they took it in cash and kept on working."

That is the part I could not believe. They kept working like the Japanese, with no vacations?

I told Harvester's lawyers. "What?" they said. "You mean some of these guys were making *$40,000* a year?"

They brought in some guy from management, who said, "Mr. Geoghegan, for $40,000, *I* would have been working in that mill."

I felt embarrassed for my clients, as if they had misbehaved.

By now, Harvester was offering $11 million and saying it was the final offer. I thought, "I can't take it. This is a matter of honor." Then I caught myself: Who am I, anyway? Sir Walter Scott? The men whom I represented, they did not care about my honor.

A Harvester lawyer said, "Why don't you just get out of the way and let me make a deal with them?"

In a way, I had become the union officer, and I began to sympathize with Tony Roque. I even had a strange desire to talk to him. I had heard he had died. There was no phone number, no way to contact him, so I put out the word through some of the men that I wanted to talk to him, maybe use him as a witness.

One day, when I least expected it, I picked up the phone

and he was on the other end. We must have talked an hour and a half.

He said, "I'm ruined now. You've disgraced me, Mr. Geoghegan. You made me look like a fool."

I said, "You were the fall guy. You took the fall. Vrdolyak, the others, they walked away."

He was quiet. He said, "Ed Vrdolyak, I don't worry about him."

I said, "You depended on him, and he walked away."

"Everybody else could hide, but I couldn't hide, you see?"

He was not the first Union officer to have blown it big. He signed something, did not know what it meant. I felt sorry for him.

"You don't know what they've said about me. What my family has heard."

I knew that people said he had been bribed.

"Mr. Roque," I said, "I've been working on this case for seven years. So of course, I know more now than you could have known then."

"I'm sure you do. I'm sure you're doing a good job. And I'm sure you want to win because you want to get paid, don't you?"

I said, "Look . . ."

"I know what you're going to say. I know, you're real noble and all of that. But look, Mr. Geoghegan, if you win, it's a big feather in your cap, isn't it? You'll be a big man. You'll be a hero. Great thing for you, as a young lawyer . . ."

"Not so great," I said.

"But I look like . . . what do I look like? You know what people say about *me*?"

"O.K.," I said, "then help us. Come testify. Say you didn't know what Harvester was doing . . ."

"I didn't know? I didn't know? A blind man could have seen what they were doing. They were trying to cheat us."

I could tell Roque was trembling with anger, and I admit to feeling bad when he slammed down the phone.

At some point in the settlement discussions, I decided to leave it up to Frank. He was almost seventy now, and I figured he knew when to hold them and when to fold them. Thank God, he folded them.

We settled for $14.8 million. He called it, and he made the right call.

My friend Joel, a lawyer, said, "I'm glad for you, Tom. I'm glad it was your client and not you who had to decide."

I admit, $14.8 million is not enough. But it was not such a bad settlement either, for the case we still had left against Harvester. The $14.8 million was more or less all that Harvester owed the workers up to the point of sale (I do not count all the money being paid to us by the PBGC, which Harvester had also owed).

Even so, to Harvester's horror, Frank wanted a vote. He had promised people a vote for seven years, a big monster meeting to vote a settlement up or down, and nothing else mattered to him as much as that vote.

The Harvester lawyers said to the judge, "This is not supposed to be a democracy. They're supposed to be the class representatives. They're supposed to decide for the class, not let the class decide for themselves."

I stood up and said to the judge, "This is America. Here the people rule. We don't make decisions for them . . ."

I stopped in my speech. I was being ridiculous.

Judge Moran said that we were the class representatives and we should settle for the class. But he was wise enough to let us hold the vote anyway, and he probably knew how it would turn out.

The meeting was on Valentine's Day 1988. I had never seen such a crowd, not at any of our previous rallies, and we hardly had given any notice. There were 700 people or more, spilling out the door of the Local 65 hall, which we had borrowed. Union halls in the eighties do not see that kind of crowd. They had risen from the grave, these people: the deindustrialized, coming for their last vote.

I asked Frank nervously as I looked out at the crowd, "What do you think?"

He said, "It's hard to read."

"Hard to read? There are 700 people out there," I thought.

They did not clap when I stood up to explain the settlement.

They sat there stonily. There was some clapping, hesitant clapping, only once, when I said, "I'll try to get the money tax-free."

I could not tell how angry they were. I began to defend the settlement, not merely explain it, but defend it, passionately. I asked them to look at what we had done: we had taken on Harvester, Kirkland and Ellis, with a case nobody thought we could win.

And I kept thinking, "And they were right, too. They had us beat. We ran out of gas. That's why we're settling, men."

I did not say *that*, of course. I did try to tell them how hard it was to go up against a big law firm, with many lawyers, etc.

"Shoot 'em," a man yelled. About 400 of the 700 people laughed.

Then I began to praise the judge.

"Give it to Judge McGarr," a man stood up, shouting. "What did that mean?" I thought. He said it again: "Give it to Judge McGarr." Later he came over, dead drunk, grinning. "I'm the asshole who kept saying, 'Give it to Judge McGarr.' " He started to throw his arms around me.

Frank said, "You can start the voting . . ." and the meeting seemed to stop, midair, and people ran from their seats, and it was over, like that. Nobody waited to hear the questions.

The vote was overwhelming, 583–75. And it was a secret ballot, with observers. I realized later, we had not had to "argue" for the settlement, we just had to throw it out there like a piece of raw red meat and get out of the way.

But hundreds ran up to the stage, no one to thank me, or congratulate me, but they kept touching me. Waving hands. "Over here . . ." "Hey, hey . . ." There was a reporter saying, "What's the meaning of all this today?" "Well," I said . . . but the men pushed him away, I could not get to him.

I was crouching over the workers. I had crawled out to the end of the stage so I could hear them. When they came in the hall, we had handed out sheets to people so they could see how much money they'd be getting, but they kept coming up, to have me say it to them, face to face.

"What am I getting?"

"How many years did you work?"

"Seventeen."

"$8,340."

"Is that *all*?" His face fell.

Some were disgusted, others were puzzled.

A man held up a bottle of liquor to me. He said, "You drink?"

The man next to him said, "Mr. Geoghegan, he wants to know if you drink hard liquor."

Meanwhile, all this time, I could see Lori, our paralegal, talking to reporters. Since she could not bring the reporters to me or Frank, she took them to Mr. M., who was happy to talk to them. "My God," I gasped, but I was swept away by the crowd.

Later a reporter from the *Tribune* said, "Is this settlement really *enough*?"

I gulped. "Well, yes . . ."

"Look," he said, "the most anyone's getting is $17,000. That's not even a year's income at the mill, is it?"

"What kind of story would this be?" I thought. I remembered that in law school I had wanted to do a "newspaper case." Well, now I had a "newspaper case."

The next day in the *Tribune*, there was my picture on the front page. The back of my head, anyway. I was crouching over these poor men, who were looking up to me, eyes raised, beseeching. I seemed to be patting them on the head.

I looked at the picture and felt sick.

In the story, the workers, whose cause I had championed, were saying, as I recall:

"Is that all we're getting?"

"Boy, I'm disappointed."

"It's not very much, is it?"

That night, after the stories, I went out with J., my then girlfriend. We ended up by accident in a lesbian bar, and they kicked us out and we went someplace else.

J. leaned over and said, in her most silken voice, "I like the way you're handling the press."

"You do?" I said.

She said, "I wonder if they know down there, your clients, that they're a liberal cause up here on the North Side."

I just looked at her and was so touched, and I wanted to marry her.

Oh, J., it was just a liberal cause to you because you were dating me. It was not a liberal cause to anyone else.

Meanwhile, most people were not sure whether to congratulate me or not, although most did. Some said, "It was a good thing, wasn't it?" and waited for an answer. At the drugstore, I ran into my neighbor Dan, a community organizer, who said to me, cooly, "I guess it's the best you could do," and I just stood there and let him condescend to me.

Most people on the North Side thought it was good because my picture was in the paper. If my picture was in the paper, it could not be bad.

I knew that under the existing state of the law the settlement was a good one, and we were saving anywhere from two to five years of pointless litigation. Yet every once in a while, for a minute, I felt like Lord Jim jumping off the *Patna*, with the Pilgrims in steerage. Before I left the meeting on Sunday, I went over to Mr. M. and tried to explain to him, personally, why we had to settle. I said we could not take the risk of losing the $14.8 million, not so much in a trial (that did not worry me) as in the Court of Appeals. I said the case law could change and we would get nothing.

I said to him, "Do you really want to take that risk?"

He said, "I take a risk every time I get out of bed in the morning. That's life. Taking risks."

I thought, for a moment, "My God, he's right."

Now came the strangest part of the case, following the big vote.

Wild rumors swept the class that we had signed away the pensions: the money that people had been receiving for seven years from the PBGC. It was absurd, of course. The settlement had no effect on that money. But the more we denied it, the stronger the rumor became. It was frightening to get a dozen screaming phone calls *a day*, and nothing I could say made any difference. Everyone else had cheated them. So why not me? Everybody had a price. Everything is fixed. If I denied there was a fix, that only proved there was a fix. My God, everyone else had lied. Why did I have to lie, too?

Many people, who had once been middle-class, who had once had dignity, became irrational.

A man, Ron P., called up and said, "The way I read it, this settlement is giving up the benefits I already got."

"Well, it isn't."

"It sure as hell is."

"It's not."

"Are you my lawyer?"

"I'm the class lawyer."

"Well, who's *my* lawyer?"

"I'm your lawyer."

"Well, you tell me one thing, but I read here another thing."

"Well, you're wrong."

"Yeah, I don't think so."

"Well, you are."

By now, we were screaming at each other, and Lori walked in and sighed, "Oh, Tom, how do you have the patience to deal with them?"

People had been calling up to scream at her, too.

Judi, my associate, said, "You know, I don't think I like some of our clients."

We all felt guilty: we were yelling at the poor.

I thought that somewhere the Reaganites, cool, aloof, must be laughing at us. Had this really once been a labor movement?

The settlement, I believed, had not been much, just a pittance, not enough to change anyone's life, and I thought people would almost sniff at it. Instead, the men of Wisconsin Steel sometimes begged.

A man called up and said, "Is it true I'm getting some money?"

"Yes."

"Coming in a few months, is that right?"

"Yes."

"Then I wonder, Attorney, could you make me a little loan?"

I heard from the wives, too, many of them divorced now. One called up and asked, "How can I get his money?"

I said, "When he applies for it, then you can take it up in the divorce case."

"You don't know him," she said. "He won't even apply for it."

"Of course he will."

"No, he won't. Just to spite me and the kids. He won't even apply for it."

In fact, some people would not sign the claim form, which contained a general release of Harvester. No release, they would never sign a release. I think some people like Mr. M. could not let go of the case. Frank said, disgusted, "If you don't want the settlement, don't send in for it."

Sometimes I think Mr. M. was right and we should never have settled. We should have kept the case going forever: no settlement. If we had never settled, I would never have had to pat people on the head and say, "This is it, the steel industry is over." By settling, I cheated them, I cheated myself. People like Mr. M. wanted just one day in court, just to scream, just to grab us all, as the Ancient Mariner grabbed the Wedding Guest and made him listen to his story. "I fear thee, Ancient Mariner," the jury would have said. And it would be Mr. M., and he would have held them there, for three months of trial, with his glittering eye. That is all Mr. M., all some of these steelworkers, really wanted.

But not all of them. Al R. voted for the settlement.

Even Mr. M. gave up at last, made his claim, took his money, stopped sending us letters. "It's sad, isn't it?" Lori said. I told her we would take all his letters and publish them one day in a book, *The Wisconsin Steel Story*, by Mr. M., and this seemed to cheer her up.

I never knew how Frank put up with them.

He said, "If they came in here, if they were mad about the settlement, I just handed them the Roque agreement. I said, 'Read it, that's what we're up against.' "

He said, "That always quieted them down."

Frank was no longer the innocent rank-and-filer whom I had first met seven years before. Save Our Jobs had become . . . well, like a real union. We all end up staggering under the burdens of office, defending settlements of $14.8 million.

Yes, I always knew it was a good settlement. Besides, we had to get some money to people, as Judge Moran once said. And, I thought, before everyone in the class was dead. This was a real risk, too. Eight years after the mill closed, hundreds were already dead. People began to feel haunted, cursed, doomed to die, their foreheads sealed when Wisconsin Steel went down.

Most were happy with anything. Everything was lost now. The steel industry *was* over.

Not even Frank Lumpkin could save it. A reporter once said to me, "In this whole history of scoundrels, he was the one good man, wasn't he?" Yes, but it would be romantic to think one good man could save South Chicago. After all, one good man did not save Sodom and Gomorrah either.

When the case was over, Frank said to me, "I never thought we were going to win."

What? I could not believe it. Why had he put me, and Mr. M., and the others, through all of this, then?

"The main thing was," he said, "just to stand up. You see a man like Salinas? All his life, he and Williams, they'd just accept whatever they get.

"But those guys, I mean . . . they changed. I mean, we went out and marched, and we fought the thing, and that's all I wanted to do. I just wanted to teach people they could fight."

I am not sure myself that Salinas changed all that much. He was the guy who always said, "Whatever you say, Mr. Tom G." But if Frank wants to think he changed, O.K., then let him.

Frank changed me, anyway, or at least as much as he changed Salinas. Sometimes I saw myself, in the case, as a hero. I would bring justice to the city. Which is a joke. I cannot even bring justice to my own life, much less the whole city of Chicago. And the settlement, $14.8 million, was not nearly enough to be the justice I wanted, romantically.

I could not bring justice to the city, then. But I did not make a total fool of myself either, because of Frank, because of the judge, and yes, I hate to admit it, even because of the Harvester lawyers.

For the next few months after the settlement, I kept waking up and thinking I was free. The case was over, and I could go to New York now, or someplace else, and do whatever I liked.

But then I found I could not, and I am still here, still practicing law.

Years from now, I will still be here, an old man, flipping through old press clippings. The picture of the back of my head. Another article saying "Attorney Quashes Settlement Rumor."

Maybe I am still here because Frank Lumpkin is still here. Frank is old now, over seventy, and he has stopped riding his motorbike. But he is organizing a new Save Our Jobs, a union of the unemployed, and they are trying, against all odds, to get a steel mill going in South Chicago. Frank still sees everything, even South Chicago, in the light of resurrection.

I wish to God he would give up.

Still, I notice, with each year, as I continue living in Chicago, I seem to move further and further north. Up to Evanston, to bigger homes, bigger lawns, where my friends are. While the Santuccis and my clients seem to move further and further south. Down to Lansing, etc. As if in the city there were a Big Bang in the early eighties when the mills closed, and ever since then, the two sides of the city, North and South, like two galaxies, have been hurtling away from each other, faster and faster.

Now, on the North Side, when I walk along the beach, I cannot even see South Chicago, except on a clear day. Even then, I just barely see the mills and the smokestacks far, far to the south, and the whole steel industry like a ship slowly sinking into the waves. I think of the men of Wisconsin Steel who are still on it, who could not get off.

It was a shipwreck. And nobody planned it, it just happened.

CHAPTER 6

Rank and File

When I walk around the city, I can't tell if I'm seeing union members or not.

Sometimes, at dawn, I think I see old steelworkers sitting in the court cafeteria. I think I recognize one or two of them. Now they've become clerks or guards, and they're down here at six-thirty in the morning, two hours before the job starts, still keeping steelworker hours. They smoke cigarettes and sip coffee, and sit with the old women with the bouffant hairdos, and it's this quiet hour, especially in winter, when it's still dark, an hour of darkness, a precious time, when people are so gentle. And getting on the El early, and going downtown, I feel like a child stealing down the stairs to see them . . . and no one else is up yet, and I could be waking up in the Rockies at dawn, on a mountain trail, I feel so far from the world, except the air is full of cigarette smoke.

It's 8 p.m., and I'm in a bar. It's one of those chic city bars, up around Armitage and Halsted. And on the walls, there are old photographs, pictures from the 1930s, or before, of workers and mills and stockyards, the old Carl Sandburg Chicago. Pictures of coke, and ash, and hissing rivers.

Now all the coke is in Lincoln Park. I sip white wine, and

look at the photographs, at the pale, haunted faces, staring out of the past. I think, "What clients I would have had then."

The workers look down at me from the photographs. Some of them are children.

If I go to the Hancock, up to the 95th floor, I can look west over the city and see streetlights, in straight lines, blasting out into the suburbs, out to where the rank and file live. The lines are so straight, they're almost frightening, like the lines on a chart when the patient's heart has stopped beating.

Some writers claim we're at "the End of History." Most of them don't put it so pompously or mean it literally. But they do mean that the old nineteenth-century problem of the "working class" has been solved, at least in the Western industrial countries, and there will hardly be any politics. And not much voting. And indeed, there's nothing to vote about, since the problem that was "History" has now been solved.

Looking out from up here, I think maybe it *is* over. Looking at the lines, perfectly straight, I think of all the people out there watching TV.

And not just TV. But cable TV, satellite TV, wide-screen TV. It's as if every home is its own little bar. Its own global village. Why would anyone, now, leave the village for the city? In fact, didn't that start all the trouble two hundred years ago?

This is the kind of thing you think about when you're a labor lawyer and haven't seen a worker for days.

Is there "class" in America? To me, it's such a stupid question. A *hopeless* question.

Unfortunately, I'm obsessed with it.

This past year, I've been reading *Huckleberry Finn* and *Moby Dick*, and while doing so, I've had this idea that most American writers, like Twain and Melville, go nuts thinking about this question. Is there "class" in America? Impossible even to discuss, without seeming weird. Impossible to write a book about. It's the book they'd all like to write, but none of them can. And they try, and try, and after a while, they go a little nuts, like Twain, or just stop writing, like Melville. Sometimes it's put not as a question of "class" but as one of "fraternity." But isn't it the same question? Except no one really knows what the question is; or knowing what it is, everyone is helpless in the face of it.

Maybe it's better to ask, "Why do people wear union windbreakers?"

I've thought about this a lot since I came to Chicago. Out here, west of Ashland Avenue, everyone has a windbreaker. Some say "Roadway," some say "St. Rita's," and some say "Local 65." Why would anyone wear one that says "Local 65"?

. I'm a labor lawyer, and I don't know.

This is no light decision either. You have to live in that windbreaker from October to May. Eight months of darkness in a windbreaker that says "Local 65."

One could say: Oh, what's the big deal? So what? Maybe it's a spare. Maybe the other one, "St. Rita's," is at the cleaners. It's not meant necessarily as a statement about the End of History.

Yet every time I see one, I want to go up to the guy and say, "Look, I'm a labor lawyer, and I'd just like to know why you are wearing this."

But I can't do this. I can't just go up to them on the street.

Lately, I've been representing the Carpenters. Friends call me up for dinner, and I say, "I can't, the Carpenters are coming over tonight."

They're shocked. "You mean you're rehabbing?"

"No, they're my clients."

"Well, ask them what they charge."

Ray S., who came to see me, was not a carpenter in the literal sense but a millwright. A millwright is a troubleshooter, a man who can work twenty-four hours straight repairing a blast furnace or a moving part of a steel mill.

Ray was from Munster, Indiana, and was in his fifties: bald, solid-looking, an ex-sergeant who still might pass for one, at first glance. He and his friends had founded or started a millwrights' local in the early 1970s. Then the millwrights' local became part of the United Brotherhood of Carpenters. It was one of five local unions in the Northwest Indiana District Council.

Ray didn't hold any office in his local, but as one of the

founders, he was like the vestryman of a parish church. He was worried about what was happening in the District Council, and he wanted to see a lawyer.

For years, the Northwest Indiana District Council had been peaceful and democratic, like a Swiss canton. The members could vote for their business agents. This was an important right, because business agents assigned the jobs. They could also vote for the secretary-treasurer, who was the chief executive officer of the District Council.

For years, the men knew each other, elected each other. Men passed back and forth from the rank and file. The secretary-treasurer was Jim Donella. He kept the dues low, and would personally do the books, and would stay late at night to account for every nickel that was spent.

Then suddenly, in 1986, the International Union put the District Council in "trusteeship," or "supervision." In a trusteeship a lower or subordinate body like a District Council loses for a time the right of self-government. The members can't vote during this time. The International Union makes all the decisions.

The International Union told Donella he had to resign as an elected officer, and he could now serve only at the discretion of the International. Then, a few months later, the International told Donella he should get out. No reason was given.

Then the International changed the bylaws. First, it doubled the assessment, which is a form of dues, from 2 percent to 4 percent of the members' income. This tiny District Council, which had only 3,000 members, was now awash with money, with a revenue of roughly $2 million a year. Second, the International put in a new man, Joe Manley, as secretary-treasurer, and changed the election rules. Under the new rules, the members lost most of their voting rights, including the right to vote for their business agents and the right to vote for the secretary-treasurer.

I said, "How could you just let that happen?"

Ray said, "We were told this was just a temporary thing. We were told, if we just kept quiet, then things would go back to the way they were."

I asked him to explain the voting rules again.

He said, "Well, we lost the right to vote for business agents. Now Manley appoints them. And we can't vote for Manley either."

"How does he get elected?"

"The business agents elect him."

"I thought he appointed the business agents."

"Well, what happens is, he appoints the guys on the executive board to be the business agents, and then they vote for him to be secretary-treasurer."

I got the idea. And nobody fired a shot. People were scared. The officers all resigned. Donella asked the union lawyer, Bernie, if there was any way to fight the trusteeship, and Bernie said, "I think you better cooperate with these guys."

"Where's Donella now?" I said.

"Hawaii. He got out."

Then one day Ray went to a seminar in Indianapolis at the Department of Labor. He came back all excited, because he said that he'd been told by someone at the seminar that the members did have the right to vote. I think Ray misunderstood. That's not what the Labor Department usually says, but I suppose someone could have told him that.

It's still a little depressing that in America people have to go to seminars to find out they have the right to vote.

I met the men secretly, at night, at a restaurant called Spiaggia's, next to Wolf Lake. Now, Wolf Lake is down by the mills, and it's the most toxic-looking pond of water I've ever seen. Spiaggia's is right next to it, on a little beach.

It was Monday night, and the restaurant was dark and almost empty, except for four men at a table. The only light seemed to be coming off the lasagna I had ordered. It was glowing just enough so I could take some notes.

It was in the fall. Two of the men were in T-shirts, sweating, pounding out beer after beer. Ray and his friend Dan sipped coffee.

At first I thought they were upset about the dues, which had been doubled. I kept saying, "We've got to do something about the dues."

No one spoke. Then Dan said, "You don't seem to get it. We don't care about the money. We want our voting rights back."

I was a little embarrassed. I said, "If we choke off the money, that'll help us."

Dan leaned over, close to me, and said, "We're going to hire you. But we want results."

I said, "Of course."

"Your job is to get back our *voting* rights, O.K.? Forget the dues."

"Yeah, forget the dues," someone said.

We walked outside. One of the men said, "You know, my wife has opposed me all my life. This is the first thing I've ever done where she's been on my side."

I've never worried about the Teamsters, but the Carpenters case was scary. I heard this story from Ray:

One night, some millwrights had gone down to the District Council. They met with Manley and some of his people.

Dan kept asking, "When do we get our voting rights back?"

Manley's people said there was nothing they could do, and they started to leave. Dan stepped in front of the door, put his foot on it, and said, "When do we get our voting rights back?"

I asked, "Did anything happen?"

Ray said, "No."

Now, in Chicago, that kind of story wouldn't bother me. Some people think Chicago is a tough town, but compared with Indiana . . . well, it's like Burlington, Vermont. And if there is trouble in Chicago, it's Indiana where they dump the body, where it's so routine, at least around Gary or Hammond, that people don't even notice for a couple of weeks.

Ray and Dan were the only men who thought they could risk signing the letters I wrote to the International, to start the legal process. As soon as they did, they were both fired from their jobs.

About this time, there was a murder of a whole family down in Indiana, and one Monday, Ray called me up to discuss something, and then mentioned in passing, "The phone was ringing off the hook here all weekend. It was that murder in the paper. The guys in the local, they thought it must be us."

In November, the millwrights' local voted to hire me as their attorney. I was to be paid $15,000 to get back the voting rights.

But the local's president, Gene S., had voted against this. He was a business agent appointed by Manley, and though once he had been a friend of Ray's, now he was on the other side.

The question then arose whether the vote was proper if Gene S. hadn't approved.

The International Union sent a letter saying the local's vote to spend the money, even if the vote was almost unanimous, would be an "embezzlement" of the local's funds, as if the men had voted to "embezzle" money from themselves. The lawyer for the District Council said we better return the money, or the members and I would be in serious trouble.

Then the prosecutor for Lake County, Indiana, sent the local the following letter: If the members didn't return the money, he would prosecute them for embezzlement.

Ray said I'd better come down and talk to the men, who were wavering. We agreed to meet at a certain restaurant, and then I was supposed to follow him to the Union hall. But we each went to different places, and when I didn't show up, and it was getting late, Ray went off to the meeting.

Meanwhile, I was calling Ray's house, then Dan's house, and finally I got Dan's wife. She said, "Where *are* you? You're supposed to be at this meeting."

I said, "I'm lost down here. I don't know where the hall is."

"Well, I'll meet you, and you follow my car."

I followed Mrs. D. to Porter, Indiana. She then began pointing to a gas station, or what used to be a gas station. The millwrights had bought it and turned it into a Union hall.

As I waved goodbye to Mrs. D., I thought I could smell gasoline, but I wasn't sure.

Now, I'd not met the members of this local, but I was expecting a hero's welcome. They were my clients. But no one was expecting me to come, and union meetings were secret. No outsiders. Secrecy oaths.

A few millwrights were at the door, but they wouldn't let me in. No one had told them I was coming.

I said, "I'm your lawyer."

They looked at me very suspiciously.

Then one of the officers came out. He seemed frightened.

"You can't come in. You'll have to wait out here."

I said, "Where are Ray and Dan?"

"They're in the meeting."

I waited outside, and finally Ray came out. "Boy," he said, "am I glad to see you . . ."

I wondered when they had converted this place from a gas station.

Ray said, "Things aren't going too good in there." He now told me, for the first time, about the prosecutor's letter, which I hadn't known about. Then Manley had called in some of the local's officers, who had been friendly to us, and got them to sign a document repudiating the vote to hire me.

Everything had collapsed, and every one had "recanted," as if Indiana were a Stalinist state.

But Ray said I was going to be allowed to speak anyway. As soon as the meeting was over "officially," the men would stay around and listen "unofficially."

There were about fifty men in the room, and some of them were young kids, with long hair, who looked like they had driven here on bikes from a Grateful Dead concert. Yet they were shy and polite, and very much like their dads, who sat next to them on the folding chairs.

I always give the same speech at a union hall. I never have to prepare. It's not "canned" in the sense that I use the same words. What's "canned" is the emotion, which is never what I really feel.

At least, I've never stood up there and said:

"I don't know if I want to be a labor lawyer."

"I wish I lived in New York."

"I feel like, in my own personal life, I'm doomed . . . and I'm trapped . . ."

No, I can't get up there and say that to a group of millwrights. Instead, I give a big speech about having hope, and how justice is on our side, and how we can never be defeated. The main thing is to train your voice, and get it deep, like a radio announcer's. A Teamsters lawyer told me this.

But the prosecutor's letter had really upset me, in part because I hadn't read it and it was handed to me as I came in.

So I picked it up and said, "This is kindergarten stuff."

I said this because I was scared, not because I was brave. As soon as I said it, I wished I hadn't.

Then some people clapped. Then some people stood up and clapped. Then everyone stood up and clapped. There had been a second or two when the men just looked at me and time had stopped. I would like to know, one day, what was going on in that second or two of time. But at any rate, we got past it.

Then I went on to tell them to have hope, and how they did have the right to vote.

Jim, the vice president, stood up. He had signed the document disavowing me. He was a short man, about fifty, very big shoulders.

"That's all I need to hear . . . I've heard enough. Look, I signed this thing. But I was intimidated. I admit it. They intimidated me. But I'm taking my name off this thing . . . I'm ready to fight . . ."

"That's right . . ."

"Yeah . . ."

There was one old man who spoke against the crowd. He said, "We have to obey our Union president . . ."

Someone said, "We're the members."

He turned, furious, and said, "The Union Constitution controls this thing . . . Look, Bernie Mamet, who's our lawyer, he told me, 'Bill, there's a lot of power in this book.' "

He faced all of us and held up the Union Constitution.

One of the men stood up and said, "Well, the Constitution I follow is the Constitution of the United States."

Loud cheers.

The old man turned to me now and said, "*You* . . . you lawyers are all alike . . . You come down here and say, 'We're going to win,' and you don't know if we're going to win or not."

After the meeting, Ray came over and said, "Boy, I'm sure glad we have you as our lawyer."

I said, "Ray, I haven't done anything yet."

He said, "We could have had more than fifty guys here, but we didn't tell anyone you were coming. We didn't want Manley to come over and break it up."

He meant this in a nice way, but I felt weird. Being sneaked into a gas station in Indiana.

Driving back, I thought this over and realized I was forty years old . . .

Then one day, like a mysterious stranger, a black man named Willie Shepperson drives into Indiana. Shepperson is an organizer from the International, but he's turned rebel. He tells the men that the top officers have lost $95 million of the Union's general fund in loans to construction projects that went sour: projects that their in-laws, uncles, or old pals had stakes in. News articles have appeared. The officers sued their financial consultants, in shock, *shock*, that they'd been told to give all this money to such people.

Shepperson is driving around the country and telling people. Ray and Dan bring him to my office.

"What do you think?" they say.

"I don't know."

Shepperson seems possessed, brilliant, eloquent. He walks into union halls and stands before the men, all white men, and he's telling them to throw off their chains. This is his life's mission now.

Now, for the first time, someone has come to Indiana and explained that what is happening here is also happening around the country. Not just in Indiana. But in Michigan, Ohio, California. In every state, the International is slamming the District Councils into trusteeship, raising the dues, putting in their loyalists like Manley, and then stripping people of their right to vote.

And until Shepperson arrived, we didn't know why. But now it's all clear. Because having blown $95 million, the officers of the International are worried. For the first time, they could be thrown out of office at the next convention in 1991. Now, normally, it would be impossible for the top officers of an international union to lose. But these guys, having just blown

$95 million, at least have to worry. So they're taking over the
Districts, putting in their friends, and stripping people of their
voting rights, just so all or nearly all of them will keep their
jobs.

So Ray and Dan call a meeting in Porter for every carpenter
in America to come and hear what Shepperson has to say. They
invite carpenters from Ohio, from Michigan, from California.
For two years now, there have been carpenters running into
each other, more or less by accident, and one guy says, "Hey,
we're in trusteeship."

And the other guy says, "That's odd, we're in trusteeship,
too."

So people in Michigan, people in Ohio, get into cars and
drive to Porter, Indiana, to a Holiday Inn, where Shepperson
is going to talk. Ray and Dan send out letters to various locals,
and it's as if the District Councils in the Midwest were like the
Thirteen Colonies, and Ray and Dan were setting up Committees of Correspondence, just groups of men writing letters to
each other and trying to figure out what the British will be
doing next.

Ann (my friend the economist) is in town for a day from the
East. She says, "Do you want to have dinner?"

I say, "Do you want to go to a union meeting in Indiana?"

"Where?"

"Porter."

She says she will. Amy, a lawyer in our office, comes along,
and we start out on Holy Thursday to Porter.

My car breaks down on the Skyway over South Chicago. We
get off the road, and by luck we see a garage.

Although the mechanic is about to close, an old man (his
uncle) is standing around, and tells his nephew, "Take care of
these people. I like the looks of them."

I've given up on the meeting in Indiana, but Ann wants to
go on.

"Where are you going?" the old man says.

"Porter, Indiana."

"I'll take you there."

It's almost an hour's drive, but he insists on doing it, so Ann, Amy, and I get in the car.

Before going on the Skyway, we drive a few blocks, and he tells us about his neighborhood: the steel mills, the plant closings, the stories of South Chicago, etc.

"And the worst one," he says, "is Wisconsin Steel . . . In fact, do you have a little time? I'd like to drive you over and show you the old Wisconsin Steel."

"I've seen it," I say. I'm worried we'll be late.

He tells us the whole story of Wisconsin Steel, but finally we get to the meeting.

Shepperson is talking to about 200 people, and saying how at the International each District Council is seen as a "franchise" and given out to certain guys who are the "franchisees." The millwrights, mostly young, motorcyclists, listen with respect.

As I listen to Shepperson, I decide to take notes. I ask one of the men at the door (his name is Rippey), "Rippey, am I going to be allowed to speak?"

"I don't know. That'll be up to Ray."

"Does Ray even know I'm back here?"

I seem to be in this meeting secretly. The millwrights watch me take notes, and this makes me feel odder, like I might be a spy.

Shepperson is saying, "Everyone tells me, 'You better watch your back.' "

Then Dan introduces the special "guests."

Dan Mulford, a local officer from Ohio, tells how Ohio was "restructured."

Tony Michael, a business agent in Michigan, tells how Michigan was "restructured."

Tony Michael says, "And in Michigan, they say we're just getting what they've got in Indiana. And they say, 'It's working beautiful down there.'

"Well, I was a business agent, and I fought it. And I was fired. And I wasn't just fired as a business agent. I was denied my employment as a carpenter.

"But I haven't forgotten my skills as a carpenter. I'm not as fast as I used to be. But I'm learning again. I used to be an officer. Well, now I'm rank and file. And I want to tell you something. When you elect your delegates, be sure you send rank and file guys who won't take any jobs and who they can't get to. And now I'm running as a rank-and-filer. And it's got to be like Solidarity in Poland. That's the only way we can get back our Union."

And at the mention of Poland, someone shouted, "Where's our democracy?"

"Yeah."

"Yeah."

And after Tony Michael, every man who stands up talks about Poland or the Berlin Wall. I'm shocked to hear all this discussion of Eastern Europe, but these men in Indiana have completely absorbed it. TV, like History, goes very fast, and these guys are way ahead of me, who's reading it in *The New York Times* and not really keeping up. Wide-screen TV, cable TV, satellite TV . . . down here, in Indiana, they're ready to vote.

Now Manley stands up, and I gasp, because he's been here all along, without my knowing it, as Shepperson is describing him as a "franchisee" and a puppet on a string.

Manley is wobbly, like he's taken some blows. He's weaving, like a boxer.

He's trying to talk, and it's hard to hear him, people are shouting.

He says, hoarsely, groaning, like he's dying, "All I ask is . . . all I ask is . . . Tell the truth."

He says it again, "Tell the truth."

"Tell the truth about what?" someone whispers.

"This is pathetic," another man says.

Manley keeps saying, "Tell the truth."

"He's lost it."

A man stands up and says, "Joe, I've known you for a long time. Joe, you got me a job in this local . . . and, Joe, I *love* you. But, Joe"—he says this very slowly—"don't take away our voting rights."

Another millwright stands up and says, "Can you promise right here to give us back our voting rights?"

Joe says, "It's not up to me . . . it's up to the International.

The International has to approve. First vice president has to approve any change like that . . ."

He's nervous, squirming. "Am I right, Willie?"

Shepperson looks at him with contempt.

"Am I right?"

Shepperson says nothing.

I think how Manley might not be such a bad guy, once we beat him.

He says, almost begging, "Look, you tell me who you want as your business agent, and I'll appoint them."

Harsh laughter.

Five rows in back of me, a millwright stands up. He walks halfway to the front, and says, in a shaky voice, "Joe Manley."

Manley looks at him.

"Joe Manley," he says again.

"What?"

"Do you know what Thomas Jefferson stands for?"

Now, the man is not drunk, although he's clearly had a beer or two.

Manley says, "Uh . . . I don't get your question."

The member says again, slowly, "Do you know what Thomas Jefferson stands for?"

Manley thinks about it. "No."

"Well, Thomas Jefferson . . . stands for all men are created equal . . . and for liberty . . . and for . . . and for . . . NOT FUCKING THE PEOPLE."

Everyone cheers.

On the way home, Ann asks if this is what being a labor lawyer is like.

"Certainly not," I say.

I had tried to give a speech at the end, but I could hardly talk. My voice was gone, like Joe Manley's, and I was coming down with a cold.

But who cares? Out there, among the carpenters, it was like tongues of fire were on their heads.

And now, driving back, I think how often, at the end of these things, I feel like a fake. But tonight, everything's great: the men, the solidarity, I don't even hate television too much . . .

and sometimes when I drive up the Ryan, and see Chicago all lit up, stunning, and think of Indiana, Illinois, and Wisconsin, big empty states orbiting around the city like dead planets, I'm almost . . . happy, because I've seen something, it's out there, even if I have to be sneaked into a gas station to get a look.

And I think of what Rilke and the other poets have said, for centuries:

You must change your life.

I really do feel this way for a short time. I go wandering into bookstores for several nights.

CHAPTER 7

In the Cage

Sometimes I represent Teamster dissidents who get beaten up at the Union hall. Oh yes, really beaten up, like Marlon Brando in *On the Waterfront*. It is just like the movies, and in a way, even the goons, or the smarter goons, are weirdly conscious of their connection to kitsch. There are moments when I expect all of us to break into little half-smiles. That is the problem with the Teamsters: Hoffa, the Mob, et al. have made the Teamsters into an icon of pop culture, like Elvis. It is hard to take it seriously. Sometimes I have to remind myself, the client is really bleeding. He is really at the hospital. His wife, hysterical, is really calling on the phone.

I am in a network of lawyers who take these cases. I have a friend in New York whose client, a Teamster dissident, was recently shot and killed at work. The Union even has a group called BLAST, a private army of goons. The men from BLAST, who are all "business agents," or BAs, employed by the Union, raid meetings of dissidents, turn over tables, try to start fights, until the cops come, break it up, and blame the trouble—evenhandedly, the way cops do—on both sides.

At first, I did not know how to handle it. Horrified, when a man was beaten, I used to take him to the U.S. Attorney, the FBI, but now I do not bother. At least in Chicago, they have better things to do: prosecute judges, aldermen, clerks who take five-dollar bribes. With the FBI, we always get two twenty-six-year-old kids (and any street cop in his forties is better than a twenty-six-year-old kid: at least the cop can track down a license plate). Here in Chicago it seems even the Assistant U.S. Attorney is twenty-six, twenty-seven. The kids are polite. They nod gravely. They say, "We take this very seriously." And: "If it happens again, please call us."

Right, sure: if it happens again, we sure will.

To me, a labor lawyer, a beating at a union hall is a political act. It's like Kristallnacht, the rise of fascism, etc. To the cops, it's just a punch in the nose. Two guys in a fight. And to the feds, well . . . the feds want to see some dead bodies, and my clients are only bleeding.

Actually, the first time a client was beaten, I did not take it too seriously. The guy could still walk, and we had filed a civil suit, for assault and battery. I told his wife, "Don't worry, we have a suit now, so they won't touch him, not while the suit is pending." Being from Harvard Law, I knew all about this kind of thing. Then, a week later, one December night, she called up, from Rush–St. Luke, where Bill had been taken, unconscious and bleeding. He had been beaten up at the Union hall: it was the night they handed out the free Christmas turkeys. I came home late at night and found her message on the machine.

Thank God I hadn't put any joke on the tape.

Bill, bleeding, was a member of Teamsters for a Democratic Union, or TDU. There are today about 10,000 or so members of TDU (out of 1.6 million Teamsters). TDU was like Miners for Democracy or Steelworkers Fight Back, but there was one difference: in the Teamsters, unlike the Mineworkers, there weren't any rank-and-file elections at the international level. So TDU could not even dream: there was no hope, no chance of a total reform. It was like being in a French Resistance that could never end. Yet these TDU members kept on going, with hope or not, and if you talked to them, most of them would say, "We're the *real* Union. We're the *real* Teamsters Union." They would go to every local meeting. They would sit there in the front row. In Chicago, they'd lose, and lose, but sometimes they'd win, and they'd keep coming back, getting up on their feet, screaming, forcing the Teamsters to be a real union, whether it wanted to be or not. They were heroes, all of them. I wish I could have represented them all the time.

But now I have to confess: I didn't have much to do with TDU. Sometimes at parties I might talk it up with friends just to make my practice seem a bit more interesting. But in fact, when I first began to sue the Teamsters in the early 1980s, there were no dissidents or dead bodies. My clients then were just suburbanites who rooted for the Chicago Bears and weren't heroes at all . . . just thousands of Teamsters who were being fired, dumped on the street, the detritus of "deregulation."

In steel, it was the dollar, the deficit, deindustrialization . . . and in trucking, it was "deregulation." Under Carter and Reagan, the big carriers were no longer protected. The industry was opened up to the "gypsies," the small owner-operators. The old Teamster order collapsed. Thousands of firms closed. Old men, who had been Teamsters forever, had to get out, scramble, make the best deals they could. It was just like steel, in a way, the same haunted people, except it wasn't as much written about.

The Teamsters Union is still colossal, unlike the Steelworkers: indeed, it seems as labor gets smaller and smaller, the Teamsters is all that's left. But where once the Teamsters had been 2.2 million, now it's down to 1.6 million. Maybe 600,000 or 700,000 Teamsters disappeared into the nonunion lower depths.

One day, I was driving down the interstate with my friend Bob. We drove in Bob's Cadillac. Bob likes a Cadillac, because, being a Teamster, he gets a bellyful of road and likes a nice ride. Bob and his sister live together, in a little Cape Cod bungalow, with two gorgeous Cadillacs. Between the two of them, his Teamster income and her railroad pension, they must make $70,000 a year: there is still some big money in blue-collar life.

But now Bob was nervous, worried. He knew it could all go any minute. As we drove down the road, he counted the gypsies.

"Look," he said, "there's another one."

"How can you tell?"

"Look in the cabs."

I looked, and I saw women riding shotgun.

Bob said, "Husband-and-wife teams."

The women seemed old, like Ma Kettle, much older than the men, who looked like their sons.

"Those poor, poor people," Bob said. "You know how much they make?"

"No."

"Just eighteen cents a mile, eighteen cents a mile. Tom, how can people live on eighteen cents a mile?"

The gypsies drive eighteen hours a day. I'd just read about them in *USA Today*. "We work eighteen hours a day." One of the gypsies was quoted as saying how much he loved it all. I could just see him, eighteen hours a day, alone up in his cab, up there on Benzedrine, speed, plotting to kill us all.

Back in the early eighties, it was the Teamster employers that seemed more like gypsies. They would pull out under cover of darkness. Old terminals would close, new ones would open. I saw old men jumping from one closing terminal to another, like ice floes in a river. They had to do it, to stay on as Teamsters, to piece together those last two or three years of pension service credit. Some Teamsters would do anything, even kill, for those last two or three years of service credit, which they would piece together, job by job, year by year, like beads on a string.

The worst thing for a Teamster is a "break in service," which is to lose "Teamster-covered employment." If a Teamster fails to keep earning service credit, he can forfeit, or lose, all his prior service credit. So when a Teamster is out of "Teamster-covered" employment, he is often wild with fear. When terminals closed in the early eighties, drivers would call each other on the road and trade the names of lawyers on their CBs. Nobody ever really knows the rules: they're complicated and frightening. A driver simply knows that he has to get a Teamster job again, and get it fast.

Even for TDU members, the most frightening thing is not the Union or the Mob. All of that stuff . . . pfft, big deal. The frightening thing is a terminal closing, a break in service, a gypsy breaking in and stealing all his gold. A guy like Bob would be up there, sitting in his cab, nervous, worried, looking around . . . and there was nonunion America, pulling up in his rearview mirror, riding his bumper, flashing its lights.

Even before deregulation, the Teamster employers could seem like gypsies. There had long been a procedure called "change of operations," when presto, the old company would become a new one, with new terminals, new lines, new routes. One day the terminal would be at 63rd and Cicero, and the next day suddenly it would be in Tinley Park.

And yes, there was seniority. But it was never safe to be way up on the top of the list, swaying in the wind. A Teamster at the top of the list might make $50,000 a year; down in the middle of the list, much less; and down at the bottom of the list, nothing, zero: he'd be on the "reserve board" and sit at home "babysitting the phone," waiting for a call, unable to leave. But sometimes when a terminal closed, or there was a "change of operations," the company would try to knock the old men from the top of the list. These older men simply cost too much: they had more vacation time, more pension credit. Old men would wake up after a "change of operations" and find out they didn't have any arms and legs. And there were so many ways the lists could be combined. They could be "endtailed" (one list on top of the other) or "dovetailed" (the two lists blended together).

And that's how they'd hit the streets:

Endtailed, dovetailed, bobtailed, and . . .

Well, screwed.

Once, three of them came in to my office. These men were in their mid-forties, a bit older than me, and they all had lost their jobs, after ten to fifteen years with the company.

Often such men will come in and stand there unannounced. I always hate it when they come in this way.

I came out in the lobby and said, "I can't see you."

"We'll wait," one of the men said.

"I don't want you to wait," I said.

He said, "*Please*, let us wait." He looked like he hadn't slept.

Yeah, right, let them wait. Sitting there, coiled like panthers. Try going back to your office and getting any work done.

I said, "O.K., come on in."

These men thought that when their terminal had closed, they would have the right to transfer with full seniority: they would have the right to "bump" the younger men. Now it turned out there was no right to "bump."

They stood in my office with a thick greasy pile of papers: grievance forms, company bulletins, with tar and motor oil all over them. Somewhere in this pile, they thought, were their "rights," their contract "rights," their rights to bump.

I looked through the papers, which were worthless.

But these men didn't know that. They kept fumbling, handing me more papers.

A Union officer once said to me, "These guys know more about the White Sox batting averages than they do about their own wages."

One man pulled out a piece of paper and gave it to me. "Look, look, read this, read this . . . Doesn't that mean anything?"

"No," I said. "Look, you don't have any rights."

I said it so routinely. The man looked as if he would leap over my desk and choke me.

"What about the contract?"

"There is no contract. If we sue, they'll change the contract."

"What about my *rights*?"

I thought, "What's the matter with these guys?"

"No," he says, "no, *please* . . . look, it says right here . . ."

In labor law, before the members can sue, they have to "exhaust" the grievance procedure. And by the time I see them, they really are exhausted.

Most have just come from the "hall." They have to go down in person. Phoning the hall is like phoning the moon, and no call, in the history of the Teamsters (at least in Chicago), has ever been returned. So when members are fired, or laid off, or "bumped," they go down to Ashland Avenue, to "Teamster City," the Teamster office building, west of the Loop, and stand there on the street, with the kids selling crack, and work up the nerve to walk in. You walk through the door, and you are in the "cage." The cage is a good name for it, because when a member walks in, he feels like an animal. There are no windows, no chairs, just a TV camera aimed at the member: a police station or a Soviet mental ward would be cheerier. At a tiny windowlike opening, with iron bars, there is a secretary, who coldly asks you your business. Then she goes away for a long time.

I have stood in the cage and know the feeling: hellooo . . . ? It is quiet, but the quiet is deceiving. On the other side of the door, the BAs are breathing. Just breathing, deep in a vault. Letting the phones ring. Waiting.

The grievant goes through the door and down a hall, for a hearing. As he enters the room, he sees his employer, his BA, and the "6-Man Board." Now, I must explain a bit about the Joint Committee, or 6-Man Board. The Teamsters do not have the usual grievance-step procedure, ending in a final, binding arbitration by a neutral third party. Instead, to hear the grievance, there is a Joint Committee, or 6-Man Board, three for management, three for the Union. If the Board deadlocks on the grievance, it goes up to the next higher Board, or Joint Committee, and on, and maybe even up to the "Central Conference." But that's the big time up there: they deal with Presidents, Attorney Generals, and the Strike Force on Organized Crime.

But back downstairs, in Teamster City, there is the first 6-Man Board, which is all most Teamsters ever see. Actually, no one ever sees all six men. Two or three are always missing, out to lunch, or in the john, or wandering around the building. But then, they don't need to hear the evidence. The idea is not to decide the grievance "legally," by the contract, but to horse-trade, or cut a deal.

Always, in the Mineworkers or Steelworkers, the Union is the member's "lawyer" at the hearing. But often at a Teamster hearing, the BA says nothing, not a word. Often the member has not even seen the BA until the hearing. As he gets near the room, he hears laughing. The Union is not the member's lawyer, or even his friend. Really, it is there to handicap the grievance, "price" it, see what it's worth: the member has to present his own case. Many of the members are so scared, they can hardly talk, even when the wives, the night before, have written out in longhand, like schoolgirls, everything the men should say.

My client, Bill, was beaten up at his own grievance hearing. He had the statement, all written out by his wife, Diane. But he never got to it, because as he walked into the room, the BA said,

"Denied."

And Bill said, "I knew you'd sell me out."

The BA stared.

And then he screamed. And screamed. Eight BAs who had been in their offices, letting the phones ring, came running into the little room . . . and Bill was kicked, and punched, and jabbed in the eye, and dropped to the ground.

Yet, after every hearing at Teamster City, the member has to sign a form which says, "The grievant is satisfied with the Union's representation." This is for legal reasons, to prevent a suit. So as Bill lay there, moaning, on the ground, one of the BAs came over and gave him the form: "The grievant is satisfied with the Union's representation."

Bill said, "I'm not going to sign this."

The BA said, "Why not?"

"Because I'm not satisfied with the Union's representation, that's why not."

"Fuck you."

"What?"

"Fuck you."

"Hey, I'm a member of this Union . . ."

"Hey, don't raise your fucking voice with me . . ."

The BA wasn't even mad, really. He just wanted Bill to sign the form. For him, it was just another grievance hearing down at the hall.

One day I would like to write a book, *Fired People*. It would be short stories, in the manner of Chekhov, or Turgenev . . .

anyway, somebody Russian. I think a Russian who had my job
and liked to write could do a lot with it.

They come from the Car Haulers, United Parcel Service
(UPS), Over-the-Road, Piggy-Back, all in their forties and fired.
Teamsters fired for a million reasons, fired for scratching a
fender, fired for being late, fired for no reason but to show
they can be fired. The worst must be UPS. It fires people just
for fun.

I remember one small timid driver, seventeen years with
UPS, not an accident, not a scratch, not a blemish on his record.
Then one day someone bumped his truck, and he was fired.
The Union filed a grievance, and then, after the first step, let
it drop, indifferently, from its beak. He had been fucked for
no reason, but it was of no interest to the Union. He was too
small, too timid, to get anyone's attention: seventeen years lost,
no pension. The poor man cried, telephoned UPS, sent letters,
but it was no use, he would never come back. Maybe he was
fired just to show no one at UPS is safe.

At least he had a first-step hearing. Many members never
have one. I once dealt with a bakery that fired fifteen drivers
at different times for different reasons. Not once, for a single
driver, did the Teamsters have a first-step hearing down at the
hall. It was not that the Union failed to pursue the grievance.
It would not even let a man file one. Each time, the man called
the hall, but the bakery had already called first. Each time, the
BA came down, went into a room, soundproof, glass-enclosed,
and chatted with the boss. The men gathered around the
window, looking in, trying to read lips. Then the BA came out,
raised his hands, and said, "Nothing I can do."

The men said, "What about filing a grievance?"

He shrugged and said, "Nothing I can do."

I went to the NLRB and filed a complaint against the
Teamsters for unfair representation. The NLRB lawyer said,
"So what? So the Union didn't file a grievance."

I said, "*Fifteen* times? It's obvious, isn't it? The Union's on
the take."

He scoffed, "How do you know?"

How do you know? I should have said, "Any union that

endorses Reagan is presumptively on the take." But the NLRB under Reagan would not find this very funny. So I said, "I don't know. You never *know*. You just see things."

The lawyer shrugged and said, "Nothing I can do."

The other night, I had dinner with a friend, and I told him some of these stories.

"O.K.," my friend said, "but what about the contracts? Aren't the contracts in the Teamsters really great? Isn't that the bottom line?"

Contracts?

I was speechless. I thought, "I should be able to answer this," but for fifteen seconds I could not think of an answer. Maybe it is the price for getting lost in a job, for doing a thing, instead of thinking about it. Ask me something simple, too simple, like "What is a labor union?" and I go blank with terror.

Then I remembered why I could not answer the question.

Contract? I could never get the contract. The big game with the Teamsters is to find the contract. There is the National Master Freight Agreement (one book), the Supplement (another book), and the Rider (a third book). Little paperbacks, like Penguins. No Teamster member ever has all three books at once. How do I know what is in the contract? Nobody has all three books.

Besides, the Teamsters is the union of a million deals. The "contract" is just the starting point, the opening bid, for the serious negotiations. UPS has a fixed contribution rate, an amount it must pay into a pension fund every month. But is that what UPS is really paying? Probably not, and members have to file a lawsuit to find out what the new, true, renegotiated deal is all about. A few years ago, in the heyday of deregulation, there were so many concessions, so many "give-backs" at so many terminals, there were not enough Teamster officers to do all the deals. The BAs could not get to all the "barns." Often, the employer just called in the drivers and bargained with them directly, one on one, without the Union. Such a practice is so illegal that it's a "per se," or automatic, violation of federal law, i.e., the duty to bargain with the Union, and *only* the Union. But the NLRB, under Reagan, always looked the other way.

Often, the supervisor called the drivers into a meeting, and the men were told either to vote for wage concessions or to sign cards, individually, to "give back" a portion of their wages.

"Hey," someone would ask, "where's the Union?"

"Oh," the company would say, "they couldn't make it, but they said just to go ahead without them."

The BAs are thoughtful that way.

The company would say it needed "relief," and if the men did not sign the cards agreeing to "give back" their wages, it *might* have to lay them off. In some cases, instead of just signing the money away, the men would get shares in an ESOP, an employee stock ownership plan. It sounds socialistic: the drivers would own the company. But the acronym itself, ESOP, has the sound of a setup. The ESOP is often a corporate shell, no assets, which management will dump when it is going to open a terminal somewhere else: the ESOP goes bankrupt, and the worker-owners get dragged into court. There are so many horror stories about ESOPs that many men would just prefer to sign their money away.

So the men sign the cards, and then go home and try to explain it to their wives.

Actually, some drivers, like my clients, the TDU members, refuse to sign. "Hey, I'm not giving back my wages." So they drive around like royalty, collecting the contract wage, and the employer leaves them alone, because these side deals ("giving up your wages") are illegal, and besides, 95 percent of the drivers will sign. It makes no sense. The "good" workers, who say, "Yes, Boss," have to subsidize the "bad" workers, who say, "No, Boss." The "good" workers realize this and start waiting for the "bad" workers to come out to their cars. Some guy grabbed one of my clients, and said, "You son of a bitch, I'm paying your fucking wages."

"Let me go."

"I'm paying your fucking wages . . ."

"Hey, get off . . ."

And then the Boss would have to call the cops. And it's just a day in the life of the Teamsters . . . well, Union.

•

"Really?" my friend at dinner said. "But what about the Mob? Aren't the contracts really great because of the Mob?"

Oh yes, that's what everyone thinks . . . the magic of the Mob, and they think Teamster members love the Mob, because the Mob always gets a hell of a deal.

Actually, the Mob is terrible at collective bargaining. Of the last five Teamster presidents, no one was closer to the Mob, or supposed to be, than Jackie Presser, and his contracts were bad. The last three he negotiated before he died, Master Freight, Car Haulers, and UPS, were rejected in contract-ratification votes by margins of up to 65–70 percent. And this was with the Teamster *officers* counting the vote. God knows, in the real count it might have been 90–95. These contracts, except the one with Car Haulers, went into effect anyway. In the Teamsters, until recently, a contract was considered "ratified" if 33 percent voted in favor.

But then, the Mob would never negotiate a great contract. Or if it ever did, nothing would be nailed to the floor. Everything would be on sale. After all, what else does the Mob have to sell? Why do employers have their wallets out? I can never understand why so many people think the Mob would negotiate a great contract, because, by definition, the Mob has to be selling somebody out.

Anyway, I would not necessarily blame Teamster contracts on the Mob. Plenty of Teamster officers are free agents, and even in Presser's case, the man may just have been a bungler. Presser never negotiated a contract in his life until he became Teamster president. He was too busy, in his early career, being a double or triple agent or informer, for the Mob, for the FBI, maybe even for the contras: the FBI might have been negotiating Presser's last contracts. Presser was always in court. When the top leadership is always under indictment, nobody has time to negotiate a contract, and the Teamster members are well aware of it: there is no percentage in being a Mob union.

To me, the top Teamster officers seem disconnected from the Teamsters, almost irrelevant to it. They are bloated Colonel Blimps, not really agents of evil, more like balloons. In 1986, the latest count, at least 124 Teamster officers made over

$100,000 a year. And these salaries are just what they bank. Some of them used to draw two or three salaries, one from the local Union, one from the pension fund, one from the Joint Committee or Central Conference. At these salaries, they turn into balloons. They are not capable of collective bargaining. And the ones with the biggest salaries, $300,000 and up, like Presser, are like sultans, carried in sedans, on pillows. They are benign, almost nice, in their thievery, even to the dissidents, like TDU. It is the honest ones, who make $100,000, that scare me. They tend to be the sadists. They carry out the beatings at the union hall.

Somehow people do survive the warning letters, etc., and make it to old age. By old age, I mean forty to fifty years old. I used to see Teamsters coming in to the office, and they were *my* age at that time (thirty-seven or thirty-eight years old), and they already had gotten in their first twenty years.

There was Bill, beaten up at the union hall. Later, after the Teamsters set fire to his car, I said, "Bill, why don't you get out of the Union?"

"No," he said, "I have to get in my twenty years."

Bill was thirty-eight, married, two kids in high school. And I was thirty-eight, and single, still dating, still going into trattorias in Lincoln Park. And I'd see someone like Bill and shiver. One thing about driving a truck: it really is the fast lane into old age.

Well, it's true for some, anyway.

They go around wearing their pensions like hair shirts. Everything, all of living, is postponed for the next twenty, thirty years.

Why? Why throw away your life like this?

"I'm doing it for my family." That's what a guy like this will say.

The pension, the "thirty years and out," drip, drip, drip, building up over geological time . . . "I'm doing it for my family."

Family? Their families could strangle them. They're just doing it for themselves.

And some of these guys don't even want the money. They're going to crawl, to grovel, to throw away their whole lives, just so they can stand up at the end of it all, for one fleeting moment, and say to the Boss, to all of us, really,

"Fuck you."

That is, if they make it. There's a weird, waterless stretch, from age forty to sixty, they have to cross. Some don't make it. They stall out. They just sit there, in their cabs, ten or twenty yards away . . . someone has to get out and push them over the line.

And then some of them at age fifty still haven't figured out how the pensions work. They find it won't be as big as they thought. Or they'll never get a pension at all. And it's amazing, because they've staked their lives, their whole lives, on this one thing: and yet only at age fifty do they sit down for the first time and read the rules.

Sometimes I get calls from pay phones on tollways, and someone is saying, "I can't do this anymore. I've got high blood pressure . . . Help me, *please*, get me off the road."

Here are some "pension stories."

Well, with Ed, I feel like a doctor who's seeing the patient for the first time and knows he's already looking at a dead man.

Ed's a big, red-faced Irishman in his late fifties. And in his case, because of the transfer, he won't get a pension at all. And as I tell him the bad news, he gets redder, wheezing, veins popping on his forehead, and I think, "My God, he's going to die right here, in my office."

And if I had only written a letter to him, he could have died at home, in his own bed, and I'm starting to panic.

More for medical reasons than for legal ones, I say, "Ed, I think maybe there could be a case."

Ed says, gasping, "I'll pay . . . pay whatever you want. How much do you need?"

I make up some number.

He says, "Is that enough? Do you need more?"

I'm watching, horrified, as he fights for air.

He says, "Look, I'm not doing this for myself . . ."

I wait for the words "*I'm just doing it for my family.*"
He gasps, "I just want to get those guys."

I had to tell Phil that his pension was half of what he thought
it would be. He is one of these small, bent-over Teamsters who
can barely see over the dashboard. For years, he has been
driving, puffing cigarettes, getting smaller and smaller. He has
found out, just now, that his pension benefit will be $200 a
month instead of the $700 or $800 he expected. Phil, too, was
transferred many years ago from one pension fund to another.
In the old fund's plan there is an implication, just barely, in
small print, that the old fund can pay him, not at the current
rate when he retires, in 1988, but at the old, historic, preinflation
rate that was in effect when he left the fund in the early
seventies. Phil did not read the fine print. He went around for
thirty years thinking he would have a normal pension. He is
not a fool, he is not like a few of these old men, brains gone to
mush, like little boys sniffing glue. Phil still has his wits. Cigarettes
saved him, maybe. He put his kids through college. I can see
how this happened, and yet . . . what can I say to him now?
He gives me a weak smile, the smile of a man who knows
he has been a fool. He says, "Well, I can't keep driving a
truck."

By the way, over in Europe, they laugh at all this. They say,
"Why don't you just give them all a pension? What's all this
about 'vesting' and 'years of service,' etc.?"

But then, there is no welfare state in America. The Central
States Pension Fund is as close as we get to Sweden. In the
Teamsters, it's always just ahead . . . *Sweden*, shimmering like a
mirage, just down the road, only thirty years away. And so
Teamsters like Phil keep driving and never getting there . . .
Sometimes I think of them alone, up in these cabs, smoking
cigarette after cigarette like French existentialists.

For a man like Phil to get a pension he has to invest his whole
life, which is his "capital." It's his only stab, really, at being a
"capitalist." Some of them don't make it, just like on Wall Street.
And yes, those Teamster pensions are really great. But for

some people to win big, other people have to lose out. And there are many ways to lose.

I suppose there should be a law, and in fact there is a law, the Employee Retirement Income Security Act, or ERISA. ERISA could have been, should have been, the most important domestic law passed by Congress since Social Security. It could have transformed the private pension-fund system into a kind of Sweden, a welfare state that was wise and fair, without any tricks. ERISA: it sounds like the name of a Greek goddess, kind, beneficent. Ah, but ERISA is fickle and cruel to her favorites.

To me, the heart of ERISA was Section 404, which would appear to impose a legal duty on every trustee to act as a fiduciary, or guardian, as at common law. ERISA was to incorporate the old English common-law standards, which were strict and rigorous, for the administration of charitable trusts. For Phil, for Ed, for everybody, the law was meant to place on every trustee the duties of "care" and "loyalty" and "prudence," and really, too, of faith, hope, and love. If the federal courts had enforced this law literally, as it was written, with these high common-law duties, Ed, Phil, and thousands of other Teamsters could never have been cheated out of their pensions.

But the judiciary quickly gutted the act. Usually the trustees can merely give a reason, *any* reason, and the courts will not inquire further, and the case is dismissed. Indeed, ERISA, except for a few specific acts of treachery that are named in the act, has now become a sweeping grant of immunity that lets trustees do whatever they like. In many respects, the old state law that ERISA replaced was a much tougher form of regulation (for example, trustees no longer face punitive damage claims). ERISA, to lawyers like me, was to be the civil rights law of the eighties. But now, as to "care" and "loyalty" and all of that . . . well, to the Reagan judges, it's just a lot of poetry from Tudor England.

Often I'd have better luck just begging the BA.

I had a client, Larry, an old man in his seventies, or even older, maybe in his hundreds, older than Father Time, and when I meet him, he's still working as a Teamster. He's a security guard on the Gold Coast, guarding a warehouse from yuppies. For over forty years he's been a Teamster, but he still doesn't qualify for a pension. Most of his employers are gone, and the records are gone, so he doesn't get credit for his years of service.

I meet Larry's wife. We write to Social Security. We track down his old bosses, in nursing homes. We talk to Larry for hours, and coax, and shout (Larry doesn't hear too well), as he sits there chain-smoking, remote, indifferent.

I telephone a woman at Central States, which is the big Teamster pension fund. She says, "Where was he in 1955?"

"Larry," I say, "where were you in 1955?"

"What?"

" '55."

"What?"

"Where did you work?"

"Darling and Company."

"Doing what?"

"Hauling."

"Hauling what?"

"Grease."

"What?"

"Grease."

"Grease for what?"

"Germany."

"Germany?"

"We sent it to Germany."

I stop here, arbitrarily. I call back Central States. O.K., they say, now what about 1954?

Slowly, we document twenty years of service credit. It's not much, but enough for a little pension.

Actually, Central States is quite decent about the whole thing.

I call Larry's wife and tell her the good news. She sounds disturbed.

"Larry can't come to the phone," she says. "He has to stay in bed."

She hesitates. "I don't think Larry can go to work anymore."

At least Larry *did* get a pension. Years from now, his story may seem like a fairy tale.

As a young labor lawyer, I used to think I could ignore the Teamsters. To me, "Labor" was always the Autoworkers, the Steelworkers et al., and then there was something else called the Teamsters.

It wasn't even part of the AFL-CIO: Meany had kicked them out back in the fifties. I'd always connected it, dimly, with old men in dark Italian restaurants (which turns out to be at least partly right). And there was no point in suing them. Sue the Teamsters? It was like hitting your head against the wall. Besides, when I came to Chicago in 1980, I wanted to be a *union* lawyer. I didn't want to *sue* any unions, or do anything to hurt them. Now, I know that to people outside labor, this must sound strange. What could help labor more than to clean up the Teamsters? But inside labor, it doesn't look that way. It's a breach of solidarity . . . or even a sign that you might be just a frivolous person, a kibbutzing yuppie.

Then one day a Teamster with a pension case came into our office. I thought, "Well, just one little suit, then I'll stop." But I couldn't stop. I did another, and another . . . My God, they were so suable. If there's racketeering at the top, imagine what the Teamsters do with the little civil laws down at my level.

Oh, I knew I shouldn't be suing the Teamsters. But it was the 1980s, I was depressed, and it fit my mood at the time.

In fact, it made me feel a little better. I'd been piddling around with these nineteenth-century industries like coal and steel. Suddenly, with the Teamsters, I felt like I'd leaped into the twenty-first century.

Friends would tell me, "We drove past Teamster City the other night, and we thought of you."

But I didn't feel any hatred or bitterness or even passion in suing the Teamsters.

Or at least I didn't until the night I found Diane's message on my answering machine.

•

That night, when I got the message, I called her back at the hospital. I was trying to impress her, or someone, that I could think like a lawyer.

I said, "Diane, can you get some pictures . . . ?"

"They've almost *murdered* him . . ."

Bill nearly had his eye cut out, by a Union steward who did it with a stack of cards, which he wielded like an ice pick. It was the second time Bill had been jabbed in the eye . . . I thought, "They like to go for the eyes down in Teamster City. Like in the revenge plays of the Elizabethans."

He kept his hands in his pockets as they beat him. He wanted to show everyone there that he wasn't hitting back. It must have been a strange sight: three men in union windbreakers beating another man in a union windbreaker . . . when you'd think in the Reagan era they'd be clutching each other like orphans in a storm.

As a lawyer, I was grateful for all the blood. We did get some pictures of Bill's eye, which I could barely look at. And I didn't want to talk to Diane. I'd told her no, no, don't worry . . . and all the time she'd known more about these BAs than I did.

But I got to know Bill pretty well. In a way, I didn't have much choice. I'd practically gotten him killed.

One day he called me and said in a grim voice, "Diane's put my handkerchief in the wash."

"Oh my God."

This was the handkerchief that a cop had put against Bill's eye, to stop the bleeding.

I was upset, he was upset. The bloody handkerchief was for the jury.

And she had dumped it in the wash . . . like in the revenge plays of the Elizabethans.

I deposed the three men who had nearly murdered him.

Each of them had a letter from his doctor: bad back, arthritis, heart problem, etc. "My doctor told me not to choke or kick guys, because of my back . . ."

"Counsel, my artery, here, on my wrist, it's about to burst. Here. Feel it."

"I don't want to feel it."

"Just *feel* it . . . My doctor says that if anybody touches this artery too hard, I'll die."

Now I think, "Why didn't I just touch him on the artery and see if he'd die?"

Sometimes people ask me, "Is the Mob really 'in' the Teamsters? I mean, how do you know?"

And I used to ask it, too. Personally, I'm not sure I've ever seen the Mob. But I don't have to put my hand on their side or touch them on the artery. Not all knowledge has to come to us through the senses.

By the later 1980s, three things were clear:

First, the U.S. Attorneys had convicted *over 340* persons for racketeering crimes related to the Teamsters.

Second, four of the last five Teamster presidents had been indicted for racketeering-type offenses, and three of those had been convicted. The fourth, Jackie Presser, died before they could get him to trial. The only one not indicted, Frank Fitzsimmons, had almost surely had a hand in murdering Hoffa.

Third, Roy Williams, one of the Teamster presidents, had testified under oath that the Mob had selected him as the Teamster chief . . . and then had selected Presser after Williams went to jail.

In 1988, Rudolph Giuliani, the U.S. Attorney in New York, sued in federal court to put the Teamsters Union in trusteeship. Giuliani had been suing Teamster locals through the 1980s. In a series of cases, he showed how the Mob took over businesses by taking over the Teamster locals they dealt with. Giuliani showed that what made organized crime "organized" was, in part, the organization of labor. And one couldn't say, "Oh, that's New York, and this is . . . Kansas City." What Giuliani showed us all was a methodology. One could drop a Giuliani into Cleveland or Chicago, and he could do it all again.

At some point, Giuliani and his staff began to wonder: How do you get the Mob permanently out of the Teamsters? Slamming guys in jail won't work. They'd already slammed 340, and the Mob was as strong as ever. But a trusteeship of the Union wouldn't work either. A trusteeship or monitorship of the

Teamsters had been tried in the 1950s. The monitorship only made a martyr out of Jimmy Hoffa, and at the end of it, both Hoffa and the Mob were back, and were even stronger than before.

Meanwhile, TDU had a better idea: rank-and-file elections. No more Las Vegas conventions. TDU argued that in a rank-and-file election, with the government counting the vote, the Mob could do nothing. It couldn't count the vote. It couldn't shake down 1.6 million voters. It couldn't pick the officers behind closed doors, as it could at Las Vegas with Williams and Presser.

And there was a precedent: the Mineworkers election in 1972. That was the only time that a whole criminal leadership had been thrown out of Union office for good.

Most of the "Teamster experts" were skeptical. They said, "It's a nice, sentimental idea . . . but do you really think your rank and file is going to vote out Jackie Presser?" This was a way of saying: Aren't the members themselves corrupt? And by the way, aren't those Teamster contracts really great?

In 1988, Giuliani filed his suit, seeking a trusteeship of the Teamsters Union. I remember seeing the complaint. He was suing not just the Union but all these other guys who hung around the Teamsters: "Fat Tony" Salerno, "Matty the Horse" somebody, someone called "Nicky Fish Eyes." I was confused. Was this a lawsuit or *Guys and Dolls*?

Then, right before the trial in 1989, Giuliani made the Union an offer. No trusteeship, no jail, but rank-and-file elections . . . the TDU proposal. And the Teamster officers agreed, since the alternative for some of them might have been jail. The Democrats in Congress screamed how outrageous it was, using the racketeering laws to require democracy. So did some Republicans. So did the AFL-CIO. But it was too late: in 1991, for the first time, there'll be rank-and-file elections in the Teamsters.

This happened the same year, 1989, that democracy came to Poland, East Germany, and almost to China, and somehow I could believe these amazing events. But I couldn't believe there would be rank-and-file elections in the Teamsters. This, at last, was going too far.

Giuliani did this on his own. Congress, the Labor Department, all of them opposed rank-and-file elections. He had no support in official Washington. Perhaps he was enough of a celebrity (on the cover of *Time*) that no one in the government could stop him if he decided for some reason he liked Union Democracy. It had never occurred to me that a *prosecutor* might be in favor of the right to vote . . . but maybe no one had any better idea.

Then, after Giuliani, there was another shock. Not only would there be elections but an honest man was going to run for president. Ron Carey, president of a UPS local on Long Island, declared he was a candidate.

In 1989, I heard Carey speak at the TDU Convention. I loved the strong Irish-tenor voice in which he gave the speech. It was a fierce, nineteenth-century, open-air kind of speech. I wish I could have heard it on Labor Day in Cadillac Square.

I thought how once, in 1972, Carey had supported Nixon. Once there was a time in the seventies when maybe Carey and "kids" like me couldn't stand each other. But he's repented, we've all repented, we're all in this together now.

So can Carey win? I don't know. Nobody knows. Nobody's ever voted in an election like this. Nobody's ever run for president of the Teamsters: I mean, really *run*, instead of floating up, higher and higher, like a balloon.

Although I'm not part of TDU, I've now gone to seven or eight TDU conventions. I think I do it just to see a group that's all rank and file, no officers.

On Saturday night, there's a banquet. Usually I end up with old men, pensioners, church deacons. We sit there talking about "vesting" and "seniority."

And at the table next to me, people are laughing and popping cans of beer.

This year, after Carey's speech, I wander around the hotel and think, "How am I going to escape the deacons?"

I pass a display table, and there's a kindly Teamster wife selling T-shirts for TDU.

One shirt has a drawing or cartoon of a UPS driver: there's

a little screw screwed into his stomach. Underneath, it says, "United Parcel Servant."

I start to buy it . . . then I see it soaked in blood in somebody's file drawer.

I try to think of the popping cans of beer.

Every year at the TDU Convention, I see some of the same faces, but most are people I've never seen before. Some of them are in TDU for a while, and then they drop out. And then they come back. Even someone like Bill will be gone for a few months, or even years, and then one day, for some reason, he's back.

So what would prompt them to come here, give up a weekend, walk around from "workshop" to "workshop," making notes about grievances, pensions, their right to vote? They're not starving, after all. They can make $40,000 a year, or more, and they can afford to stay at the Hilton. They can take me out to dinner at nice restaurants. Yet I sense, with some of them, that they feel like they're in a cage, and no matter where we go, the cage goes with them, too . . . when they have to drive, through the slush, four winter nights a week, when they go to the hall, or when they "babysit" the phone. They're always in a cage, and can't get out. They can take me out to dinner and pick up the check, but there's nothing I can do to get them out.

Lately TDU has begun to win. Still not in Chicago, but elsewhere . . . even in the home local of one of the big boys, Weldon Mathis, the Union's vice president.

I think of Carey's speech. And I think that Carey could win.

I remember reading a philosopher who said that total negativity delineates its very opposite, like an x ray.

And so, too, in the Teamsters. Sometimes there is hope, a streak of light, a blur on a piece of film.

When Giuliani filed his suit, I wanted to help TDU as best I could. So I called up a big law firm in New York and asked if they'd come into it, pro bono, for TDU. I talked to a friend of mine there and told him how TDU wanted to argue in favor of rank-and-file elections.

He was excited. He said he'd talk to some other lawyers and call me back.

But when he did call back a few weeks later, he said, "Sorry, we can't help."

He said that the older lawyers who were liberals like him wanted to do it, but the younger lawyers did not. The younger lawyers didn't want to be involved with Teamsters at all.

"But we're the good guys," I said.

"That's not it. They don't like *any* Teamsters."

"Why?"

"They don't like the fact they make $40,000 a year . . . you know, just by driving a truck . . ."

I was unhappy with the decision, but I also felt a secret thrill . . . the idea that twenty-eight-year-old lawyers, driving BMWs, making only $100,000 a year, could resent these rank-and-file Teamsters, could *resent* people like Bill and Diane, and that even now, at the end of the Reagan era, when every other union has been run off the road, young lawyers could still look out, could still see, pulling up in their rearview mirrors, riding their bumpers . . . the Teamsters, coming after them, breathing down their necks, making $40,000 a year.

CHAPTER 8

Officers and Lawyers

It is chilling to look at the presidents of Big Labor now. I mean, just to look at their faces. Some are lawyers, and others, in scary numbers, have postgraduate degrees. Men like Lane Kirkland and Lynn Williams, the Steelworkers president, look and talk like the kind of professors whose lectures I used to cut.

A few years ago, Williams spoke to an audience of college students at the University of Pennsylvania. The speech was to commemorate the fiftieth anniversary of the CIO organizing drive in basic steel, and a friend of mine heard the speech. He was astounded that 900 students came to hear Williams speak. He thought, "Here are 900 kids, in the 1980s, who want to hear what labor has to say."

Williams cleared his throat, made a few introductory remarks about the occasion. Then he launched into a twenty-minute speech on . . . import quotas.

Recently I heard Williams speak at a labor banquet in Chicago. As he rattled off some numbers, I whispered to a friend: "Was this guy ever, like, a plain union member?"

My friend shrugged. "I think once maybe he had a cup of coffee."

The "new" union president seems this way: like once, maybe, he had a cup of coffee.

These people have taken over the international unions.

Maybe, one day, they will take over the locals, too. But for now, at least, the high school grads can still play with them. The local unions (and, I suppose, gas stations) may be the last American institutions that high school grads are still allowed to run. They may be the last places where such people can still rise and fall like kings, like the heroes of a Greek tragedy. Even here, I think, it is just a question of time before they are pushed out.

Already in Chicago, many members think the lawyer really runs the local. I hear it all the time from my Teamster rank-and-file clients: "Grady, or Bernstein, really runs the local." Now, I know that the lawyers do not run these Teamster locals. (I only wish they did.) But when I say that to my clients, they only scoff at me for being naïve.

They say, "Come on, he calls the shots."

I say, "Look, you guys pay no attention to me. Why can't it be just as true for the other side?"

They can never answer that one.

My clients say these things, perhaps, to belittle or show contempt for their local officers, who are their enemies. But I think some of them, deep down, just don't believe that guys like themselves really can call the shots.

Even in the Steelworkers, which Williams heads, it is widely believed that the Union is under the virtual martial-law control of the lawyers. I represent twenty-four Union officials right now, in a suit involving the Union. My clients all believe that every major Union decision, even policy decision, is made by Bernard Kleiman, the general counsel. These are not his enemies speaking: some of them admire Kleiman for it. It is just assumed now, routinely in the big internationals, that the lawyer is the real power behind the president, except maybe in cases when the president himself is a lawyer, too.

In some unions, the general counsel has dispensed with the nonlawyer union president. If he has the president's signature stamp, why does he need the president? In the Laborers International Union, it is a common joke that Tony Fosco, the president, sits all day in a Washington restaurant. Every important decision comes from Robert Connerton, the general counsel, who, to an increasing degree, simply issues them in his own name, as if he were president. Connerton uses his *own* signature stamp.

Naturally, these lawyers stop being lawyers and need lawyers for themselves. So the legal work is farmed out to outside counsel, and soon they start making the decisions, and the whole process starts over. One set of regents piles on top of another.

There is a hopeless resignation about this among the officers. Indeed, they are going to law school, too. So now, when I deal with a union, I often go through three sets of lawyers: outside counsel, inside counsel, and staff reps going to law school.

I realized how bad things were when I saw a Labor Day parade two years ago. A friend says, "You can tell a lot about the state of labor by watching that parade."

I saw very few rank-and-file members actually marching. But as the floats went by, I did see some labor lawyers. They were up there sitting on carnations, waving to the crowd. One was a lawyer I'd just seen in court.

I heard a young woman near me say, "What is all this?"

Her friend said, "I think it's Armed Forces Day."

Really, it was more like Law Day. But that's the state of labor today: no working-class heroes, just lawyers sitting on floats, waving to the crowd.

Every staff rep or BA has to function like a lawyer. The entire labor movement is like a giant bar association of nonlicensed attorneys. I have seen them in their windbreakers and ties, going into arbitrations, but they could be divorce lawyers, or DUI lawyers, or street lawyers, the kind who hustle cases in traffic court: no, I think they are more like divorce lawyers, on the 14th floor of the County Building, the kind that enraged husbands pull out guns and shoot. This is the bottom of the labor movement, eight rungs below Lynn Williams, nine rungs below Kleiman or Connerton. But this is the cutting edge of labor. This is where we pick up first-step grievances and DUIs. Actually this is where I pick up some cases myself.

There are many reasons why every staff rep has to function like a lawyer, but the main one is the Supreme Court.

In 1958, the Supreme Court decided three cases known as

the Steelworkers Trilogy. The Court held that nearly every dispute which occurred while a contract is in effect is subject to arbitration by a neutral third party. There could be no strike or other form of pressure. The Trilogy helped create this new man of labor, who is more or less a paralegal.

Here I must pause and say something about arbitration. Oh yes, arbitration. Nothing has been more psalmed, more solemnly, by more federal judges since the Trilogy, as if it were the greatest invention of man. I am so sick of judges writing psalms to arbitration. Have they ever seen one? No. All they know is, they can kick these cases out of court.

Arbitration is what people mean, essentially, when they talk about "our modern system of industrial self-government." They mean mini-lawsuits, millions of them, jam-packed in big backlogs, going back for years. Without the Trilogy, it could never have happened. And this event occurred with no act of Congress, no statutory text for it: the Supreme Court just did it, snapped its fingers, and the labor movement changed forever. Now, in fairness I must add that organized labor, or most of it, wanted the Steelworkers Trilogy. It *wanted* to turn into a bar association. It may have been an unconscious wish, but it came right on schedule, with the Zeitgeist, the flow of History, the last act of the Protestant Reformation, the Rationalization of the West. It all happened so long ago, in 1958, no one can remember organized labor being any other way.

What is arbitration? Arbitration is . . . well, let me begin with the four steps of the grievance procedure, which are . . . As I write this, I feel weak, the pen falls from my hand. This is so boring. Yet I am a labor lawyer, and I do arbitrations.

Can we go back and talk about, oh, class in America?

I said arbitration is like a mini-lawsuit. Often, however, there is nothing mini about it. It can be just as long, just as expensive as a real lawsuit, sometimes worse. An arbitrator, unlike a judge, can charge by the hour, so for the union, which is broke, there are two meters running, the arbitrator's and its lawyer's. Just one arbitration can cost a little local union (of say, fifty members) tens of thousands of dollars and literally bankrupt it.

So, does this force expedite resolution? God no. Arbitration is like a lawsuit in drag. Mainly, it drags on and on . . . One of

our union clients, Local ———, has a standard collective bargaining agreement. In the last ten years, the shortest time in
which *any* grievance has progressed to a final arbitrator's award
has been in excess of two years (let's say two and a half years).
The two and a half years include the four steps of the grievance
procedure (depending on the contract), the scheduling of
appointments, the preparation of answers, the convening of
the arbitration board, the call upon the American Arbitration
Association, the ultimate appointment of an arbitrator, the
scheduling and rescheduling of the arbitrator's dates for the
hearing, the conduct of the hearing, the filing of the briefs,
the deliberation of the arbitrator, and the final award.

It is easy for management to "jam the grievance procedure."
And during all this delay, the rule is: "Management acts, the
union grieves." And grieves and grieves. For two and a half
years, the company can have its way. It can transfer out the
work, make the discharge stick, do any kind of urinalysis it
wants.

What do we arbitrate?

Basically: sex, drugs, and rock and roll. A big issue in labor
is, Should it be twenty nanograms of cannabis or more?

No, most arbitrations are pretty dull, transfer of bargaining-
unit work, etc. I sit in a Holiday Inn in Springfield, and as the
case goes on, I remember Harvard, running along the Charles,
drinking sherry in the junior common room, the sixties . . .
back when the standard was not twenty nanograms of cannabis,
or even fifty, but anything you liked, and I would not lose my
job. My mind wanders . . . How did I end up doing arbitrations?

For some of the BAs I feel sorry. After all, I went to law
school, and I asked to be a lawyer. Did they? I deserve what
has happened to me. But these guys probably thought they
would lead strikes or something.

It is sad to go into their offices. Find a staff rep, go into his
office, and on the wall you see May Day posters, posters of
Eugene Debs, posters (in German) announcing the General
Strike. And then look on the desk and you see grievance forms:
stacks and stacks of grievance forms, most of them stuck in the
last "step."

The poor bastard. He sits under the strike posters shuffling papers. He sits in the arbitration hearings marking exhibits. He sits on the stand testifying as a witness. Mostly, he just sits there. No soap box, no stump speech, no calling out, in a beer-barrel voice, to hit the bricks. The working-class hero in our time. A miserable little career in Philadelphia lawyering.

The big issue in labor-management relations today is not who can survive a strike, but who can survive, without blinking, the arbitrator's bill. Most of the time, labor is no match for management. The company has more money, and it has a big, overstaffed personnel department. It can outspend, outbrief, and outman the union in any case, if it wants. It can do all the urinalysis it wants, and then, after two and a half years, it clobbers us in arbitration.

Then it goes out and tells the public how labor is running the company.

My friend David, a young lawyer, wanted to do arbitrations. I trained David as a lawyer when he was with our firm, although he probably knew more about labor than I did. He came from a good family, New York, socialist, Jewish: his parents had met as labor organizers in the 1930s, and his brother was a labor lawyer, too. Although our firm does arbitration cases, we did not do enough for David, and he did not like the fancy, far-out labor law I did (RICO, Union Democracy, etc.). He wanted arbitrations. He wanted them straight up, neat, no chaser, straight into the bloodstream. Real labor law.

So he went to another firm, and now, for three years, he has been doing "real" labor law. And he hates it.

We were having lunch the other day. He said, "Tom, I had no idea . . .

"It's much worse than you said. The unions we represent, they don't care if we win these arbitrations. They stopped caring years ago. They just want us to hold down the legal bills.

"Often, we go into the hearings without preparing. Really, I just wing it: no notes, no talking to witnesses. The clients can't afford to have me prepare. And the company, of course, is totally prepared. They just cream us.

"And the BAs I'm with, they don't care. They've been through so much of this stuff, they don't give a shit anymore. You know what I mean . . . they've seen too many jag-offs get fired.

"You know, they think worse of our members, in most of these cases, than the company does . . ."

Listening to David, I thought, "My God, I'm not this cynical." I began to defend the locals we represented.

He said bitterly, "Sure, those are good locals. I got spoiled. I thought they were all like that."

I felt bad about David, whose roots are in labor. He had grown up in New York, Upper West Side, where even in the fifties and sixties people wrote *pamphlets* about labor, like in Russia. I had grown up in Cincinnati and had not expected anything.

He said, "I've got to find out a way to practice labor law and not become a total cynic."

As David said, the BAs stop caring, they've been through so much of this stuff. They're no match for the company, anyway. They blow the arbitrations, or blow them off. So members, understandably, began suing their unions for "unfair representation." At first, the NLRB and the courts permitted these suits. There were so many shocking stories, even from the "good" unions. But then came the flood and the judges were aghast. They were awash in these suits. So the judges, once again by their own fiat, simply changed the law. They imposed a new, six-month statute of limitations, which few people, fired, without a job, could meet. And in my circuit, they redefined unfair representation, so that now an employee has to show more than gross negligence: he has to show that the union has a personal grudge against him. And, of course, that is rarely true; most of the time there is no malice. As David said, the union simply does not give a shit.

I used to think it so sinister, how the courts changed the law. But, in a way, the courts had no choice. What were they supposed to do? Retry all the cases? I often see, in other unions, good solid claims dropped at the fourth step. I hear of cases where the BA never shows up, and the member runs out, at the last minute, to call up his cousin, a divorce lawyer.

Yet I can also see it from the union's point of view. The union is broke, there is no strike fund, they cannot even call a strike. A union official, looking at a discharge case, has to decide: "How much is this son of a bitch worth?" And then he has to explain to the members. David is right, I guess, that labor, generally, does not give a shit, but he forgets one thing: the labor movement cannot afford a lot of justice. Too often it can seem to embittered BAs that the union treasury is there not for strikes or other good collective works but for the legal fees of these sons of bitches. They probably think that it's a good thing that the Supreme Court got rid of the right to strike, because at least they don't have to go on strike for some of these jag-offs. I guess I see the point: the man *lied* on his employment application, or he wrecked a truck, or he punched out a co-worker. Is this really worth an arbitration?

The only thought that consoles me is: We all deserve to be fired. At some point in our lives, we've all smashed the company's truck.

My greatest arbitration case came out of an asylum. It was in downstate Illinois, a strange, eerie place full of asylums and corn silos.

It was a case in which I was defending, well, patient abuse, they said. I was trying not to tell my friends back in Chicago. I had gone into law to do good, to make the world good, and now here I was, in the labor movement, defending a charge of patient abuse, my God, like in *One Flew Over the Cuckoo's Nest.* I kept thinking, as I drove to Springfield, "I hope nobody I know finds out."

But we had taken the arbitration. And the patient, L., a mentally retarded man, was a thug, 250 pounds, in his thirties, built like a linebacker, who liked to ram other people from behind. One day he made the mistake of ramming John, a nurse, as John was drinking his coffee, his first cup of the morning. John, a nurse, is six feet six, a Vietnam vet, a gentle, bearlike man. John gently "extended" L.'s neck, gently pushed him back, gently leaned him over a table, and gently said, "Don't fuck with me today, L."

And the state, not so gently, fired him. The state was ecstatic.

It fired John on the spot. Because John was our Union president and it was the middle of negotiations. The state, with one blow, had literally cut off the Union's head.

Let me tell you: A union does not lightly lose its union president. Management acts, the union grieves, but we had this baby to arbitration, final step, in five months.

John was inconsolable. For five months, he sat in a dark bar. Absolutely inconsolable. He still had hair down to his shoulders, like in the sixties. He said that in Vietnam he had come to like sitting in a dark bar. He felt safe in a dark bar. I had to prepare the whole case in a dark bar. I couldn't get the guy out of Vietnam.

In the arbitration, the state was repulsively sanctimonious. It hauled in a parade of bureaucrats who swore that no nurse in the state ever "offensively" touched a patient. No. All the nurses in Illinois submit passively, like the early Christians, and let themselves be beaten. It was quite a show. The state really wanted John's head.

Bureaucrats kept sniffing at us: "How can you defend patient abuse?"

We had our own parade of witnesses—nurses, security guards, even some doctors in management, people who loved John. Never touch a patient? Some days, our witnesses said, they had to tackle patients. Nurses, being beaten, would set off alarms ("flying pages"), and doctors, nurses, janitors, would come running down the hall. Sometimes a nurse, or even a doctor, would sit on top of a patient. It was not in the book, of course, but sometimes, in real life, a nurse, 105 pounds, would have to kick a 250-pound gorilla like L. in the balls. On average, in this asylum, there was one tackle squad a day.

Our witnesses were great, because people loved John. We asked the arbitrator to love John. That was our whole case, in the end. Yes, John did wrong, he should not have said "fuck," not even gently, not even to L. He was sorry. But the state was full of evil, deceit, and hypocrisy, coming in here, sniffing at us: "How can you defend patient abuse?" We asked the arbitrator to love John, and coldly, impassively, he adjourned the hearing, mailed us an opinion, and reinstated John, with almost all his back pay (except that John lost two weeks for using the word "fuck"). John is now back in the asylum, with all the other nurses, back in flying tackle squads, routinely violating the rules. These are the dark victories you win in arbitration. Unions protect the right to reasonable patient abuse.

As I write, the current big battle in the arbitration world is over urinalysis. Every company seems to be doing it. Com Ed, at its Zion nuclear power plant, is doing random drug testing of our clients, the members of Local 1461. It is just picking people out randomly, with no grounds for suspicion, and forcing them to give urine specimens. Last December, Com Ed picked out six of our members.

What for? the Union said.

Anonymous phone call, the company said.

Where? From the men's room?

The Local was furious, and it asked us to file a lawsuit. The hell with waiting two and a half years. The Local wanted an injunction, immediately, pending arbitration.

But labor law is not set up this way, and it would be very hard in our circuit, we said. The Court of Appeals had just upheld random drug testing for high school cheerleaders in Indiana. What chance did we have at a nuclear plant?

Still, the Local said, "Sue. Spend the money. Go for broke." The whole executive board was enraged.

This is as close as you can get, under the Trilogy, to going on strike. It is not clear, at this writing, how our case will turn out. I mentioned it the other day to another lawyer. He said, "Is the ACLU helping? It sounds like an ACLU case."

For some reason, I was annoyed and said, "We *are* the ACLU." Even the Teamsters, in its sphere, acts like the ACLU. I suppose it's true of any International Union, more than thirty years after the Trilogy: facing outward, to the employer, it's like the ACLU. And facing inward, to its members, it's like the Vatican in Rome.

After a while, in the world of the Trilogy, the dream of being a lawyer haunts the staff rep or BA. Some of them print up business cards, like lawyers. I think of Jill Dempsey, a BA, a *Teamster* BA, in San Francisco, of all places, who is in TDU, of all things. Her business card says, "Jill Dempsey, BA," like "Jill Dempsey, Attorney-at-Law." If you flip the card over, there are typed out your Miranda rights as a Union member:

(1) In the event you are reprimanded, you have a right to a union steward;
(2) You have a right to a phone call;
(3) My emergency number is _____.

I now forget her emergency number. I was so impressed with her, and I thought, "Why don't all BAs have cards like this?"

But I was suspicious of her. "Are you really from San Francisco?" I said. "I didn't know they had unions out there, just affinity groups."

She bristled. "Just because you're from Chicago, you don't have to be a snob."

As she walked off, I thought, "Why am I still chasing women from Wellesley? Why not date a Teamster BA?" But I, well . . . there may be some ways I will never know the rank and file.

Now, not every staff rep or BA wants to be a lawyer. There is Sue, for example, who thinks union members are sheep, who has a different style, who does not belong in the Trilogy world. She once told me, "I love to pick out some little twerp . . . some company personnel guy . . . some little yuppie . . . and then I just target this person, I pound the shit out of him . . . pound, pound, *pound* . . ." She begins cackling, smacking her lips, like a child thinking of a turkey dinner.

This woman is never going to law school. Thirty years ago, she would have been leading a strike.

As a general rule, though, the good ones end up in law school. A typical career is to join the union staff; grieve, grieve, grieve; then go off to night law school. Deborah, Pat, all of them: we have lost all our best staff reps this way.

But then, it is the only way to rise to the top in some unions. The Steelworkers, which is riddled with lawyers, makes its staff reps do arbitrations, so they literally have to learn to practice law. I know union grievance handlers who, when their layoffs came, took the LSATs. One of them, unemployed now, with seven kids, is in night law school.

At the UMW, in the seventies, the first miner I ever met was a lawyer. He was my office mate, Rich Trumka, and back then, I thought of him as a freak, a curiosity. I often wondered why he was a lawyer. I told him once, "Why didn't you run for union office?" Back then, I had the dumb, naïve view that there were the "officers" and the "lawyers," and they were two different things. Trumka just looked at me and puffed his cigar. I was about fifty years behind the times.

Trumka is now president of the UMW. He is an officer *and* a lawyer. And I, who am just a lawyer, do arbitrations in asylums in downstate Illinois.

Not long ago, I was in a nasty argument with a shop steward. He was not even a staff rep, but just a steward, at a can factory, and his name was Fred. Now, I knew staff reps who were as good as lawyers, who could hold their own in a court. But Fred was just a steward, and I had to pretend in a superior way to condescend to him. I had to pretend, because he was beating the shit out of me. Not just on the contract issue, which was seniority, which he might be expected to know, but even on points of federal law: I cooed at him, patted him on the head, praised him for his knowledge, but it was very unnerving.

I kept thinking, "This guy could be a lawyer. What's he doing in a can plant?" But in a way, he already was a lawyer. Being a full-time shop steward, he never did a bit of work: he did third-step grievances. Technically, he was a heat-treat feeder, a working stiff, but when I looked at his hands, they were as soft as any lawyer's.

The stewards really throw me, I never know what to expect. I put a technical point in baby language, and I forget these guys have been to more arbitrations than I have. By now, I should know better than to condescend, but the other day I was with Phil, a Teamster, and I was trying to make something simple, so he would understand. Phil just sat there, calmly listening, in his white, *G.Q.*, neo-Milan Italian suit, like any other average rank-and-file Teamster who might dress in the fashion of Tom Wolfe. He listened to me talking to him in baby talk. Then he took what I said, shredded it, tore it apart, used all the correct, adult legal terms. Once again, I had been a fool. Too late, I tried to recover, rev back up, talk like an adult, but no, it was too late, I kept losing altitude. I crashed into a babble of baby talk. Phil looked at me the way Trumka would, at the UMW. Then he snickered and walked away.

Sometimes, I want to lean over and whisper, "I don't get it. What are you doing down here?" But that is the one question you can never ask. They are watching, waiting for you to say it. They are waiting to see if you fall into the trap.

I meet people like Phil all the time. I know it is rare, and I know how dumb and naïve I sound here, but I dare you, if you take my job, not to become obsessed about it. It is a scandal of the democracy that even I, a labor lawyer, can be scandalized. Why should I be shocked? Yet I am shocked.

I wonder how much of it is luck. The officers, the staff reps, who go to night law school, they must look around and wonder how much of it is luck. There is birth order, environment, genes . . . yet somehow, at the first step of the grievance procedure, we all seem to start out pretty equal.

While I have no special bond with the rank and file, I do sometimes have one with the *officers*. Or put it this way: the rank and file, when they run for union office, become . . . well, like me. They stop working nine to five. As officers, they become bohemians, artists, they can hang out in coffeehouses: now, at last, we become brothers and sisters. Nobody can find us. We set our own hours. All of us in organized labor, we sit on the rim of the world, the rim of the GNP, and watch the other people, the "members," go to work. I often think, "We are not selfish about it . . . we would save others if we could . . ." In some deep, indescribable sense, none of us are at work.

We are on "lost time." Technically, this is not the name of a psychological state, but the name for a payment from the company to the employee for the time that the employee spends performing legitimate union business (handling a grievance, etc.). Many locals budget for only one or two full-time salaried officials. The others, such as the stewards, are supposedly part-time officials, who continue to receive lost-time wages from the company. As a result, for example, GM and not the UAW pays many of the officials of the UAW for the work they perform. This practice may look like bribery, or at least like a flagrant conflict of interest, but nobody seems to mind it.

At some big plants, there may be one full-time steward, on lost time, per thirty workers. Think of it: one full-time, company-paid agitator for every thirty rank and file. Once in Wisconsin I saw it: a local that had a one-to-thirty ratio. It was like England or Germany. And many of the stewards were dropouts from the sixties, guys who had been in grad schools. Now, as stewards, they were on "lost time" just as in grad school, too, they had been on lost time. There is a deep, almost libidinal pleasure to be on lost time, to be AWOL, to roam around the plant without permission. This may be what draws people into the unions, to be stewards, vice presidents, recording secretaries. They are the people who cannot hack it anymore at work. A few years ago, when the layoffs came and work forces began to shrink, there was no need for so many stewards. So while other members lost their jobs, the stewards lost their lost time. After years of being stewards, they faced the agony, when the layoffs came, of really going back to work and taking their place on the line. The stewards may have suffered more than the members who were unemployed.

Some of them claimed, desperately, that they were disabled now. Men shot themselves in the foot, like in wartime. Jimmy T., who had been on lost time for fifteen years, said he fell out of a tree while deer hunting with a bow and arrow. I represent Jimmy T. and I know him well, and I cannot imagine him in a tree with a bow and arrow in Indiana, but Jimmy T. is a hell of a steward, after fifteen years, and he shrugged like it could happen to anybody, and U.S. Steel bought the story. He was out of work for twelve months. The guy is a legend around the plant.

All over Chicago, at any moment, thousands of people are on lost time. In a sense, I am on lost time, too: I mean, why do I practice labor law and not take a real job, as everyone else has done? No, most of us in organized labor are lost, lost on lost time, and would like to stay lost and never be found.

A man or woman starts to change on lost time. I see local presidents at summer concerts at the University of Chicago.

Outside at night, for the string quartets: they sit with their wives on the lawn and look up at the stars.

To me, there is nothing harder than to run a local union. Stay up all night bargaining a contract, then go to a plant gate at 6 a.m. People call you at night, every night, and talk to you through the night. Every local president has two or three phones at home. When I go to Ed Sadlowski's house, he is always on the phone. There is no place to hide; there is never a time when you are not at work, especially when you are at home. From "work" to "politics" to play, there is no line that separates one from another. After a while, how do you know what you are doing? Often they do not know what they are doing. They seem to sleepwalk, splashing, through a river of coffee. And the coffee is terrible, always being reheated from the bottom of a tin can.

It was in the Steelworkers, in the seventies, that I came to know about local officers. I met the Steelworkers officers, the new men, the new progressive local-union presidents who had come to power in District 31 with Ed Sadlowski. The Sadlowski campaign in Chicago swept out all sorts of local-union old guards. Progressive Sadlowski supporters took office. Jim Balanoff, Local 1010, at Inland Steel; Joe Romano, Local 15279, at Danley; John Chico, Local 65, at U.S. Steel.

I had never met such men. They were shrewd, tough, Tenth Ward-type Chicagoans. They were street-smart, yes, in the mean-street sense, but they also knew something of the world of *The New York Times*, of Washington, D.C. At least they knew it was out there, like Five Gateway Center, and they knew I was from out there, and it did not freak them out. It was not like the Mineworkers. They knew exactly who I was, and we could sit down and talk.

I saw the big existential kick of being a local-union president. Back then, being just a kid, I was a sucker for living on the edge. A local president, it seemed to me, had everybody after him, if he was doing his job: Inland, Pittsburgh, the Daley Machine, Vrdolyak, the Labor Department in Washington, the assholes in his own local. And the setting of it was so existential, too: South Chicago, always winter, the beer bottles in the snow.

Everything about it was so melodramatic. I wanted to spend my whole life representing these guys.

The most existential was Alice Puerala. She was a woman and had to wait for her shot. She succeeded John Chico at Local 65 when John turned on us and went over to the other side. She was the first woman local president of a big U.S. Steel mill and was kind of a Mother Jones, or Emma Goldman, in the early eighties, in the battles on concessions. Soon she was dying of cancer, in good South Chicago style. And in the election, they said, "She's dying of cancer, don't vote for her." But she was tougher, dying of cancer, wearing a wig, than anyone else in the local, and everyone was after her, U.S. Steel, Mayor Byrne, Vrdolyak, Pittsburgh, the Department of Labor, shrieking at her: to the moment she stepped into the grave. When she sat in my office, I used to think, "All this shit is keeping her alive a good extra year."

It is odd that these people, who are politicians, almost never go into general politics. A Sadlowski, a Romano, a Puerala, they almost never run for any public office. To them, I guess, it is not the same kick, or the same high. It would be like switching from heroin to methadone. Charlie Hayes of the Meatpackers went to Congress, Frank Lumpkin ran for state representative, but there is something flat about general politics, not the same sense of . . . oh, danger.

I exaggerate, of course, the sense of danger. But it is not an ordinary politician's life: there is a strange hunted quality to it. This is as true for a Jackie Presser as it is for Cesar Chavez. A good union officer must give the sense that if he had to do it, he might break the law. Not in a crazy, wacko way like in the Mineworkers, but in a goddammit-you-leave-me-no-choice way, the sense that he knew the law and could normally follow it, but he could say, once in a while, fuck the law. The whole labor movement is tied up with lawyers, but a good officer, once in a while, could break himself free. Back in the seventies, the ones I met, they knew about lawyers, they knew about ducking subpoenas. They always were willing to get a clean pair of underwear and duck across the state line. They used to beg to do it. They would beg to do something illegal, to show they were free. The tragedy is that most of them, even in the

Teamsters, go through their whole lives begging, hoping for the chance to break the law, to be officers and not lawyers, and after marking exhibits in a million arbitrations, finally, at last, to be in jail and to be free. But they know, deep down, just the way it is set up now, it can never happen. They will always obey the law.

Now it seems almost boring to me to be a union officer, at least in South Chicago. The big existential appeal of it is gone. It is the nineties now, and no one is after them. Alice is dead, Jim Balanoff is retired, John Chico is somewhere. I do not know the new guys. The other night, I went to a meeting of four Steelworkers local presidents. We were supposed to discuss starting a new project, job training for unemployed steelworkers. Only one president, Willie Ross, showed up. Ross said, "I called the others, they said they were coming." He was irked, I could tell. He sat at his desk, which was a mess, and ate stale old cookies past nine o'clock at night.

We were in the Local 65 hall, and in Ross's depressing office, at nine at night, eating cookies. There is a lot of downtime in organized labor, waiting for meetings to start. Sitting here, waiting . . . it gets you in the mood for the Great Depression.

Every union office is a dump. Is it possible, really possible, that letters could be written from this office? I look around Ross's office and try to figure out how it could happen.

John Chico sat here, Alice Puerala sat here. How had they done it? Styrofoam cups were everywhere. Back issues of *Steelabor*, six months old, and Ross was saying something about the company, U.S. Steel.

"God, they must think we're stupid . . ."

I hear these words a million times from local officers.

We waited, and waited, and waited, and there was no meeting. The other local presidents did not come. This is the 1990s, meetings never happen. People sit around for a while, and then they go home.

Are local officers, or staff reps, really capable of collective bargaining? In other words, are they smart enough?

When I was at Harvard, or the Department of Energy, a standard question in my circle was: "Is he, or she, smart?" You know: *smart*. It was a way to check someone out, to decide, even, whether he or she should be your friend. I always hated the question, since I could imagine them at Harvard asking it about me, and I was pretty worried about the answers. So when I heard someone say, "Is he smart?" I would give strange answers. I would say, "I don't know. Does he have a good heart?" I was probably more obnoxious than if I had just answered the question straight.

A friend of mine, H., has been a labor arbitrator for years. Recently, he told me, he had to deal with a strike, and he got to know both the union president and the company president.

"You know," H. said, "I kept thinking these two guys should switch sides. It was one of those rare, rare times when the union guys totally outclassed management."

I was pleased to hear this. And then, in a way, I was offended. What did H. mean, "one of those rare, rare times"?

I thought of John L. Lewis, who ran the coal industry for decades. There were no big companies in coal in those days, just thousands of small operators cutting each other's throats. Lewis, through collective bargaining, brought order out of chaos. He set the wage levels, the production targets, the safety standards, and he really planned the whole industry. He showed the world that he could do a better job, consciously planning, than the market could do, with its invisible hand. Lewis not only totally outclassed management, he totally outclassed the market. For a generation of planners, Lewis was the man who proved you really could, sometimes, outsmart supply and demand.

Then there was Walter Reuther, of the Autoworkers, who saw the industry's problems more clearly than it did. Would Reuther have kept building those big, crappy, unsalable cars? No, Reuther, a social democrat, would have made Volkswagens, cars for the people, cars that would last forever. He, like FDR, would have devastated the Germans and the Japanese.

Then there were Sadlowski, Balanoff, Puerala. What if they had run the steel industry? Maybe they could not have saved it, but they would have invested in research, pushed new product uses, bought the new technology. They would have done by instinct everything the critics say the steel companies did not do. They would have done so because they would have had to answer, not to stockholders or mutual funds, but to workers and their families, men and women who had their twenty years and dreamed of "thirty years and out." They would have had to act, instinctively, like textbook Japanese, not out of some Jungian impulse buried in Asian culture, but out of the need to protect their voters, their constituents, like any rational Western politicians.

It was in the 1980s, ironically, when organized labor fell apart, that with the rise of Japan et al. we needed the instincts of labor the most. Are they smart enough, in labor? In light of all our wrecked industries in the eighties—auto, coal, steel, just to name a few—it is hard to see how the union guys could have done any worse. At least they think of Americans first as producers and only second as consumers. That fact alone would orientalize the country, no matter how dumb the union guys otherwise might be.

And where were Sadlowski, Balanoff, Puerala? Handling grievances at the fourth step, marking exhibits. Our big mistake in the eighties was not to put these people in charge, let them bring in the fire department, turn the hoses on the bonfire of the vanities.

So what did H. mean? "Rare"? "Rare" for the union guys to outclass management? It annoyed me.

But I said nothing. He was right. It was pretty rare.

True, in a sense it may take more genius to run a union, or even a local union, like Local 65, than it does to run a Ford or a U.S. Steel. Because a Ford or a U.S. Steel is there, on the ground, in the world, like a ton of rocks, while the union that is its counterweight has the lightness of a dream. But if it is genius to conjure up a union, it is not the kind that counts for much in this country, and besides, there are not many people, like a Sadlowski, or a Romano, or a Balanoff, who have it.

But these three men, for example, would never talk about it as I have here, as a matter of genius, or being "smart," or even "having a good heart." Jim Balanoff once told me, "It's your belly."

He said, "Does the guy have a good belly?"

Sadlowski told me the same thing, "That's what I want to

know. Does the guy have a good gut? How does it sit in his gut?"

Jim Balanoff was talking about American Bridge. He drives past the place now, all shuttered along I-90, a big spooky place. When Balanoff was district director, there was a chance, maybe, to save American Bridge. The company wanted concessions, the workers voted no, and American Bridge closed. Jim said, "I could have saved it, but hell, I let them decide.

"And you know, I drive past that place all the time, and it still sits right in my gut."

He laughed like a Bulgarian ("we got that good Turk blood in us"), and I like his philosophy. In my reading, only Nietzsche and the Desert Fathers discuss a man's belly the way people do in South Chicago. "What's his belly like?" I could never be a union officer because my own belly, in the 1980s, has been weak, queasy, not Nietzschean enough. I could never drive, like Jim does, past American Bridge and laugh.

My friend E., an investment banker, is a consultant for Steelworkers locals in collective bargaining. He flies out from New York, rents a car at O'Hare, and drives down to 1010 (pronounced "ten-ten") in Indiana for collective bargaining with Inland Steel.

E. is from Lazard Frères and is a genius. Once I asked him, "Are these guys, well . . . are they able to follow you?"

"Oh," he said, "you should see how sophisticated they are. They ask how the new issuance of the Class D preferred will affect the restructuring of . . ."

I started to lose him here.

He said, "I mean, this is a pretty sophisticated local."

It must be just like Manhattan. You can bet that at 1010 they do not waive millions of dollars in pension rights, and it's good to remember that there are some locals like this. In 1010, in fact, they even have their own Union calendar (which I receive). There's a different picture for every month. For January there's a photograph of a contract clause.

But E. works for the International, not the Local. Technically, at the top, labor does seem to be getting smarter. In its dying hour, it is calling in Lazard Frères. With ERISA, ESOPs, leveraged buyouts, proxy fights, labor has no alternative. Yet there is an eerie sense that organized labor seems to be slipping away, not only from the members but even from Lane Kirkland and Lynn Williams. It's even slipping away from the lawyers, people like me. It's as if the "smarter" labor becomes at the top, the faker the whole thing seems to become.

Maybe when it all goes, they'll finally murder all the lawyers. But for now they still have to work with us. Once, a union officer told me about a kid he had scared. The "kid" was a management lawyer whom he ran into downtown at the NLRB.

"So," he said, "I went up to the kid, who was a young kid, your age, and I said to him, 'How come a nice kid like you trying to *fuck workers?*'

"Kid jumped back, and said, 'Oh, *oh* . . . what did you say?' "
He imitated a kid shaking with fright.

Upset, I said, "You can't *say* that."

"Why not?"

"I don't know, you just *can't.*"

I wanted to say: That kid doesn't mean anything by it. He's just being a lawyer . . . probably he goes home at night and listens to the Talking Heads and "Burning Down the House." And he probably *likes* you, even, and then you come up like that . . .

In short, I was upset.

Well, I'm a lawyer, too, and there have to be certain rules.

Chapter 9

Life in the Theater

To me, the best part of being a labor lawyer, or the only part that is any fun in this dark age, is to be with the dissidents. It is also the part that a union lawyer should avoid: we are not supposed to side with the rebels. And to my shame, this is the part I most like, the part that weakens the labor movement, everybody says. But I like it down here, in the cellar of American labor, where people crawl out, desperate, to be stewards and officers.

This is the place in labor, down here, at the very bottom, where I think, romantically, I will "cross class lines." I keep swearing off dissidents, yet I am always waiting for one, a new one, to walk into the office. I think, "Maybe this is someone I should follow." I am fascinated by whether he can do it: whether he, a rank-and-filer, can turn himself into a union officer. Then, if he does do it, does it make any difference? I am fairly passive, waiting for a new one to walk in the office. It was said to me once, a lawyer has to wait for the right client, latch on to him, see where he takes him. But it is perverse in a way: I am the one who went to law school, I work downtown in the Loop. Yet I am waiting expectantly on some guy who works in a mill.

If a dissident walks in the office, how do I know I should sign up with him? Is he the guy who can build a movement or bring a crowd?

A few months back, I remember, Jerry came to the office.

He was running for business agent. Should I take a chance on him? He was in a pin-striped suit, that was O.K., but no socks, and that bothered me. He seemed to be wearing black silk stockings. He was cross-eyed, too. He had a little, intense, screwed-up red face. And he smelled of gin. In fact, he looked a little demonic. And he kept saying, in a loud voice, "Oh boy, they *know* me down at the hall."

A TDU member once told me, "The guys who start out running for Union office? Don't trust them. They're out for themselves. And if they get elected, you can't trust them in office. No, the good ones, they start out fighting the Boss. They don't even know about Union office. They just keep going and going, and fighting the company, and doing more and more things. And then somebody says to them, 'Hey, there's this other thing, Union office,' and they think, 'Oh yeah, maybe I should do that.' "

I used to wonder: Why do they do this? Why go for Union office instead of, say, trying to become a foreman or a supervisor? Well, in the Teamsters, the money's about the same. Besides, as I said, you are free, a bohemian, you can hang out in coffeehouses: as a foreman, you're just at a different level of UPS hell. Who wants to go into "management" when there is this "other thing," Union office?

There are no lawyers who want to take these cases, so I should have a clear field. Yet I still pick the wrong guys.

Actually (this is a chilling thought), in all these elections, my side has *never* won.

In Local —— I've represented the dissidents in the last three Union-officer elections. We ran one time as the Lion Slate, and another time as the Inter-Slate. The name for our slate keeps getting worse.

But our side, by whatever name, always loses. Two to one. When you lose in Local ——, it's *always* two to one.

We lose, yet I've never seen a local so ripe for winning as Local ——. There are now 15,000 members in the Local and the membership seems to dislike the officers, who have been in power for decades. These are old men now, in their seventies, Irish, bald, red in the face, at the age that Irish old men start to go "pop," with a stroke or aneurysm, like old Mayor Daley, their hero. Recently, one of them did go "pop," but another old man replaced him. There is an occasional grand jury investigation of the Local, but none of us can tell if it is "mobbed up" or not. Anyway, the real issue in the Local is not the Mob or corruption. The real issue in the Local is hardening of the arteries: these are old men, like "your old man," cranky, irritable, still fighting rock and roll, who still look on people my age as kids. They can still negotiate contracts that look good on paper, at least for the high-paid, over-the-road drivers (for them, maybe, anybody could). But there is no follow-up, no enforcement, no servicing of the contract. Too many discharges, bungled grievances, unreturned phone calls. This is a rank and file that should be restless.

Nobody likes them, this old guard, but nobody can get them out. Even though the Local is about 15,000, the most these old men can get, in any election, is 1,800 votes. Just think of it: with 1,800 votes, out of 15,000, they can run the Local. They can control a pension fund with a third of a billion dollars in assets. They can draw individual salaries of up to $250,000 a year or more. Why would any young man, seeing all this, not want to take his shot?

To be sure, my clients wouldn't take the salaries of bandits . . . our side would settle for the salaries of yuppies. But in this Local, that's real reform.

Yet our side, mysteriously, can't even get the 1,800 votes. In a local of 15,000, we can't even get 1,801. Or if we have, the votes have somehow disappeared.

It is true, in general, that unions do not have permanent opposition parties. Every local union is like a one-party state, and normally, one gets into power like an apparatchik, by going to night law school, becoming a son-in-law, and then murdering someone. But there are some that come close to being opposition parties, like Jim and his friends. Of course, they're doing it the hard way . . . running for election.

The worst part is always election night. Every three years I tell myself, "This time, dammit, don't go down to the hall. It's too painful." But then, like an idiot, I go down. It is always the same. As the votes are counted, we get the numbers, and I stand there with the clients, and feel so helpless. It is the worst, most helpless feeling in the world. We stand around expressionless, as they kick our brains out.

Two to one. It seems that when you lose, it's always two to one. All I want to do is scream.

I see the men, they hold it in all night, then at midnight, after the count, they walk out on 47th Street, look up at the stars, and that cold wind on the South Side just blows and blows. I know what they must think: "Three more years of those assholes. Oh, God, God, *God* . . ."

Not to mention three more years of driving a truck.

After election night, the worst part is the morning after, when we have our slate meeting to go over the results. I have to go, because here we talk about what went wrong, what violations the other side committed. It's always the same. We meet in a basement. There is a treasurer who lists expenses. The other men pull out their wallets and pay up their shares. Everybody is thinking the same thing: "I can't believe it, I can't believe we lost." They gave up their vacation time to campaign. The wives are furious.

Jim chairs the meeting, and at the end he looks around the room. "Hey, this time we showed them we're a force to be reckoned with."

Then he goes outside and throws up.

So the campaign drags on to the next election. It's like the Hundred Years' War in this one little local. Our election protest also drags on through the Labor Department and the courts. I would love to be shed of it, but then I think, "I have to help Jim." He *did* walk into the office, and I did bet on him. By this point, I am caught in it, trapped, partly by friendship now, but also by the fact that I am running, in a way, for union office, too. I'm in the same boat with them, and they know it. I guess, whether I like it or not, we're all running on the same ticket.

So we file our protest, and we say the elections are rigged, and I think they are. But after three defeats, I ask myself, "Did we really win, or did we lose?" I can accept the cheating, the rigging, etc., if I can only *know*. Sometimes I wish I could say to the other side, "Come on, what was the real count? Seriously, off the record. I promise not to tell."

One time I'd like to know, just for the hell of it, if we really did win.

In fact, this last election, I thought we had won. The Labor Department finally had acted on one of our protests, and as a result, the Department struck a deal with the Local to have a loose supervision of the 1988 election. It was not the full supervision we sought, but it was better than anything we had ever had.

It was sobering for all of us to think, my God we could really *win*. None of the men, Jim or Bill or the others, had any experience in running a union. They had never run a pension fund with a third of a billion dollars in assets. Now, for the first time, they had to realize they could be elected, and they became odd, dreamy, distant, thinking of their inaugurations.

I remember Jim once, for no reason, blurting out, "I can *run* it."

"Run what?" I said.

"I can run it, I can run this Local, I know it, I've thought about it."

Then he began a speech, and it could have been iambic pentameter. It is the kind Shakespeare puts at the very start, in Act I.

"Tom, that last contract, the ratification . . . I was the guy. I called the meeting. And I know, after that . . . well, the other guys at work, they see me differently."

Then he said, "Yeah, I should have gone into management. I could have been a foreman . . . . I know I could have done that. I don't know, maybe I will do that. I don't know, though, there are things I've got to *do*."

Anyway, what could management offer that was half as good?

Jim is a married man, and so are most of the men on our slate. It is a good sign to have married men, with kids, on the slate. When the married men are involved (not the bachelors, the monks, the professional dissidents yearning for self-immolation), maybe the incumbents can be knocked off. The married man is different. He is careful not to be beaten up. He is a careful, cautious man, who in a careful, cautious way has become desperate enough, at last, to lunge for "lost time," in a big way, in one wild roll of the dice.

I envy them for getting to roll the dice. So often I think, "They're blowing it, they're blowing the campaign," and I would love to step in and do it for them. Sometimes, without thinking, I almost pick up the pen and start rewriting our campaign literature. My God, even the flyer . . . it's so crude. I see a couple of typos. No wonder we lose . . . But no, no, at the last minute I stop. I put down the pen, because this would be the great, unforgivable Miltonian sin. I'm only the lawyer, I can only serve.

But still I think, "Why don't we get a professional to do our literature?" I whisper, "Can't you do something about this?" The members must think . . . well, for all they know, we're a bunch of LaRouchies. And how else *would* they know, if they don't go to the meetings?

Yet still, this last year, I thought we could really win it at last. The Labor Department would be supervising. I thought the members had been waiting, just waiting, for the chance to throw the bums out. And the chance to vote us in: men like themselves, rank and file, to run the pension fund, negotiate their wages.

I had a horrible feeling in the pit of my stomach. This is the election, the "honest" election, which, of all the elections, I dread the most.

Around 9 p.m., I went down the hall, and to my shock, we were in the lead. I could not believe it. I had come from a wedding. Then for a while I had dawdled across the street, where I watched part of a bullfight. It was in the International Amphitheatre, and there had been a big controversy about it. The bull was under the protection of a court order. I stayed as long as I could: I didn't want to cross the street.

But when I did, we seemed to be winning. The count had been going on for two hours. The voters were gone. My clients, in three-piece pin-striped suits, stood around, statesmanlike, and some had big, happy grins. They looked ready to be inaugurated.

Jim came over and said, "See our numbers?"

The numbers looked great. Jim was beaming.

He said, "Look at those guys over there, they're shitting in their pants."

I looked and saw four or five huge men, who seemed to be bouncers, with big key chains on their belts. One of them was staring at me.

"They don't look worried to me," I said.

"Ho, they're worried, believe me."

Harry, one of our candidates, came up and said, "Hey, the other side's been saying to me, 'Looks like you guys are going to elect some business agents.' "

On a local-union election night, there are no such things as projections, so we wait, in the prehistoric state of our grand-parents, when they simply had to count every vote. On election night, without computers, it is all a dream world: for hours, everything can be seen, even to the losing side, in the light of resurrection. But we really *were* in the lead, and we did know, this time, we were not getting our brains kicked out, and that sense alone could give a certain light-headedness, even dizziness. We were on laughing gas, with our lead, and even to me, after a while, the bouncers looked worried.

There were six counting tables, and there were two counting stations at each table. The Local, not the Labor Department, was running the election, but four or five women from the Department stood near the various tables. We had observers, and so did the government, yet I had the strange sense that no one was really "observing." Nobody out on the floor can know what is going on at all the tables, with all the ballots (used and unused), all the time. I walked from table to table, visited our observers, took down their reports: I work in Chicago elections, union elections, I know how to do this pretty well. And I have *no* idea what is going on. I just walk around the room, the way Bloom walked around Dublin, sometimes stopping for an epiphany or to have a chat.

As observers, we only were looking at the walk-in ballots from Saturday's voting in the hall. No one, however, had observed the Local's handling of the mail ballots from members living outside the Chicago area. There had been 3,400 personal requests for mail ballots, and now, on election day, only 1,700 ballots had come back. The other 1,700 ballots were missing.

I was stunned: 1,700 missing ballots.

A woman from the Labor Department said, "You can protest it." She thought it was normal.

All Saturday, during the vote, we had been depressed about the mail ballots. But tonight it didn't seem to matter. With the walk-in votes, we were going to win anyway. All of us (well, most of us) were elated.

I went over to talk to Francis, our candidate for trustee. He is a big bony man, with a big white handlebar mustache, like that of a lieutenant in British India who had fought at the Khyber Pass.

I said, "Francis, we're ahead."

He looked disgusted. "We should be way ahead."

I thought, "Hm . . . this must be his first election."

"What is it with the members?" he said. "My God, the apathy out there is incredible.

"When Jim and I went around . . . well, I think Jim got mad at me. Everywhere we went, I kept getting in front of him, and grabbing these men, and I'd say, 'Hey, the Labor Department is supervising, you've got to vote. Hey, we're holding the door open. Hey, me, Jim, we're holding the door open. Vote, vote, vote.' "

Then he said, "And now, look at this turnout."

I thought the turnout was good: 3,100 members voting out of 11,000 or so. Not counting the 1,700 missing ballots.

I said, "Francis, that's 28 percent of the Local. It's the highest it's ever been."

Francis looked at me in disgust. He said, "The apathy out there is incredible."

To me, it is clear why more of them do not vote, but it is hard to explain. You have to stand outside the hall. It is not frightening, I guess, but not the most pleasant thing you could do on your day off. Sometimes, when I am out there, on the sidewalk, a business agent comes up to me, two, three inches away, in the most calculated, precise, microscopic invasion of my personal space. They must go to grad school to calculate it. Because, after all, he is just being friendly. He wants to see if

I am friendly, too. He is so friendly, in fact, I want to call the cops. And if he is friendly with me, a lawyer, imagine how friendly he is with the rank and file. Who wants to drive in from suburbia for that?

Besides, who should they vote for anyway? They must think we are nuts, with Francis running around UPS docks screaming, "Vote, vote, vote," a man they have never even seen before. The goons, compared with us, have so much more poise.

At 10 p.m., we were still ahead. I was talking to Harry, our candidate for business agent. Harry really did worry the other side. He was our war hero, an ex-Marine, who had won a Silver Star in Vietnam.

I asked him about it. He said, "I could have won the Congressional Medal of Honor. But, you know, I was just a kid. I didn't know politics."

Harry was my age, but he still had the body of Rambo or something. He was shot three times, he said, but I wondered, looking at him, how the bullets could have made a dent.

All day long, the Local sent over punks, young kids, to bait Harry, to get him to throw a punch. The kids were foulmouthed, nasty, but it was just a game, and everyone knew it. Harry just laughed. Nobody was really going to throw a punch, not out there, on the sidewalk . . . not with the ladies from the Labor Department inside the hall.

I said, "Harry, you're going to be a business agent."

He shrugged, he seemed indifferent. He said, "Really, I'd like to go to law school."

I thought, "Oh God . . ."

"Where did you go?" he said.

I told him. We got past it.

He said he had tried to take the LSATs last year. "I just couldn't do it, though, I . . . my buddies had to come and take me away." He was making it sound like Vietnam.

He kept talking about it, like a dream. Then suddenly, at all the tables, the counting stopped. The tellers began wrapping up the ballots in brown paper and masking tape.

The election was over.

I thought, "We've won."

There was conferring among the election judges. Then the

union president stood up. He seemed to be about eighty or so and frail. He read the results in a frail voice. My heart stopped.

We lost, our whole slate. We got creamed. The results were the same for all candidate positions: about 1,800 votes for them, about 1,200 votes for us.

My mouth fell open. We lost. It was not even close.

Then the people in the hall, the goons, the BAs, the secretaries, all the Local employees, began to applaud. It was not applause, really, but a jeer, a form of assault: it was their way of saying, "So, assholes, you went to the Labor Department, and you still lost."

One of our group said, "Let's get out of here, fast." I think I said it.

Jim said to me, "We're going to protest this thing, right? This isn't the end."

I didn't know what to say.

There was no meeting the next day. The idea of it was unbearable. Even later, the men were still in anguish. I did not want to meet or file any more protests. I had been so depressed after the vote I had stopped at midnight at a Mexican restaurant. By myself. What was I doing with my life?

Del, our chief observer, was not a candidate. He was our numbers guy, low-key, unemotional. He was observing as a favor, he had nothing at stake: he could be unemotional.

At the meeting, Del was emotional.

"Look, if we lost, we lost, that's O.K. by me. But don't tell me that the count was over by 10 p.m. I was watching the tally sheets. I watched them as they were done. Tom, I saw eight tally sheets for the 'slate' votes and only two for the 'splits.' And there were a lot more 'splits.' There had to be eight more tally sheets. At least eight. I couldn't have missed eight tally sheets . . . I could have missed one, maybe two . . . but don't tell me I missed eight."

But I could not believe it. I had been there, the government had been there.

I thought, "They wouldn't have had the nerve to steal it right in front of me."

Then Jim said, "Tom, I was watching you, you were quiet, but I knew you were taking it all in."

I nodded modestly.

My father had told me once, when I was a boy, "Look out for the fast count." And now maybe I had been fast-counted.

Still, would they have stolen it right in front of us? No, they had too much respect for us, they . . .

As I thought about it, I became more and more offended.

We asked for a recount, but the recount showed nothing. Del was still not convinced; neither was Jim, Harry, or Francis. They now thought the tellers, during a commotion, had switched a stack of ballots.

A woman from the Labor Department said, "I feel sorry for your guys, I really do. For a while there I thought they were going to win. But now, well, I think they're reaching."

Yes, maybe we were reaching. But it was one way to go on believing, to keep up morale, so we could gear up, in three years, and do it all again. Besides, 1,700 mail ballots were missing: I did not think 1,700 missing ballots was "normal."

Yet it was possible that the members had simply reelected the hacks.

Even if they had, I think the Lion Slate would have filed a protest. We would go on believing in union democracy. We would not trust the evidence of the senses.

I'd still like to ask, off the record, "Come on, what was the real count?" But lately, I admit, I'm not sure I want to know.

I just read in the *Economist* magazine that people like Jim and Francis will be gone in twenty years. There will be no "hand" workers, no steelworkers, no Teamsters on docks, just "brain" workers, punching things into computers. The hand workers I know, running for union office, are being bred out of existence, even as crypto-yuppies. They are high school grads, dinosaurs. Their kids will be taken away from them and raised by computers. So it is poignant, to me, that in Local X there still are goons in the Union hall on election day. In twenty years, when we're productive and New Age, there'll be no place for goons, or for anger, or for cursing. There will be no union elections. No one will push anyone else off the sidewalk.

Even now, in Local X nothing ever really happens. The word "fuck" is all that's left. This is just as true of the Steelworkers, the Boilermakers, etc. I think it's impossible in some unions even to have an election without the word "fuck." It's everything in a man's life, his sword, his buckler, his shield. Sometimes, a man's whole career threads in and out of that single word, like the eye of a needle.

I could classify the different unions by the use of the word "fuck." Try to imagine labor as a spectrum, with discrete, quantumlike gaps: at one end, the Teamsters and the Boilermakers, and then the Steelworkers and the Carpenters, and then all the way to the other end, to AFSCME and the Teachers, where the word isn't used at all. Not all of labor is like the Teamsters. There's a whole section of it where there are English teachers, vegetarians, men and women who send valentines to each other and swoon on the Eve of St. Agnes.

But I want to stay for a moment at the dark end of this spectrum.

Some day a philosopher, or linguist, or deconstructionist, can explain to me how people can do business, conduct public affairs, by saying back and forth, "Fuck you" and "Fuck you." Was this how they did it in ancient Athens, the first democracy? It's the most degrading thing about being a labor lawyer. The whole English language drops away, and this "fuck talk" takes over. A few years ago, I had to present a case to a jury, and relate what went on at a union hall. My client, being a literal man, got up and told his story, literally, and didn't leave out a single word.

"So, Mr. X, can you tell us what was said?"

" 'Fuck you.' "

"And was there any response?"

"Yes. 'You scum-shit, fuck you.' "

We went through days of testimony this way. And I kept seeing two or three suburban matrons on the jury, looking at me.

"What have you done with your life?" they seemed to be saying with their eyes.

And I felt, standing before them, like their lost little boy.

But who knows? Maybe it's our national language. Isn't it the language of our theater? David Mamet, for example, is our great national playwright, and Mamet writes this way. English teachers teach it. It's the language of the American stage, and even the English stage. It started out with Shakespeare, and it's ended up with "Fuck you."

And Mamet is the son of a labor lawyer in Chicago. And the stepson of another labor lawyer from Chicago. And I'm a labor lawyer in Chicago. So I know where David Mamet gets his characters and his dialogue. Except David Mamet lives in Vermont and makes a fortune, and I'm still here in Chicago, standing on a sidewalk in front of a union hall, and watching grown men dancing up to each other and dancing back and saying, "Fuck you," and "Fuck you," and each "fuck" is like a fist punching in the air, to no real point.

But here I can watch it for free. Off-Broadway, it's $40 a seat.

I have clients who are beaten up at the hall, but mostly they aren't. Instead, it's a pseudo-violence most of the time, and in some locals it's so . . . choreographed, like in the theater, they should have "fight captains" as BAs.

For example, a few years ago in a certain Local, the Teamsters hired the El Rukyns, an insanely dangerous black gang from the ghetto, to provide "security" for the election. Now, this Local is mostly white, so this gang of black kids was brought in to be the "muscle."

It was sad, though, that the old white officers of the Local couldn't call upon their own kids to help. I can just imagine these kids, soft, effete, sucking on grapes out in the suburbs, while poor, young El Rukyns back in the city have to put the sticks of dynamite under the cars.

On election day, the old Teamsters stood there, with megaphones, shrieking at our guys, "You scum-shit, fuck you . . ." and the El Rukyns would press up and surround some of us, and shriek, too, shouting something in El Rukyn.

Yet nothing happened.

The woman to whom I told this story said, "How do you know they were El Rukyns?"

How do I *know*? Of course they were El Rukyns . . . Why do women always want to ruin these stories?

So even the El Rukyns do damn little, for all the money they get. It's all playacting. Yet it seems that the playacting, the "fuck talk," keeps building up, year after year, like a pressurized vessel building steam.

I'm surprised, by the way, how much I've been writing about violence. I'm not a violent person. I haven't hit anyone since grade school. Yet after all these years as a labor lawyer, standing outside union halls, I think I've been building up to take a swing at someone. I know that, as a lawyer, that's not my job: my job is to hold the client's coat.

Yet I feel like a Boilermaker under pressure. Or a Teamster. Or a Steelworker.

The other night at a party, I met a woman who was a psychiatrist.

"Say," I asked her, "what *is* a neurosis? I've never really heard it defined."

"Well," she said, "it's like when you want to hit someone, but you don't, and you do something else instead."

"Oh," I said, "like . . . practice labor law?"

And she smiled this Mona Lisa smile that women psychiatrists have.

Of all the "fuck talk" and pseudo-violence, I think the kinkiest I've ever seen was in Local Y, a Steelworkers local in Gary.

The president of the Local was a man named Phil Cyprian, who had a crush, it seems, on Mussolini. He used to show up at the Union hall like a head of state, sitting in a police squad car, siren light flashing. Then an honor guard of off-duty cops would escort him into the hall. Machiavelli says in *The Prince* that the prince should always keep a militia. Well, Cyprian had two of them. Not only did he have the cops, but he would deputize certain Union members to walk around the hall with guns.

I represented the dissidents, and some of them got guns as well. If a man didn't have a gun, at least he'd put a bulge in a pocket where a gun might be. If you didn't have a bulge, you just weren't a player, politically, in Local Y.

Cyprian wanted absolute power, but my clients stood in the way. Some of them held office as stewards or grievance men.

One day, Cyprian called for new elections for steward, even though the old terms had not expired. The purpose was to rig the vote, and throw out his enemies, and then Cyprian would feel . . . safe.

All day long, as members voted, the off-duty cops twirled their guns. Our men patted their bulges. As night drew near, Cyprian must have known he had lost, or he had planned this anyway:

Suddenly, about midnight, the off-duty cops pulled their guns and told our observers, Jimmy and Troy, to raise their hands. "Slowly, slow, slow . . ."

Jimmy and Troy raised their hands. The cops pushed them into a small room. Now, you'd expect the cops at this point to put a bullet in each man's head.

But instead, they took the ballot box, and got in the squad car, and roared out of the parking lot and onto the highway.

Jimmy and Troy ran to their cars, and roared out after them.

Remember, this is an election for shop steward.

They lost the cops. They cruised all night through the streets of Gary, and went from police station to police station.

In the morning, the cops came back with the box, and the seals on the box seemed broken. But the cops wouldn't let the observers look.

As soon as the count started, it was clear that our side had lost.

Anyway, the point of the story is: there was *no violence*.

In a way, I don't blame the Cyprians, or the others, for stealing elections. Boyle killed Yablonski. Someone killed Hoffa. They do it, in the end, to save their lives. Because the loss of union office is unthinkable. It is down, straight down, into the rank and file, and there is nothing to break the fall. There is no private law firm where the defeated candidates can retire. No, it's back to the mill or the plant. Perhaps in no other political career is defeat at the polls so dreadful. How can you go back there, to the shop floor? How can you give up the skybox at Soldier Field and instead take a lot of shit from your foreman? How can you take your family back to all that?

It's easy to talk about union democracy, the right to vote. But even the good union officers, the honest ones, who believe in all this, must also think, deep down in their hearts, "My God, you don't know what you're asking." It's inhuman to ask it. It's about as thinkable as going through the last act of *Oedipus Rex* blinded and screaming.

But then there's the story of Tony Mazzochi, an officer in the Oil, Chemical, and Atomic Workers. Mazzochi was a legend in labor, as the man who pushed through Congress the Occupational Safety and Health Act (OSHA). He lived in Washington, a professional man, as much as anyone else in that town. Then, in the early eighties, when he lost an election, he moved back to Long Island and went back to the plant. He was in his mid-fifties, at the height of his skills and powers, and he went back to the plant. No one else at his level of organized labor would have dreamed of it. It still gives me the creeps to think of it. I wonder what it was like to be the foreman of Tony Mazzochi.

On the other hand, at the UMW, after six months in coats and ties, these men who had been ordinary miners . . . well, anyone could see that they couldn't go back. There was a saying at the UMW: "He's tasted the forbidden fruit." Every officer, the day he takes office, tastes the forbidden fruit, and it seems as if from then on, whether he knows it or not, he is a sworn bitter blood-enemy forever of union democracy.

Even in the UAW, the good, progressive UAW, they stuff ballot boxes and fix elections. Just recently, in 1989, the Secretary of Labor sued the UAW over the vote fraud in the election loss of Jerry Tucker, who was running for vice president of the International. Now, the UAW in labor is like the League of Women Voters. And if they steal in the UAW, they do it idealistically, out of principle. But then, to some extent, all the union officers who steal do it out of principle. They look at their opponents and think, "Who are *they*?" Sometimes they're just rank and file. No background, no training, to run something like the UAW.

And sometimes it's true. They aren't fit to hold high union office. They are high school graduates. Somebody *should* steal these elections.

So I don't blame the Cyprians, and all the rest, for stealing these elections. No, I blame the Congress, and the federal government, for letting them get away with it.

In one afternoon of work, the U.S. Congress could fix not only the problems of American labor but the entire cultural crisis of the West, by passing a law that requires an outside neutral agency to count the ballots in local-union elections. Well, perhaps there should be a few more provisions:

Require a rank-and-file vote for all officers.

Give all bona fide candidates a copy of the membership list.

Provide "public funding" from the union treasury for all the candidates.

I guess it is madness, delusion on my part, to think that simply changing the law would make so much difference. The cultural crisis of the West would continue unabated. But I'm a lawyer, so what can you expect? I think everything can be fixed by a law. A writer of any depth, like an Orwell or Camus, wouldn't be so shallow or mechanistic, or tell their readers to write to Congress. But then anyone with depth, anyone serious, wouldn't have thrown away his life dealing with the Department of Labor.

It's true that there is a law already that requires union democracy, the Landrum–Griffin Act. But the Act is something of a joke.

First, Landrum–Griffin does *not* require rank-and-file elections, at least of the International officers. To the contrary, it expressly approves of indirect elections, delegate conventions . . . and with all of that, the corrupt boroughs, the brokered deals, the parties in Las Vegas at the Sands Hotel. The delegates to these conventions don't even have to be elected. They can go "ex officio," by virtue of being union officers. There are no national candidacies, or national campaigns. In most unions, the rank-and-file members don't even know when the elections occur. Nor is there any real need to tell them.

Second, although Landrum–Griffin does require rank-and-file election of local officers, there is no attempt to require an honest ballot. This is partly the fault of the act itself, which should simply require that a neutral outside agency count the vote. But it's also the fault of the Labor Department. For example, the Act says that all candidates have the right to place observers. If the right to observe is denied, the Labor Department in theory could require a new election.

But over the years, I've had several conversations with lowly Labor Department officials in Washington that go like this:

"They kicked us out of the room," I say. "They denied our right to observe."

"Well," the man says, "that's a violation of the act. But did it affect the outcome of the election? As you know, that's what you have to prove."

"What do you mean?"

"Well, after they threw out your observers, did they do anything wrong?"

"We don't *know*, obviously. They kicked us out."

"Well, then how do you expect us to bring the case?"

Most of the time, I can't even find out who to talk to. The field investigator in Chicago says to me, "Out here, we wanted to bring a case, but the General Counsel's office in Washington said no."

"Well, who said no? Maybe I can talk to him."

"We can't tell you *that*."

"Why not? I just want to call him."

"We can't give that out."

So one or two people, whose names I don't know, are making these decisions in Washington. And if they don't help you, you're out of luck. Federal law forbids a union member from taking his own case to court.

I bet that at the big marble palaces of the AFL-CIO they know who to call. The Labor Department was set up to be their spokesman, their champion, their liaison to the White House. If that's so, how is the Labor Department supposed to sue these same people? It's not.

A few years ago, I did get through to a lawyer who had turned down one of my clients. I said, "How do you decide ever to bring a case at all?"

"We only bring cases," he said, "when there aren't any facts in dispute."

"You mean, if ten people saw Mr. A. steal a ballot but Mr. A. said he didn't, you wouldn't bring the case?"

"No, there would be a fact in dispute."

Meanwhile, men and women plunge into union politics, and become the tragic heroes of their own lives, all because of a mistake, or a delusion: the delusion that the Labor Department will enforce the law. Or the "Labor Board," as many call it, because they mix it up with the NLRB.

I've seen people sit in my office, and chuckle, and say, "One day, all this stuff I've been seeing all these years, I'm going to take it to the Labor Board."

"The Labor Department," I say.

"That's what I said."

The "stuff" is usually a rumor of some kind which has grown up over the years and is probably false.

The old man sits there, and chuckles. The years go by, and he tells himself, over and over, "One day, I'm going to the Labor Department."

I don't know whether to be bitter at the Labor Department or not. On the one hand, it doesn't enforce the law. On the other hand, if it didn't exist as a kind of mirage, I suppose people wouldn't dare to run for union office at all.

It's annoying, though, to see these men and women become obsessed with ballot fraud, stealing, etc. "Don't worry about that," I tell them, because it only distracts them from campaigning, which is what they should be doing. But they think about it anyway. They obsess about it, the black art of stealing elections. They come up with wild fantasies. They stay up all night outside the hall, or the post office, and the wives come and bring them food in covered dishes.

They weep in the dark. I eat all the apple strudel.

Sometimes I wonder if the UAW, the Teamsters, and all the rest of them aren't right. These rank-and-file members, truck drivers, or waitresses, or whoever, are they capable of running the local? I'm talking here about a *big* local, maybe 10,000 members, where the officers will be full-time and will wear coats and ties and sit on pension boards with billions of dollars. On the other hand, where did the Teamsters officers we're running against come from? They didn't *all* come from MIT . . . no, and they hire John Climaco, lawyer for the Mob.

So isn't our side just as capable? They'd simply hire different lawyers and accountants. Isn't that what it all leads to . . . union democracy, the right to vote? The right of the members to switch law firms?

The right to switch lawyers. There's a depressing thought . . . not whether they're capable of running the local, but whether I am. And yet . . .

Better me, I think, than John Climaco.

There is a good case to be made against union democracy, and I'll try to present it as best I can.

First, the people in Big Labor would say there *is* union democracy, and they'd cite the frequent turnover in union offices. Academics with ties to labor tend to cite these figures. But the numbers are fake. They include the thousands of little locals, no bigger than sandboxes, with 100 members or less, where it doesn't really matter who holds office at all.

But then the people in Big Labor will say, "But we *do* elect our International officers," and they drag out the constitutions and bylaws and say, "See, look at all this democracy." But they had elections all the time in Stalinist Russia, too: the Central Committee, the Politburo, etc.

Then after a drink or two, they tell the truth. They weep, they tear their garments, and say, "Look what happened to the Mineworkers."

For God's sakes, will they stop with the Mineworkers?

Yet I think that, secretly, some of them would like to see more democracy. Right now, they'd like to see something, anything, any sign of life in the labor movement. They know labor is in decline, they must sense that their own power is draining, and they must know that if the rank and file did start to care, did come out to vote . . . then maybe their own power would increase.

But elections, democracy, turnover in office? No, no, they are not willing to drain that cup of hemlock.

•

I could make large mystical claims for democracy. I could try to talk like the people in Plato's *Symposium*. I could cite the moral beauty of it and how, if labor had this moral beauty, we could procreate in beauty, and our numbers would increase. The whole dreadful "fuck talk" would drop away, and we could procreate our brains out in moral beauty.

But forget the moral beauty of it. It's simply more efficient to give people the right to vote. Without it, organized labor is like a giant S&L, completely unregulated, with all that must follow, and that's why unions are crashing, one by one. There's no trade-off between beauty and efficiency. I think all these trade-offs turn out to be illusory. For example, at least where unions are concerned, there is no trade-off between having more "rights" and having more "community." It seems to me that the more you have the right to vote, the right to assemble, etc., in a local union, the more community you have as well.

Isn't that the damnedest thing? Only liberalism can deliver us from isolation.

But I doubt there will be a change in Landrum–Griffin. In Washington, there is no organized constituency in favor of union democracy. The presidents of the unions are against it, of course. Business is against it, because it's disruptive. Congress is against it, simply because the people who control the union PACs are. The Labor Department is against it. There was the freak case of Rudolph Giuliani, the U.S. Attorney in New York, but his only interest was to get rid of the Mob.

Most of the labor experts, academics, etc., say nothing about this. They don't know, or want to know, what's going on. And there are others who do know, and are appalled, but they can't speak out, because they're *in* the unions. I can talk about it, but then I don't have a skybox at Soldier Field. That's why the subject of union democracy never comes up. If a big local in Chicago came along and said to me, "Here's our business," I'm sure I wouldn't have written this book.

In fact, sometimes I'm not even sure I am a labor lawyer. Every year in Chicago, there's an event called the Lawyers Conference of the AFL-CIO. Technically I should be invited, but I never am, and I think it's because I sue the Teamsters. Sometimes my labor lawyer friends try to sneak me in, but lately I've gotten nervous. I'm afraid another lawyer will spot me, and storm over, and say, "What are *you* doing here?"

One year, some of my friends called me and said, "Hey, we're at the Hyatt. Come up for a drink."

I met them in the usual Hyatt-type bar, with the waterfall, the jungle, the birds. And one of the lawyers said, "Come on, we'll get you into this."

And another said, "Why won't they let him in?"

"He sued the Teamsters."

"You're kidding. That's the reason?"

"Look," I said, "I don't want to go in."

"What?"

"Come on . . ."

They looked at me. "Prima donna," they probably thought.

Of course, I do want to go in. And if one of my clients had ever won an election, then I could have gone in there. I could have swept into their little conference as T. E. Lawrence swept into the British officers' club in Cairo, and people would have whispered, "Who's that?"

"I don't know."

"One of ours?"

And they would have bought me drinks, and cleared a path for me.

But I told my friends no. Just leave it alone.

And the truth is, I'm secretly afraid that they *could* get me in, and no one would give a damn if I was in there or not.

CHAPTER 10

Free Trade

Some of my own friends say to me, "Do you really want to take food from the tables of starving Third World workers?" My *own* friends. Often they have their money tied up in real estate or cappuccino and would never, any of them, even put a nickel into steel. But they look at me, the labor goon, as if I was taking money from the poor box. "Will he, or will he not, attack Free Trade?" Then, the question hanging in the air, they wait, wait for the moment when they can pounce, when my Dr. Jekyll turns into Mr. Hyde, when I say the slightest little negative word against . . . Free Trade.

Oh yes, I drive an American car. So what? Is it against the law? I drive a Ford Escort, because it is cheap, and I get no credit for it, either, from anyone in labor. No union official told me to do it. They warn me *against* American cars. Ed Sadlowski did, early on. He said, "Drive any damn thing you want."

Even Frank Lumpkin drives a foreign car, a Volkswagen. I said to him, "Frank, don't people around here, in South Chicago, give you a lot of grief? I mean, you being a steelworker?"

He said, "Yeah . . . But you drive a Mercedes, and no one says anything . . . because that Mercedes, that's an all-American car."

I drive the Escort, I guess, just to rattle people, make them think I am against Free Trade. Sometimes I drive it up to Evanston (a place where an Escort is something you give to your kid), and I park it pretty shamelessly, right out on the public street. And when people come out to stare, to see an adult male, a forty-year-old lawyer, getting out of one, I say, "What's the matter?" Of course, I know what they are thinking. But I am violating no law . . . except the laws of Free Trade. Oh, I could attack Free Trade. It's tempting to play the devil. I might even get away with it now, as I could not have two or three years before. Many nasty things can be said about Japan now, even in respectable circles. Politicians, writers, and economists who used to be Free Traders have now, hesitantly, started to switch sides.

I *could* attack Free Trade. I could say how it's not really "Free Trade." Other countries, like England, give billion-dollar subsidies to their steel companies. My friend Ann, the economist, who has studied the steel business in Brazil, says that the industry there isn't a natural economic activity. "It's not a 'real' steel industry, in the sense that it's for internal development, or raising the living standards of the people. It's strictly an export industry. It's just there to earn foreign exchange, so Brazil can pay off the IMF and the New York banks."

But what if she's wrong and it is a "real" steel industry, or as real as ours?

I wouldn't take a chance. Let Brazil have it, I say. Maybe it's their turn to get cancer in coke ovens. This could be what they call, at the University of Chicago, "comparative advantage."

No, I'm in favor of Free Trade. I would lay down my life for it. Seriously. I know steelworkers, too, who would shrug, light cigarettes, and step in front of a firing squad, all for Free Trade.

Because Free Trade did not kill South Chicago. In 1976, about 25 percent of our steel came from abroad. Now, after the Reagan years, the high dollar, the closing of the mills . . . 25 percent of our steel comes from abroad. Yes, there were import quotas, or "voluntary" ones, but at least it shows Free Trade is not the reason so many people lost their jobs. If we backed off making steel, it wasn't because we were forced to. We backed off making steel because we backed off making everything.

Indeed, the United States is now one of the low-cost producers of steel in the world. Not Brazil, not Chad, not the Ivory Coast, but the good old, high-wage, unionized U.S. After 1984, the steel industry was rebuilt, and $10 billion in new capital was invested. Productivity gains have been enormous, four times the national average, especially in the improvement of yields from raw steel. It's remarkable: every mill is now a high-tech mill. Even the fork lifts have computer screens. Frank Lumpkin said to me recently, "You know, a man laid off at Wisconsin Steel in 1980 wouldn't even know how to work in a steel mill now."

Yet it's a strange kind of automation. Not like investment in the past. Automation always seemed to lead to more jobs, somewhere, at some point . . . now it seems to lead nowhere. Workers used to think: It's O.K., it's leading to the next industrial revolution. But now the word on the street is: There isn't going to be a next industrial revolution.

The steel companies seem to want to shrivel, to disappear. For example, Inland Steel had 20,000 Union members in 1976, and now has about 10,000; Gary Works had 12,000 in 1976, and now has about 4,000. Yet Inland and Gary produce more steel today than they did in 1976. This could be good, of course, and steelworkers are not Luddites: they love robotics, high-tech, automation, and being a steelworker was starting to be fun, with a worker doing not one but four or five different jobs. But this is a bleak, stoic, death-wish kind of automation, with no hope of being great again. Down on 63rd Street, where 18,000 can workers used to be, Continental Can is still going, still punching out a million cans a day. "But now," my brother (who sells there) says, "there's no one in the parking lot. Can you believe it? A million cans a day, but no one in the parking lot."

The steel companies automated, *but then did nothing else*. The whole point of capitalism, I thought, is not just to cut costs but to keep coming up with new products, new product uses. Japanese steel companies do. Nippon Steel, for example, spends more on research and development than all U.S. steel companies combined. It's as if we forgot the most important part of competitiveness: to innovate, find new products, new product uses, and new markets, too. For some reason, maybe just an existential weariness, U.S. steel companies stopped doing these things. It was not because of labor, or high wages, or the Third World. These companies could have come up with new products, new product ideas, just as our old Calvinist fathers used to do. No one seemed interested. America sometimes seems like the third or fourth generation of the Buddenbrooks family in the Thomas Mann novel. Nobody wants to go into the old family business, because it is too hard, too much trouble, and no one really believes in it. We want to go into real estate and cappuccino. We could have preserved our industrial base. But was it really worth doing? To people like me, my generation, growing up in the sixties and always knowing we were the superpower, what was the point of just proving, over and over, that we could keep doing it? We had done it. Thanks. Very enjoyable. Now what?

Sure, they did need to close down some of the old mills. But they didn't just tear down the old, inefficient ones. They tore down brand-new ones. They tore down the $100 million No. 6 Mill at Wisconsin Steel, which Frank Lumpkin tried to save. Next door to No. 6, there is a $40 million rail mill, built by USX, brand-new, which just sits next to Lake Michigan and is rusting away. Why did people give up?

I can hardly blame those who run USX, or any other steel company, when I never met anyone going into the steel business, or manufacturing at all, except my own brother. Even my own connection with steel seems a bit affected: an East Coast Harvard graduate representing the workers. Sometimes, in this mood, I think of the people with whom I went to school, especially those whose lives, I think, turned out rather sadly: who should have stayed in the Midwest, grown up, run a company, got on the local school board, done something serious with their lives, in short, but who, instead, left Ohio, Illinois, Michigan, and are stranded now, high and dry, up and down the East Coast, lost somewhere in law or investment banking.

It has always been a mystery to me why in the 1980s the industry sector of the Republican Party let the financial sector roll all over it. Why did the manufacturing people not scream when the banks, Wall Street, Paul Volcker, et al. began liquidating them? Maybe a whole generation of screamers had been lost, a missing generation, a lost generation, nobody to raise the cry, because the most eloquent, who could have done it, had gone over to the other side or expired long ago on the fields of Flanders.

The problem was not so much with labor or management as with the failure to *be* management: to stop being lite, to stop drinking lite beer, to do nothing that was serious, or substantial, or Churchillian with our lives, when our country came under attack. We were not much of an upper class, i.e., me and my friends. Even some of the statesmen of Wall Street, like Felix Rohatyn, seem disturbed that we could not even behave properly on the night of the Great Crash.

For me, the strangest part of the "Crash," in October 1987, was the giggling. All evening, on October 19, I saw TV reporters talking to brokers and bankers, and these men would break into little giggles. They could not control it, just the thought of it, the Dow dropping *500* points . . . The reporter would say, "How about that?" The man would look at him, smile nervously, then out would pop a little giggle.

In 1929, men like these crawled out on ledges and jumped off. Now, it seems, they go on TV and giggle.

The next night, October 20, a friend of mine came to town, for a client who had lost millions. We went out to dinner. For a brief time that morning, the Stock Exchange had almost closed. It had been a frightening moment, almost a total meltdown, and I thought the heat of it, the intensity of it, would have a chilling effect tonight. For once, I thought, the big restaurants on Michigan Avenue would all be deserted.

I was wrong. They were packed. We couldn't even get a reservation on a Tuesday night. I must have called two or three places before I found one, Convito Italiano, which said it could take us, maybe, only if we hurried right over.

Every restaurant on Michigan Avenue must have been a dramatic scene that night: many people thinking, "This could be the last chance, in our lifetime, to have dinner on the client." It was not so much the size of the crowd at Convito Italiano as the feeling at every table of intense, excited talk. Something was happening. People seemed awake, alert, full of a real event, the way people might seem, or used to seem, on a presidential election night.

Indeed, that night President Reagan was on TV and telling the country to "keep spending." It was our only hope, "keep spending." Tonight he truly was the Commander-in-Chief. There was something more feverish than patriotic about the spending tonight, though, as if the Crash had given everyone a bit of an erotic charge, or as if we wanted to prove that our clients could be shattered, bankrupt, but for us, the money would still flow. For us, the plastic would never stop. We were Depression-proof.

I spoke about it to my friend B. He said, "You're being ridiculous."

B. thinks I am a socialist, which I am not.

He said, "You'd like to see a depression, wouldn't you? You'd feel justified."

"No," I said.

"Well," he said, "if everything collapses, it won't be you or me who suffers. It'll be your clients, the steelworkers."

I almost said, the steelworkers have had their Depression and maybe this one is just for us. But he was right, I knew: they could always have another one.

As I looked around the room, I wondered if some of us did not secretly want a crash, or a 1930s, or a world war, to straighten ourselves out, to give some weight to our lives. And the fact is, we can never "crash," and this is not like the 1920s: we are trapped in these lives forever. It will never come to an end.

It might seem different, of course, if one has children:

A few weeks after Black Monday, a friend, R., was showing me around his law firm. All these firms seem to be eight miles high, with the same numbing view of the lake and the mills. I often wonder how people can do any work here. As we stood in this enchanted place, R. began to talk about that day, October 19, when he and many others, perhaps for the first time, looked straight down into the abyss.

"That afternoon," he said, "I sat at my desk in my new office, and for the first time, I realized, I had *no* work to do. Every deal in the world was on hold. Every bond offering. Every merger and acquisition. There was nothing to do except watch the Dow drop. And drop. And drop.

"It was spooky. Nobody here had anything to do.

"And I thought, 'What if this is it? What if this is the end?' I began to think of my wife, my two sons, how the birthday of the youngest was coming up, and I thought, 'How will I feed them if everything collapses?' "

R. stopped and said, "I know this sounds silly . . ."

"No," I said.

"So I tried to remember. What did people do during the Depression? What did my father do? Once I read somewhere that Disney stocks had done well in the thirties . . . you know, *Snow White and the Seven Dwarfs . . .*"

"Huh," I said. I made a mental note.

"Then I thought . . . If only I could become a judge. In state court. Because then, no matter what happened, I would be safe, and my family would be safe. They never lay off a judge.

"It's not a lot of money, but I could feed my family."

He said he had never told this to anyone, not even his wife. But once, on Black Monday, he had thought about becoming a judge.

And if my family were starving, I'm sure I'd do the same.

When the Crash came, I thought, "There goes the money for the next industrial revolution." Just in one little 500-point drop in the Dow. In fact, I think it made no difference. We had blown that money already. We blow it every day, in a sense, just on dessert at Convito Italiano.

Down in South Chicago, they are powerless to stop us. In a way, we are powerless to stop ourselves.

I keep reading in the press about the "new" economy, the "information society," etc., and I assume that something really big is happening out there. Then sometimes I wonder if it is. A while ago, for example, a reporter from *The New York Times* called me. He said he was doing a piece on the new postindustrial economy, and he wanted to find a worker, like a steelworker, who now had a white-collar post-industrial job, using a computer or something.

I said, "Why are you calling me?"

"Well," he said, "I can't find anyone like that, and someone said you could help me out."

Because it was *The New York Times*, I did everything I could. I talked to union officers, members, ex-members, but nobody had heard of such a person. I even asked Judy, my own secretary, if she had any ideas. (Judy is a daughter of a steelworker, and she also married one.)

She snickered. "You want to find a steelworker who's working with computers?"

"Yes."

"Hey, these guys need a foreman to tell them what to do."

Then Susan, my friend at the City, called me with a lead. She knew of a woman steelworker who had taken a job as a secretary.

"No," I said, "we want someone who works with computers . . ."

"She can type on a word processor . . ."

"Susan," I said, "you're a genius."

So I called the *Times* reporter, who talked to the woman steelworker and called me back, with evident relief: "She'll do. Thank you. You've been a big help."

This is how I helped produce an article on the new post-industrial economy. First it was in the *Times*. Then it was probably picked up and rewritten by *Forbes* or *Business Week*. Then I probably read the *Forbes* story four months later in the dentist's office, and I must have sat there puzzling, as I always do, "How come I never know anyone who's got one of these jobs?"

So you tell me: Is there a post-industrial economy or not?

It may sound odd to say, but I am one of the rich. Compared with many of my friends, I make very little money. Yet in personal income I am still in the upper one-fifth of the country: I make, on average, $60,000 a year, which is a laughably low salary to my friends, who take me out to dinner, pick up the bill, and regard me as a kind of monk. It frightens me to realize I'm upper one–fifth, for several reasons:

1. It is frightening because I can do it by defending the poor. That seems wrong to me right there.

2. It is frightening because I really am poor. I can barely get by on $60,000 a year.

For now, I can keep up appearances, go out to the same restaurants as my friends, even walk into Convito Italiano on the night after the Great Crash and spend eight dollars for a glass of wine. But I know if I ever get married, the jig is up. I would be exposed, my world would collapse, because then I would have to buy some $400,000 house. Sure, I may be upper one-fifth, but I am not really a serious person. A friend of mine put his hand on my shoulder and said, "Tom, what if you want to get married and have children?"

I crawl at the very bottom of the upper class. This makes me a natural political radical or malcontent: $60,000 a year is probably what Lenin made just before the Revolution. Or what George Orwell made when he was down and out in Paris and London. This is the income bracket that starts all the trouble and keeps a person on edge. Somewhere in a Raymond Chandler novel, I read that Marlowe did not make a lot of money either and it helped him as a detective to stay in touch with real life. I flatter myself that on $60,000 a year I can be like Marlowe himself and look deep into the heart of darkness.

In fact, I have no idea how anyone else lives, how the bottom four-fifths of the country gets along. When I hear that the median family income in America is $29,000 a year (in 1986), I take out my passport and wonder what country I have wandered into. Did you know that? $29,000 a year? That means the income of roughly half the families in America is below that. Why isn't this fact on the front page of *The New York Times* every single day? Imagine what it would be like on $29,000 a year, or less, just you and your family of four—with both you *and* your spouse working. What would you do? Eat out at Pizza Hut once a week, that would be it, or so I used to think. A Teamsters member told me once, "Pizza Hut? You can't even do *that*." When I think of that number, $29,000 a year, I feel as cut off from the U.S. as someone living in Malaysia. I cannot even begin to guess what the real, unwritten life of my own country is like. And I am a labor lawyer, too. I represent them. My friends rely on *me*, as if I were Marco Polo, a traveler in Malay, and other places, to come back to tell them what the pizza at Pizza Hut is like.

And if that's so, we're all in trouble.

I was at the ball game the other night with a friend of mine who said, "Come on, it's not that bad, $29,000 a year . . ."

"For a family of four?" I said.

"You're thinking of Chicago, where the cost of living's really high."

"I don't think it is high here."

"I bet $29,000 goes a lot further in Des Moines . . ."

"Not that much, I bet . . ."

We ran out of things to say. As we did, I looked out in the bleachers, which were totally empty.

It is not the low median income that is so shocking to me but the fact that we (i.e., me and my friends) do not even know about it. In *The Ancien Régime and the French Revolution*, Tocqueville says that the great evil in France on the eve of the Revolution was not the existence of class but the fact that the classes never saw each other. The French upper class, isolated, lost any feeling of responsibility for the common people, or, indeed, for the nation.

Maybe that is happening here. I notice it in the way we talk about the "economy." In fact, it is impossible to talk about the American economy now as if it were a single, seamless thing. If I try to talk about the "economy" with anyone in my "class," it turns into a wild lunging conversation, and I talk about A, and he or she talks about B, and both of us end up utterly frustrated and angry. In the old days, it was pretty clear when the American economy was "good" and when it was "bad." Now, with the growing class division, this is a much trickier exercise. "Good" or "bad" for whom?

Of course, this has been true before. In his book *The Age of Empire*, E. J. Hobsbawm writes that in the 1870s, when wages rose but profits fell, the period was called the Great Depression. Then, around 1900, when profits rose but wages fell, the period was called the Belle Epoque. Now it seems true again. In the 1980s, profits rose but wages were flat or falling in real terms, and this period is called the Reagan boom. It is eerie how even in South Chicago, even as people were being laid off, they still assumed that, well, yes, this is a "boom." And in the Reagan years, it is true, for most people, not steelworkers but most people, it was a much slower, subtler, not unnerving kind of decline, like cutting your wrists and bleeding into warm bath water.

For labor, the "boom" was the "crash." Our "boom" was their "crash." But even in my "class," not everyone thinks it was the Belle Epoque. Robert Reich and James Fallows are two of the best writers who worry over the new class division in the country. Both men are not so much economists as *moralistes*, who both write in the *Atlantic* for a large educated audience. Even when the two argue with each other, they seem to share a sense that we are being driven now, not by the old Newtonian economic laws, but by new forces, to some new, unknown, probably terrible place, past the last moon of Neptune, into a cold and lawless beyond.

Reich, quite grimly, says that the new global economy has turned the U.S. into a class society, and there is nothing we can do but watch. There will be three kinds of American workers: (1) symbolic analysts, i.e., those who process information, like lawyers, bankers, scientists, and consultants; (2) routine production workers, like steelworkers and miners; and (3) routine personal service workers, like secretaries and shoeshine boys. Reich claims that those in the first category, symbolic analysts, i.e., the lawyers, bankers, yuppies—have cut loose from the American economy and are no longer dependent on it. They are now part of a global economy, which will always need their services and always enrich them, even if the American economy falls apart.

So, Reich says, America's industrial base can disappear and people at the top will still get richer and richer. For them, i.e., for "us," the American economy is as meaningless a concept as the economy of Delaware.

Now this, to Reich, is a new development. Formerly, the rich depended in some way on the well-being of the whole nation.

Henry Ford paid his autoworkers good wages, Reich says, so they could go out and buy his Model T, and he knew his prosperity was tied to theirs. But now we can let the workers shine our shoes, and it will not hurt "our" prosperity one bit. Other countries will pay the bills we run up at Convito Italiano, because other countries will always need the fancy postgrad services we provide, with our fancy postgrad educations. There is no such thing as a national economy.

Fallows, writing from Japan, has a different view. He says that once, like Reich, he, too, thought a national economy was a meaningless concept, like the economy of Delaware. Then he went to Japan and saw that in Japan a national economy is not meaningless at all. The Japanese elite, their upper one-fifth, sure as hell have a national economy. Indeed, to Fallows, the Japanese economy is a kind of super-Delaware devouring the world.

So who is right, Fallows or Reich? Maybe both of them. Maybe there are two paths open to an "upper one-fifth," namely: (1) love your country and build up its economy, or (2) throw in with the world economy and send your own people into Third World hell. This is the choice facing us. And in a way, so little was asked of us, historically, as an elite: simply that we not make America any worse than it was, any more of a class society. And we blew it, we could not even do that.

It may not be a question of free will. I know I should save money, and I even have saved some, but I could spend it any minute on a condominium. I often think that tonight, at Convito Italiano, I will pass up dessert and maybe, if I push myself away from the table, just once, for one night, and put what I save in a bank, there could be money for a steel mill in South Chicago. I feel guiltier than most, I suppose, because I made my money off steelworkers. It is horrible to be sitting at a wine bar, looking in my date's eyes, then suddenly to see the apparition of a steelworker before me.

In Tom Wolfe's *Bonfire of the Vanities*, supposed novel of our time, the hero, an investment banker, discovers the "other class" when he takes a wrong turn and runs over a black kid in a ghetto. Imagine if Wolfe had written a novel in which an investment banker runs over a middle-aged steelworker. It would not even have occurred to Wolfe. Nor would it sell. Yet it happens every day.

I would be in favor of Free Trade if we had an upper class like Japan's. I would be in favor of Free Trade if we, my generation, the Reaganites, could be more patriotic, if we could go out and make something, if we could save a little and not keep forcing ourselves to throw up, like the ancient Romans, so we could go out and consume more.

I would be in favor of Free Trade if we were not so corrupt.

Recently I spoke to my friend Ann, the economist, and asked her the following:

"Look, Ann, I know all about the economic reasons for deindustrialization. I mean, the high dollar, the high interest rates, the debt crisis, the loss of markets in the Third World. But isn't the real reason just that we're corrupt? I mean the upper class, people in the upper one-fifth?"

She looked at me. "Are *you* in the upper one-fifth?"

"Yes."

"Isn't that amazing? So am I."

"As an economist, do you think it's silly for me to say, 'It's corruption'?"

She said, relieved, almost in a whisper, "I think it *is* corruption. When I talk to groups, and talk about the steel industry and its decline, I think some of them feel ashamed. They feel embarrassed."

I know this is true. More people are feeling embarrassed. I feel embarrassed, now that I let adult men kneel before me and shine my shoes. I just started having my shoes shined. Sometimes the man who shines them looks up at me and gives me a horrible grin, and I feel sick, but I keep going. I tell myself, "It's good discipline," and he is a personal service worker, and I should not cringe, this is the way it's going to be from now on. But still, I feel like I have one foot in Babylon.

My friend Len said to me recently, "In the 1950s and 1960s, things always seemed to be getting better. Every year, it seemed, wages were higher, there were more civil rights, more social justice. You had this sense of progress . . . Now it's gone, this whole sense. Now, each year, there's more racism, more poverty, unions get busted. Everywhere you look. We're headed *down*." A friend told me that his sister, a medical researcher, was being courted by a big drug company. She turned them down, but they persisted: "How much do you want? $150,000? No? $200,000? How about $300,000?" O.K., she said, she would try the job for a week. Every day, at her door, there was a limousine waiting for her, driven by a Teamster. As she came to know him, and they started talking, she found out he and the other drivers had not had a raise at this company in three years. The company had tons of money, it was doing great, it was just stiffing these guys because . . . well, why not? Labor is weak now.

The role of these people, in the global economy, is just to drive around the upper "one-fifth."

Reich says there is no way we can stop this from happening. Real wages will keep falling. All we can do, he says, is to change the tax code to increase transfer payments from the rich to the poor.

When I reached this point, I thought, "What a wimp this guy is." Americans do not like to use the tax code this way. No Democrat is even talking about making the income tax more progressive, and it was luck we had as much tax reform as we did in 1984. If people on the left want to redistribute income, they can only hope the economy, and not the tax code, is going to do it.

But Reich says there is no hope. So maybe we can have voluntary transfer payments from rich to poor. There are several ways we could do it:

We could take more cabs.

We could leave bigger tips at restaurants.

We could give presents to them. For example, a friend of mine at Skadden, Arps just gave his secretary a car. He really wanted to give her more money, but he couldn't: it would have upset the firm's salary structure. So, in lieu of that, he gave her a car and set an example for us, in the century or so to come: just pick out the workers we like down there in the lower four-fifths and give them new cars.

•

In this new global economy, I worry about the Third World. Not the Third World "over there," but the Third World down the street. This is the real threat to organized labor: not Brazil, not Korea. Indeed, why is there such a problem competing with *that* Third World when we have such a large one of our own here at home?

I speak now of the "underclass," a growth sector of the economy, the people who are under the personal service workers. The whole class did not exist as such twenty or twenty-five years ago. If I call them Third World, it must seem for rhetorical effect. This is still America, not Brazil, etc. But the Third World recognizes its own, and in little gestures, almost invisible, it is welcoming us to the club.

Mother Teresa has even sent her nuns over from India to work on the West Side of Chicago, to feed people. When she came here, she said Chicago was *worse* than anything she had seen in India. A priest I know said to me, "And she wasn't kidding."

"I don't believe it," I said. "That woman is shameless."

"Go see for yourself," he said.

So I did. I went to a kitchen run by the little nuns brought by Mother Teresa. The hardest part is just getting there, to the West Side. While it makes up a quarter or even a third of the city, it is not quite clear to me where it is. It seems to me like Brigadoon, shrouded in mist, occupying no real "place." Although it is only four miles or so away from me, it does not seem possible to get in a car and drive there, any more than it would to get in a car and drive to France.

One point I have to clear up: The kitchen to which I went, at St. Malachy's, is not like a homeless shelter one might see in a white, liberal church. This is India, not Lincoln Park. The nuns serve food here every day, at ten in the morning, and the most ordinary people come in to eat, not bag ladies, not weirdos wearing winter coats in August. Neighborhood people, you know? Of course, there is a cop in a squad car around the corner, not quite in sight of the kitchen, and he sits there all morning as food is being served.

To get in the kitchen, when I arrive on Sunday, I have to

push through a crowd of fifty or so men who have been waiting for the nuns to open the door. This is the part I hate, the two or three minutes waiting for the nuns to open the door, when it is just me and fifty young, desperate black men: and I have my back to them. They say, "Knock louder," then they laugh.

Then a little nun from Calcutta opens the door, just wide enough for me to get through, so I can go in and they can't.

On Sunday, which is the big day here, about 200 or more people will go through the line. There is a Gospel reading at the start. The first Sunday I came, it was the passage in which Jesus is telling the disciples to give up everything, to take nothing with them, when they go out to preach the good news. The men in the room looked blank. I thought, "This is not the Gospel I would have picked . . ."

There are very few women or children. Most are young men, twenty to thirty-five years old. While the men are thinner than steelworkers I know, slighter, even gaunt, many of them seem very strong in their upper arms, as if they work out in a gym or on a Nautilus. They looked darker, more Ethiopian, and yet I had a feeling that I *knew* these men . . . I had seen them before. This was the shock for me: I could have seen these people in my own office, I could imagine them in a mill.

Now, maybe, if organized labor had not collapsed, they would not be steelworkers. They would be busboys or dishwashers, and the men who are busboys or dishwashers now would be working in the mills instead. Everyone would advance in the queue: the part-time dishwashers would be full-time, the full-time ones would be in mills. And the little nuns could go back to India.

We could not have created this soup kitchen without busting the unions.

Going through the line, most of the men say nothing. If they don't want green vegetables, for example, they shake their heads. Or they make grunting sounds. Once in a while, someone says, "Thank you." It is always the two words, "Thank you," not "Thanks." Mostly they say nothing, but then I don't say anything either.

The nuns did not exactly swoon over me when I volunteered. But they did put me to work. Sister Arjay, the boss, told me where to stand and what to do. She and Sister Colleta are both about four feet eleven and probably they are peasant girls from villages. They talk in that furiously fast way that Indians can, and the men talk back as slow as molasses, and it is impossible to understand anybody here.

My first time, it was a brutally hot morning, in the mid-90s. The smell in the room was overpowering. The T-shirts seemed pasted on the men with fourteen days of sweat. I would stink of cabbage and ammonia and sweat for days after I left. Waiting for the nuns to open the door, I had almost gagged, and I wondered how the men could even bear to eat. As I watched them sitting and eating, in dead quiet, I thought, "This could be a prison cafeteria." Except a prison cafeteria would not smell this bad.

I was at the end of the serving line. My job was to pour the iced tea into cups, which were mostly old Dannon yogurt cups. I was told to fill up the cup by two-thirds, *no more*, because it was hot, and we might run out. Sister Colleta watched me carefully, to make sure I was not too generous. A man would ask me, please, to fill it to the top. I would say, "No." I felt like a guard in a concentration camp.

A child came up and asked for more. Sister saw me hesitate, so she came over and said, "No."

"Gee, I thought she'd let the kids have seconds," one of the volunteers whispered.

I almost gave Sister twenty dollars and said, "Let's give the kids some iced tea," but it was a bit late to wave my money around, like a big shot.

Anyway, Sister was right. It was a big crowd.

I would later ask George, an unemployed man who acts as a volunteer, "George, why is the crowd so much bigger on Sunday?"

"Because the men who work during the week are here."

"You mean, some of these men have *jobs*?" I said.

George looked thoughtful. "A few."

Just as the last man came through the line, I ran out of iced tea. The nuns were impressed. Sister Colleta came over and gave me a big smile. "You're very good," she said.

But now I knew I would have nightmares all night: Did I give one little child too much? And maybe his sister not enough? I felt like Sophie in *Sophie's Choice*, standing behind the iced tea.

I had expected, at the end of it all, to love the poor, to be filled with a warm glow. But I didn't feel any love for the men here. Around the room, on the wall, I could read the sayings of Mother Teresa, like New England samplers. But there was something hollow about the whole experience. I complained about it to my friend the priest.

He said, "You're not down there for self-actualization."

I said, "I didn't feel any love for them."

"So what?"

"Isn't that the point?"

"No. The Church says nothing about that."

"I thought Jesus did."

Look, he said, these nuns aren't liberals. They are conservative, semi-cloistered, probably in Opus Dei. They don't care about "love" in our modern, interpersonal way. We, the liberals, want love: we go to soup kitchens to *be* loved. The nuns go there to feed people. That's it. Give them something to eat. Period.

I wish I had talked to this woman, Mother Teresa, before I had gone into labor law.

One saying of Mother Teresa I did not see on the wall was: Chicago is worse than anything I have seen in India. Now, I admit that things are bad in Chicago, but I just can't believe they are worse than anything she has ever seen in India. I know, of course, what she means. India has been struggling with a caste system for centuries, whereas here, in the United States, we have created ours, the "underclass," etc., in just one decade, the 1980s. But what is this woman's problem? Is she against Free Trade? Does she want to take food from the tables of starving Third World workers?

Sometimes it is depressing to be there, on the West Side. But now when I am depressed, I think of Free Trade. That beautiful idea, that noble thing, which does such credit to the human race, which binds the nations and the peoples together. And

/ 221

when I think of Free Trade, I do not mind filling the Dannon yogurt cups two-thirds of the way. I always feel, in my own little way, I am doing something for Free Trade.

Last summer I met an undergraduate at Columbia University, and she told me, "I worked in a soup kitchen, and what's the point in it? It just seems hopeless."

I wanted to say, "Then join us, organized labor. If we had had strong unions, they wouldn't have let this happen."

Then I realized it was 1989 and she was only twenty-two. She had probably never heard of organized labor.

Anyway, in the 1970s, there had been strong unions, and everything I deplored had happened in any event. This is the problem that torments me.

Planning could have saved the basic industry of the United States. I have no doubt of it. Just as Germany, Japan, and many other countries saved their manufacturing sector through planning, we could have done the same.

Now, the U.S. has a tradition of *not* planning, or of not using industrial-type planning, the way other countries do. But when I was in school, in the 1960s, I was convinced we would have to change. I read books like Andrew Schonfield's *Modern Capitalism*, Charles Lindbloom's *Markets and Politics*, and Samuel Beer's *British Politics in the Collectivist Age*. From all these books, I learned how Western Europe and Japan engaged in industrial planning and how the U.S. would have to do the same to survive. By "planning," one meant not centralized Soviet-style planning but something like the Ministry of International Trade and Industry in Japan or the Commissariat du Plan in France. These "plans" were really proposals for capital investment, for letting some industries grow and others die.

I believed in this kind of planning fervidly. It was one reason I became a labor lawyer. It seemed to me that the U.S., with its excess of individualism, with its shortsighted brand of liberal capitalism, had no constituency with any interest in the long term, or in long-term economic planning, except organized labor. Indeed, in the 1930s, John L. Lewis had been one of the few who supported the kind of industry planning that Western

Europe and Japan now routinely do. When led by Lewis, labor saw its future tied up with planning. It was one of the unknown tragedies of American history that Lewis lost out in this battle in the early stages of the New Deal. Lewis, Rexford Tugwell, and the other American planners were routed, in an early power struggle, by Felix Frankfurter, Louis Brandeis, and others on the left who abhorred the idea of planning and were urging a strong program of antitrust and laissez-faire.

So the great opportunity for planning had been lost. But I was convinced, from reading all my books, that the opportunity would come again. It had to, or we would deindustrialize and lose much or all of our industrial base. When the opportunity came again, organized labor would again be the champion. America would find itself in its own desperate "Battle of Britain," and it would at last realize it would have to go to war and *plan*, just like our enemies, Germany and Japan. And a Winston Churchill would come out of exile to lead us. And he would have as his strongest support the leaders of organized labor, who would naturally support long-term planning and responsible actions to save our manufacturing sector. This is how we would steer ourselves through the storms of the rising global economy.

Now I wonder if planning in this country could have ever worked. The whole culture is against it. In the U.S., even organized labor would be walking into Convito Italiano on the night of the Great Crash. It is not just the yuppies, I found out, to my horror. Everybody in this country has the same disease.

I am thinking of 1979, that damned, horrible year, the last year organized labor could have saved itself, although not many in labor may realize it now. This was the year, 1979, when Iran imposed the oil embargo; when OPEC then tripled the price of oil to $30 a barrel; when the U.S. economy then crashed in flames, with double-digit inflation *and* unemployment; when mobs started forming to throw Jimmy Carter out of the White House; and when Paul Volcker became chairman of the Federal Reserve Board and could more or less run the country under martial law. After 1979, everything was lost. If it were not for that year, the Democrats might still be in the White House;

some people might still call themselves liberals; we might still have an organized labor. Everything began in that one horrible year.

It did not have to happen either. None of it was inevitable. For, oddly enough, just at that moment, 1979, we had, for the first time, an Administration willing to *plan*: and plan European-style, too. Not every industry, just one industry, which was energy. But energy would have been enough. The Administration had a plan that would have saved just enough oil to stop a catastrophe: to keep OPEC at bay, to head off Reagan's election, to hold off the darkness of the 1980s to come.

I know, I was there. In my one brief departure from being a labor lawyer, I had joined the Department of Energy in 1977. My two DOE years make no sense in terms of my career, if that is the word, but there was this much logic to it: I had tried the mystical, populist approach to changing the world by being in the Mineworkers and then in the Sadlowski campaign, and neither had worked. I thought, "Look, if I want to change the world, why not try the direct approach?" Like any normal Harvard graduate, I would do it from the top, work for someone in the White House, be a special assistant to some special assistant. But I would not work just anywhere. In the Carter Administration, "energy" was the one and only thing I would have considered. It was the only thing that was new and exciting. I would even work for that . . . mandarin, James Schlesinger, who was a hawk, too, Nixon's own Secretary of Defense, although I admit, for a liberal like me, this had a slightly adulterous thrill.

Anyway, I had always wanted to be a planner. And Carter was proposing in his plan just the right answer to the problem. We were consuming too much oil, because oil was too cheap. Our domestic oil had been price-controlled since 1973, to keep oil companies from reaping a windfall at the higher OPEC price. The National Energy Plan, or NEP, would have solved the problem in a neat manner. NEP would tax the price of our domestic oil up to the higher OPEC price and thereby discourage consumption. Then NEP would rebate the proceeds of the tax back to consumers, American citizens, on an equal per capita basis, so that consumers, the middle- and lower-income ones especially, would not be any worse off.

In other words, NEP was a redistribution of income. A fairly major one, too. So NEP would have saved us from destruction, made our society more equal, and kept the Democrats in power. Also, NEP had a special benefit for organized labor. It would have raised energy costs in Texas and the South, to which anti-union employers were moving from the North and Midwest.

NEP was the first time since the thirties that the federal government had tried to "plan" for a whole industry. If successful, NEP could have led into a new era of European-style industrial planning. It could have realized Lewis's dream in the 1930s. Organized labor, at last, could have a greater role in planning the economy. It could have been the start of a wider, bolder program to save our manufacturing base and plan our way through the perils of Free Trade and the Global Economy.

So you might think that in that fateful year, 1979, organized labor supported NEP. Spent millions in pushing it. Took its last stand in supporting it. Said, "This is it, on this one we live or die."

Actually, labor opposed it. Yes. Opposed it. Teamed up with the oil companies and the Republicans to kill NEP in the Senate. The AFL-CIO, in its wisdom, set out to kill the very type of thing for which John L. Lewis had fought. Seemingly, labor does not want any kind of economic planning.

I couldn't believe it. I gasped. I was dumbfounded. I went to meetings with labor people, to explain NEP. They wouldn't even listen to us. I remember one of them, a lobbyist, was especially contemptuous.

He said, "Now, this NEP . . . you're going to tax people, and then give the money back to them?"

"Yes," we said.

He sneered. Crazy Harvard liberals, he must have thought.

"You people," he said. "Do you think you can just play with people's lives like that?"

Yes, actually, we did think that. We, the Kennedy School graduates, the Rhodes scholars, etc., the second lieutenants in

Schlesinger's army, we had thought up NEP, and it had sprung full-blown out of our heads. Yes, this was elitist. But what was our alternative? Work with these chuckleheads?

NEP was giving these people *free money*. And they still were against it. They just wanted to gas-guzzle, keep driving their cars, keep driving and driving and driving until they went over the cliff.

I had known labor was dumb. But until now, I had had no idea how dumb it was. Now I was not fighting for the rank and file but fighting them, and it was quite chilling to see them from the other side.

Boy, they were dumb. And to think I had believed, once, in *democratic* planning?

Lewis would have laughed at me for being such a fool. Labor, plan? Lewis thought all the leaders of organized labor, except for himself, were a bunch of rubes, bunglers, and self-serving idiots. He called them, regularly, the worst purple-prose names. And as to my idea, democratic planning? By the rank and file? Poor, ignorant people in coal mines and steel mills? Lewis never even remotely thought of democratic planning in that sense. To him, the whole notion would have been cruel, to turn such matters over to the rank and file. I may have believed in these people, but he didn't.

So after the defeat NEP, we had nothing, no "plan" at all. The clock ticked away, Iran exploded, and the rest is history.

I knew I had to get out of D.C. Anyone could see the Democrats were through. I remember the summer I left, 1979, going to a party, and someone asked me, "Don't you work at the Department of Energy?" When I said yes, I could hear my answer ricochet around the room, and I could hear people whisper angrily, "He works at DOE." Who could blame them? It was not our fault, but . . . At this point, it seemed everything I touched in my life had been a disaster: the UMW blew up, too democratic; Sadlowski lost, too honest, maybe; and my dream of democratic planning was in shambles, because organized labor was so damned dumb.

So I went far, far away on a long journey. I went to Chicago and became a labor lawyer again. But now I would live simply.

No changing the world. I would stay away from the East for at least ten years, all through the 1980s, and I would do little cases now, with little local unions. Because here, I thought, is where it starts, with the little people, in the local-union halls. Here is where I can get back my faith again. Maybe one day I can come back to the East again, after years in the mysterious Midwest, with faith, with knowledge, like Carlos Castaneda.

And now that the 1980s are over, now that I've been out here in the local-union halls, and been out here with real people . . . did I get back my old faith?

Well . . . I've only been here ten years.

In fact, I did try to change the world in the 1980s. It was the suit to recover the pensions for the men and women of Wisconsin Steel. The suit in itself was no big deal. But I now believe that anything that consumes a person, any one of us, whatever it is, has a greenhouse effect: it changes the earth's atmosphere. Anyway, here is what I wanted to say about planning:

Once a year, the "women of Wisconsin Steel" invited me to speak to them. Until now, I have referred only to the men of Wisconsin Steel, but there was also a large group of women, who were union as well, most of them "office and clerical." Every spring, about fifty or sixty of the women took over a restaurant in Lansing, rented a private banquet room, and had a reunion. You would expect that these women would eat a lot of salad, but in fact, the food here was "chicken, beef, and sausage," or "CBS." It was just as carnivorous here as in a union hall. The women never went to the rallies with the men, even when the settlement was voted on. They stayed apart, in their own private banquet room.

There were no men, except Frank Lumpkin and me, as the honorary male guests, to report on the status of our case. Then one year Camille, who organized the banquet, said that I should bring a date. "I don't know . . ." I said. (It was always a problem getting a date to the South Side.) Oh, she said, bring your girlfriend, and she made a point of pressing the idea. So I asked J. if she would come to the banquet. J., who had never been to Lansing or anywhere near it, was very troubled by it all. "What is this thing?" she said, and I tried to explain it. "I don't think this is appropriate," she said, and she seemed rather upset.

"Oh, it is appropriate," I said, so she finally went.

I wish I could describe what it is like to have dinner with "the women of Wisconsin Steel." You see women like these in the Loop on State Street, at 5:05, pouring into the buses, headed for the South Side, or taking the South Shore train, and I almost envy them some nights, especially in winter, when it is cold and already dark, and they are off to the bungalows and to a long, drowsy evening in front of the TV. I think, as I go back to work, how much I would like to be on that bus or train.

Most of the women of Wisconsin Steel have jobs, and they seem to be doing much better than the men. For them, the 1980s could have been worse. Sometimes I think the rank and file have switched sexes, and now the women, not the men, should be wearing the union windbreakers, because they are the real "proles" in the new global economy.

Yet the women of Wisconsin Steel miss the mill, almost bitterly. They seem to miss the idea of working with their husbands, who were in the mill, not in sight perhaps but nearby. Often, the women would work for a few years, then leave to raise the kids, then come back to their old jobs. The men, their husbands, would keep working steadily. And all through the sixties and seventies, the wages of the men, their husbands, kept going up and up.

At every banquet, the program is the same. At the end of the meal, going around the room, one by one, each woman stands up to speak a little about herself. I explained all this to J.

The first woman stood up and said, "Hi, I'm Millie N."

Someone laughed. "We know, we know."

Millie got the giggles. "And I'm a receptionist at Leo Burnett . . . and, uh . . . uh . . ."

"Tell us about your grandchildren, Millie."

"I have two lovely grandchildren, two girls . . ." One of them was in a fashion show recently, and she's only four.

"And two years ago . . . my husband, Bill, passed away . . ." Millie stopped.

Some "oohs" and "aahs" from the crowd here.

"And I love my job, I really do . . . but oh, I miss the mill, and I miss you all, and I miss all the great times we used to have there . . ." Millie just burst out with this, very rapidly. Many women speeded up at the end.

Then Millie sat down, and the next woman stood up. Her name, I think, was Irene, and she was a big, fat woman who had a wonderful laugh. She was very funny talking about the jobs she had after the mill closed.

"I had a job at McDonald's," she said, "at $3.25 an hour . . . and I was the *boss*." She roared with laughter, and so did everyone else.

I should add, everyone had been drinking.

Then another woman stood up, and she froze. Stage fright. Could not speak a word.

Other women yelled, "Come on, Grace, speak, *speak* . . ."

Grace tried to speak, but nothing came out.

Some of the women laughed. "Next, next . . ."

Grace sat down, but as she did, she gave us a look that was full of . . . well, love.

It startled me to see it. I don't know who else did.

Then the next woman stood up and said she had a job with Waste Management, Inc., which owns several dumps in the area.

Some women booed.

She said, "Well, you know our slogan . . . 'Better us than in your backyard.' "

"It *is* in our backyard," a lady snapped.

More women stood up. More grandchildren were described. More alcohol was consumed. Some of these women, with their bouffant hairdos, looked like the old babysitters I had as a child.

As the women spoke, I looked over at J. to see how she was doing. She seemed to be very moved. Later, much later on, she said to me, "I didn't know anything about people like these . . . who are in unions, I mean."

I must have seemed blank, so she went on.

"I grew up as a Republican, remember. Oh yes, I'm a liberal now . . ."

"Like everyone," I said.

"Yes, but I still thought people in unions were grubby, materialistic, just concerned about their wages . . ."

"Well . . . they are," I said.

"No," she said, "they're *not*. That's not what I saw. These women, they have . . ." She was looking for a word. "They have . . ."

She gave up. She didn't want to be corny and say ". . . nobility of character."

I know this, because the same corny thought has come to me.

But that night I had a quite different, perhaps cornier thought: What if these women who stood up and told the stories, what if they had been in charge of the economy in the 1980s? What would they have done with all the money we drop every night at Convito Italiano?

I feel that somehow they would have spent it on their grandchildren. They would have spent it on education. They would have looked to the future, the long term, etc., not in the priggish, self-conscious way of a planner, but more like a family member, a grandmother, one whose husband was dead, and who herself might soon face death. I am convinced they would have spent it not on themselves but on the kids. These women ask for little and lead very simple lives.

Chapter 11

Bread and Wine

I rarely hear of strikes now, except those that end in disaster. No union I have represented in Chicago has gone on strike in ten years, and I wonder if any of them ever will. Until the Eastern Airlines and Pittston strikes in 1989, I thought I might never see a strike again.

Strikes in the U.S. in 1988 fell to their lowest level in four decades. In 1972, which was no great year for strikes, there were 443 of them. In 1989, there were just 43, which is about the same as the number of prison riots.

One day I saw my friend Dan who's a lawyer at the Mineworkers. As labor lawyers we sit and gasp in horror that no union's on a strike. Our friends in other professions do not quite see the Orwellian horror of this.

"No strikes? What's so bad about that?"

The question is so stupid I can hardly deal with it.

Dan and I, being labor lawyers, are different. We're forty years old, but we "remember" the 1930s. That was our formative experience: I've almost forgotten the sixties. I guess we "remember" the 1930s the way even a few years ago little Dondi in the comics could still "remember" World War II.

I'd hoped at the Mineworkers that at least they were still going on strike. "Dan," I said, "you ever have a strike now?"

He shook his head. "Only in eastern Kentucky."

That didn't count. A few scattered miners, up in the hills,

. . . like Japanese soldiers who didn't know the war was over. "Nowhere else?" I said.

He shook his head. "It's a bad time," he said softly.

Most people in labor say it that way, softly, mantra-like, "It's a bad time." As if one day it will not be a bad time. But out here in Chicago I don't see how there'll ever be a "good time" again.

Out here, organized labor is busted. It's out of the game. Even when the economy in the Midwest came back in the late eighties, labor was still flat on its back. No local out here, it seems, can pull off a strike.

No one can strike now because there have never been more scabs. The scabs now are not just the unemployed, but those *with* jobs, too—people getting $3.75 an hour frying burgers, people who can triple their wages by helping to break a strike. In the old days, if unemployment was 5 percent, there would be strikes all over a "union" town like Chicago. But now, I hear less about strikes than about "lockouts," when the employer locks out the union after the contract expires, and dares it to strike.

When some people talk about labor's decline, they mention PATCO, the political climate, etc., but PATCO as a cause pales next to Reaganomics. Reaganomics created a pool of scabs as big as Lake Michigan. The U.S. in the eighties lost one out of three jobs in heavy industry, especially the old high-wage industries like steel and machinery. Reaganomics put these industries in a double bind: the high dollar made foreign imports cheaper and the high interest rates made it harder to borrow money for modernization.

It was the Midwest, labor's stronghold, that really suffered: it was demonic of the Reaganites to do all their wrecking in one place. It was like an earthquake here, for a few years, with a press blackout. The Midwest lost steel, machinery, and other industry, while it also lost the big new dollars in defense spending, which went to the South, New England, California. I wanted to write letters to friends back East, get them to start a Marshall Plan, to send us a little money to rebuild the Midwest.

Now the wrecking is over, but in the post-Reagan economy, the scabs are still everywhere. The ex-steelworkers, for one thing, have not gone away. In the Chicago area alone, the Union lost over 50,000 members in the 1980s. Under Carter they were Union men, and under Reagan they became boys, such as bell-boys or messenger boys running around the Loop, where I still see one or two of them, who seem lost now like Reagan himself in some post-industrial second-childhood.

Some of them are still in . . . uh, "manufacturing." They dip their hands in strange chemicals, for $5.00 an hour, with no health insurance. A few once made $15.00 an hour and worked for a company that had health insurance, pensions, etc. Back then they were "union." And now they would scab.

Well, some would. It's amazing how many don't.

But there are many, many others, who were never in unions. Younger ones, kids . . .

We call them "scabs," but they are just being realists. They read *The Tribune* looking for strikes as if they were want ads. In the old days they wouldn't scab, because they'd hope one day to be in a union, too. But labor's dying now, or it's dead . . . better get what's left. There's no sense now to hold back, and to hope one day, like in the old days, to graduate "up."

And sometimes people apologize. In the football players' strike a few years ago, the scabs were interviewed on TV, and some even said that the players, the ones they were replacing, were their heroes. Hey, one of them said, good luck with your strike.

So the unemployment rate may be 5 percent. But for any union out on strike, it might as well be 50.

I remember Frank Lumpkin telling me about a "job" that paid $4 an hour.

"You call that a job? You call that *employment?* Man, that's *unemployment.*"

The city is full of them, men with "jobs," begging, praying, salivating for a strike.

And as I write this, the Midwest is now regarded as one of the bright spots of the economy.

I read in *The Wall Street Journal* (June 29, 1988) that despite a strong economy unions that year might have to negotiate wage concessions. The *Journal* asked, almost incredulous, "How can unions be so ineffective, when the economy is growing steadily and living-cost rises would seem to justify raises of 4 percent or so?"

The reason is that any union member who goes on strike now can expect to lose his job permanently, in twenty-four hours.

Take what happened at CDS. CDS Midwest is a shipping company in Chicago. It had 90 or so employees, many of them over forty years old. As a result, CDS was facing a big pension bill. CDS kept prodding the employees to go out on strike. But the employees, terrified, and being no fools, refused to strike. CDS, annoyed, had to lock them out: then, after the lockout, it reopened again, in just a few days, with a brand-new complement of fresh young scabs. It had replaced all the old workers who had the audacity not to strike.

Any company like CDS that wants to dump the union or dump the pension fund must be kicking itself, because it's so easy. In twenty-four hours, it can start saving a ton of money. A union cannot save itself anymore, by refusing to strike or going down on its knees, crying, begging, willing to sign anything. There's no right in the Reagan era to unconditional surrender.

Sure, I know: How can they replace "skilled" workers? I once said that to a local-union president, and he laughed.

"Skilled? These guys have no real skills. A man's got his seniority, and that's all he's got."

His local, by the way, really *did* have skilled workers, but I was missing the point: when a man goes on strike, he is betting his whole life.

Here's another "strike" story I heard:

Aurora Meat-Packing had 90 workers or so, all Mexican and most of them illegal. The company thought it was a big joke to have Mexicans who spoke no English. You call them the worst, scummiest names, and they are supposed to look blank and not understand. They were part of a Teamsters local, which ignored them, but slowly the Mexicans learned how to use the contract. They elected a steward, Herrera, who spoke English, which by itself had a chilling effect. He filed grievances. Suddenly, for the company, having Mexicans was a lot less fun.

So Aurora decided to fire them. When the contract was up, it refused to negotiate. The Mexicans took the dare, went on strike, but I am still not sure why. Maybe it was Herrera who was behind it, or maybe it was a lawyer who had crazy notions of labor law and told them they had "rights."

Anyway, the Mexicans went on strike, probably as a favor to Herrera. I think they did it glumly, without hope: as if they knew they were dead men.

As soon as they walked out, the company and the Teamsters made fast work of them. The Teamsters BA signed a new contract, without telling the men: so the Mexicans, without knowing it, became illegal strikers, in violation of their own contract. Aurora then could, and did, fire them all as illegal strikers. Then it reopened in a day or two with a whole new work force, and this time there were many more whites and blacks. Aurora had decided to try some new races.

Now, even though the strike was lost, the men wanted to see a lawyer. As if they thought a lawyer, an abogado, like a priest, should perform some last rites over them.

So I stood in a room with forty or so strikers. I had a translator, Lozano, an organizer from another union. Lozano was a wry, funny man. I'd say a sentence or two, and Lozano would translate, and translate, and keep talking for five or ten minutes.

"What are you doing?" I said.

"Hey, don't worry. I'm just putting it in context."

So, as Lozano spoke, I just stared out at them.

Welcome to America.

They looked back at me as if I might be one of their bosses.

Sometimes at dawn, if I can't sleep, I get up and drive to Las Villas Bakeries. It's in the writer Nelson Algren's old neighborhood, full of Polish drug addicts back then but it's all Latino now. The bakery has a coffee bar, and cappuccino is sixty *cents*! At 6 a.m., even on a Sunday, the bar is packed with men, in work clothes: no women. Everyone is quiet. It's like an early

Mass. Everyone is going to work. I can drive the long city blocks here and not see a union windbreaker for miles.

I always think, at this hour, of the men of Aurora.

The strike at Danley was the old-fashioned kind: it was the good war, the old cause, lasting nine months, like trench war in France. It was a strike of suburbanites, and maybe only suburbanites now are capable of such a strike. They drive Ford Tauruses to the picket lines, as if they were normal middle-class people. But a strike that lasts nine months changes people utterly. A strike this long is like a sea voyage. Men get sea legs and become catlike and grow beards. Under the beards, they may still be suburban, but now they are starving, picking up bricks . . . This is what happened at Danley.

I knew Joe Romano, the local president, well. Once, in the seventies, we had worked together in the Steelworkers election. But I felt involved in the Danley strike for more than this personal reason. The Danley strike became a cause for most of us in organized labor in Chicago. First, it almost broke the best local in the city. Second, it was such a long-drawn-out public agony. But most of all, because this was the one local that despite Reagan, despite everything, still wanted to fight, just like in the seventies, the rest of us in town, who did not want to fight, felt that at least we should go out there to Danley and give witness.

Danley Machine Tool, in Cicero, makes machinery for the auto industry. In 1985, in machinery and in steel, employers were demanding concessions, and Danley, like everyone else, went to Joe's Local with a long list of "give-backs." It was not a big deal: all the unions were expected to go along.

Joe said to me later, "I took their demands, and then I went to our guys, and I laid it out to them. And I said, 'Look, here's what they want.'

"And one guy after another stood up and said, 'We've got no *right* to give that up. Our fathers, our grandfathers fought for that. We *can't* give that up.' "

So the Local voted to strike, when almost no other local did. It was going to be a nightmare.

Laramie Avenue in Cicero, where the Danley plant is, would

be a good place for a prison riot. There are miles of machinery plants, wire fencing, and grim Gestapo-like signs that say things like "Solvent Building in Rear." The suburbanites who drive in and out of here every day seem to be on a kind of work release, in reverse.

The Danley strike, like many others, was a waiting game and a numbers game. Every day the two sides, Danley and the Local, counted up the "crossovers" and the strikers, like two armies facing each other across a field and counting up their dead. The Local kept count of the union dead. The Local had 400 members: about 350 of those went on strike and 100 or so of them later crossed over to the plant. Danley also hired some new, unskilled scabs.

But Danley could not operate until it had a hundred or so more crossovers, or new hires, who were not just "skilled" but "highly skilled." These were people who could not be easily hired off the street. But it was not such a large number. Danley had to wait for the number of crossovers to add up, until the balance would tip and Danley could start up, like a crippled battleship, and sail away from the strike.

And every striker would think about this, all day, for fourteen months: "What's the magic number? When does this fucking thing tip?"

They also thought about the cops.

Throughout the strike, Danley had its own private security force, as well as the Chicago cops (off-duty, in theory), to go up against the strikers. They were like the old Pinkertons who used to bust strikes in the 1890s; it gave Cicero a certain *fin de siècle* charm.

They know how to push, to bait, to provoke the strikers, and then they call in the cops to make the arrests. They know "strike judo," and the suburbanites, who do not, who are amateurs, lunge and fall flat on their faces. Then the cops pick them up.

By the way, the Pinkertons are still around. But there are young yuppie rivals, like Asset Protection Service. ASP even gives a seminar for busy executives. It's called "Arms and the National Labor Relations Act."

Sometimes at the office, I get brochures from these union-busting seminars. The brochures never say "union busting."

They say instead that there will be a "frank discussion of de-unionization." The "frank" part, I suppose, is where they talk about the Pinkertons and baiting people.

Which is "frank," I guess, but not very original.

Over nine months, the men learned how to be strikers and how to use "strike judo," too. A man would wear a T-shirt that said SCAB HUNTER, under the big open barrel of a gun, and he would stand there in front of the scabs, his T-shirt pointed at them. The T-shirt is the real picket sign in a long strike, when there is time to print them up. It is a way of whiling away the time, wearing T-shirts, while staring across the street at the cops.

There was only one real act of violence in the strike. One day while sitting in his car at a stoplight, Romano was attacked and beaten. Two men in the car ahead of him simply walked back, smashed the car window, tried to pull him out.

Joe did not do too badly. He had a sawed-off pool stick in the back seat, and it was a good weapon. Still, it bothered me that as a young lawyer, in the seventies, I had wanted to get people like Joe Romano into union office. Now, in the eighties, they were being pulled out of their cars and beaten.

Hunger is the biggest problem. While maybe miners in a rural area can grow food, Danley workers in Cicero could not. They had no right to food stamps or unemployment benefits. They only had the strike fund. Sometimes, on Sunday, there would be a rally at the gym, and other unions came and gave what they could. I was vaguely aware that some of the people in the gym were hungry.

Then the Local got the cheese. Or as I hear it, the cheese almost eucharistically came from a Catholic priest. Nobody knows. I am simply told that a big truck, with several tons of cheese, pulled up to the hall and began unloading. The Danley management, the cops, stood across the street, watching in horror.

But too much cheese is bad for you. One man said, "It stops you up, you can't take a shit. We had guys rolling on the ground."

Too much cheese could have stopped up the strike. The

Local began swapping it, bartering it: their main goal was apricots, prunes, anything with firepower.

The strike went on and on. Families went hungry, lost nine months of income, and for what, really?

There is a point when strikers know that even if they "win," they can never make up for all the loss. Here they are, going hungry, and what is the point? No concessions? Everybody else made concessions. Why not them?

But by now, they were no longer suburbanites. Now they were hunger artists.

At last, Danley and the Local signed a contract. While this was a victory and there was even a small wage increase, the Local had barely survived. Many strikers had lost their jobs, through permanent replacements. The strikers who came back were a minority, a rump faction, of the Danley workers.

Then, as soon as the strike was over, Danley attacked. Some of the scabs had previously filed a petition with the NLRB to "de-certify" the Union as the bargaining agent. Danley said that the Union no longer had the majority support of the employees. The Board would conduct the "de-cert," and if the majority voted against the Union, the Union would be out.

The "de-cert" should have been easy. In a way, the settlement of the strike had been a trap. Now the Local, depleted, seemed to be doomed, because it needed the votes of the crossovers and scabs. The scabs should have hated the Local. Every day they had been called "shit," "asshole," and other names, too, unspeakable even to the children of Cicero. Now back in the plant, the strikers out of hatred would not even speak to them.

Yet when the "de-cert" vote was announced, the Danley workers had voted, by two to one, to keep the Local.

Danley management was stunned. The Danley lawyers were stunned. Joe Romano and his friends were stunned, although they had gone through the plant fighting for every vote. Danley should have won, but it lost. And it was not even close: it was a landslide.

The scabs had voted to keep the Local. We call them scabs, but who are they, really? Often they are the blacks, the Latinos, who would love to be in labor. Often they are, in a sense, the poor, and maybe it is only as scabs that the poor can inherit the earth. All the better if, as at Danley, they can inherit the Local, too.

Now the strike was over, and it was time for a party. March 18 is the Feast of St. Joseph the Worker. Since the strike, on every St. Joseph's Day, the Local has had a banquet, or party, to remember the strike, remember its dead. Joe Romano sends out a letter of invitation, which is grave and dignified. Everyone who gets it tries to go. The food is astounding. This must be the only local in America that deserves two Michelin stars.

Every year, when I call the hall to check the time, I hear an old man's voice, with a thick Italian accent. Already, my mouth is watering. At the hall, people spill out on the sidewalk, and I squeeze through them to eat. I try the lasagne, the linguine, the lamb, the eggplant, the olives, the apple cake. And there are still two tables of food I have not even reached.

And I think that all over the world, this day, people must be eating like this, on the Feast of St. Joseph the Worker.

I remember the first St. Joseph's Day best. People kept coming up to Joe and hugging him. I had never seen so much embracing. I always wish at times like this I could have been born Italian.

People kept walking in and out of the hall with two, three plates of food.

I asked Joe, "Do you think people's politics changed as a result of the strike?"

He said, "Oh yes, oh yes . . . it was wonderful what happened to people . . . I mean, like the wives. At first, they hated the strike. No money coming in, all of that. They came down here to the hall and said, 'Jesus, what's going on?' Then they saw what was happening. They saw the cops pushing around their husbands.

"After a while, the wives were the biggest supporters of the strike."

Joe looked out at the crowd and said, "You know, in a union you've got to give people something."

I was thinking about getting lasagne.

"You know," he said, "during the strike, we had Thanksgiving dinner here. We had to. People didn't have any money. It was someplace to go . . ."

I knew what he meant. Once, before the strike, the families here had been strangers to each other. Then they starved together, and now they were friends. They took trips together, went to dinners together. It was this experience of starving together which the Local had given them: paradoxically, on St. Joseph's Day, it had them coming back for more.

Now some of the men in the Local, on weekends, drove around to other strikes, to visit strikers, to give them food. They remembered how other people had done it for them. On the first St. Joseph's Day, the men from the other locals came back here to eat. Joe introduced them, and they stood up, embarrassed, and everyone cheered. Mostly they were old men, retirees, not from the Danley Local, but just from the "Union," the big one. It was all one "Union," I realized, sitting there full of pasta. These old men had taught us a lesson, and now the rest of us had to carry on.

I felt such peace and contentment. "My God," I thought, "the Danley strike was wonderful."

It also was a nightmare: 200 people lost their jobs.

And not long after this the UMW went on strike.

In 1989, when democracy swept the world, the Pittston Coal Company tried to destroy what was left of the United Mine Workers. Pittston had cut off the health insurance of the retired miners and had withdrawn from the UMW's Health and Welfare Fund, the great social-insurance fund that John L. Lewis had created in the 1940s. If Pittston had been able to win the strike, other employers would have withdrawn, too, and the Health and Welfare Fund would have dissolved.

Yet even though Pittston tried to provoke the strike, the miners at first refused to go out, knowing how easily Pittston could replace them. For two years, they worked without a contract, and then in April 1989 they went on strike, because if they were still going to be the UMW, there wasn't any choice.

It seemed at first that Pittston had won. The governor of Virginia was on the company's side. He flooded the area with state police to protect the scabs. The courts limited the pickets and picket signs. The state of Virginia paid over a million dollars a month to maintain the state police like an occupying army around the mines.

And my friends kept coming up to me and saying, "Isn't it wonderful about the Soviet Union? Can you believe they now have a coal miners' union, just like *ours*?"

Yes, Secretary Dole did intervene to settle the strike: at least she did when it became clear the miners would fight on. And why did she do it? In part because the State Department was putting pressure on her. Our NATO allies were beginning to complain. They pointed out how bad it looked in this year, of all years, to smash the miners' union in America. The center-left parties in France and Italy were even sending observers to Camp Solidarity, the strike headquarters set up near the Pittston mines.

Even the Japanese businessmen who were the customers of Pittston were beginning to complain. They were shocked that an American company would cut off the *health* insurance of retired coal miners. They said to Pittston, "Hey, we like your coal, but do something about this strike."

O.K., I admit, even in America it's still possible to win a strike . . . but only if NATO and Japan decide to get involved.

In Washington, D.C., in the big unions, they are working now, late into the night, on alternatives to the strike. The strike is dead. It cannot stop management; it cannot close the plant, even for twenty-four hours. Now, instead of strikes, a few unions are trying "corporate campaigns." Instead of pickets, they may try lawsuits, proxy fights, or other approaches. The union, in other words, fights the strike like a shareholder. This is post-strike America: the rank and file stay home and send out their lawyers.

A friend of mine in D.C., a labor lawyer, has been teaching me about corporate campaigns.

I said, "It's too much corporate law. I can't do it."

He said, grimly, "We've got to learn it. Look, if I can do it, you can do it."

The D.C. lawyers who represent the internationals are ahead of the rest of us who represent locals. When I come back from D.C., I feel like such a rube. What am I doing out here, dinking around with locals, instead of doing "corporate campaigns"? As we start to land, and I look out the window, it seems like Bedrock down there. Somewhere down there, I know, Fred Flintstone and Barney Rubble are still holding picket signs. It seems so primitive.

To me, the "corporate campaign," replacing the strike, is very East Coast. It's like the iced decaffeinated cappuccino . . . it's already in New York. Next year it will be out here.

Well, we live in a new age. Old-fashioned labor law doesn't work anymore. So we need a new approach for the new kind of American boss, for men like Pickens, like Icahn (why are they always in the same deals?), for the new men, who make nothing, who, unlike the old robber barons, have no earthly estate, who appear in amber on computer screens, for just a few seconds, and then they're gone. It is hard for the old labor movement even to know where to put the pickets.

Once I tried to get some clients, rank-and-file union members, to think about a "corporate campaign." I told them that if we bought stock, we could file lawsuits, etc.

They looked puzzled. "O.K., we'll buy stock," they said.

A few days later, one of the men called and said, "My stock went up."

"So?" I said.

"I want to sell."

"Don't you *get* it? This is a corporate campaign."

But why should I blame him? I don't know what I'm doing either.

Meanwhile, slowly over the years some unions were buying stock.

Today the Machinists should be no more powerful than, say, the Mineworkers, but their stock ownership sets them apart. As a friend said, "Fine, give us more stock. When you own as much stock as the Machinists or Pilots do, it gives you a lot more options. Then, when you go to the bargaining table, the other side has to listen."

The rest of the labor movement blew it. It passed up the chance to own stock. It was an incredible blunder.

I recently tried to explain this in Chinese. It was a few weeks ago, when I spoke to a delegation of Chinese officials. Believe it or not, they wanted to talk to a labor lawyer. The Chinese were touring the U.S. and going to only three places: to New York, to see Wall Street; to Los Angeles, to see Disneyland; and to Chicago, to see . . . well, a bunch of rusted old steel mills. This is our Disneyland, I guess.

The Chinese were shocked that our steel industry had collapsed. They could not believe our Union members had permitted it.

One of them asked, through an interpreter, "Why are American workers so powerless?"

I thought, "You guys are the Marxists, you tell me."

Another asked, "Why don't American workers own more stock?"

This was a very good question. I thought about the Pilots and Machinists. It was daunting to try to answer the question through a Chinese interpreter. But often when I am talking about labor to those outside it, even to my friends, it would be useful to have a Chinese interpreter.

The question was: "Why don't American workers own more stock?"

I really don't know. The easy answer is, they were stupid, and it may be the real answer, too. There is something about organized labor, even now, that is peasant, squint-eyed, greedy, stuffing cash in mattresses because we do not trust the banks. I represent steelworkers who used to make $40,000 a year, and every week they cashed the checks in bars. It was inconceivable that they would ever take stock, or any funny money. In the seventies they would have snickered in the bars. Stock? They would have said, "Come on . . . ," "They must be in trouble," or "I'm holding on to my wallet."

Stock? Co-ownership, co-determination, co-anything, that was all right for Europe, for labor in Germany or Scandinavia. But here it was better, more "American," to be an outsider. Better to be outside the stockholders' meeting, with a picket sign, with a cigarette dangling from your lips, like Bogart, like James

Dean: better that than to go inside and get conned. They would take your wallet. You would be a chump. Get the money up front. The attitude in labor was: collective bargaining is for adults, stockholder meetings are for kids.

I remember a UAW official who told me, "I could never go into a stockholders' meeting."

"Why?"

"They're so undemocratic. I'm a trade unionist. I'm not used to being treated that way."

Yeah. We like our Union meetings. Like in the Teamsters, where they beat the shit out of people in parking lots.

Perhaps it was a deeper insecurity. "We're just high school grads, we could lose our shirts." It's like the way I feel about corporate campaigns. "We're just high school grads . . ." Except on Wall Street, the Board of Trade, some of them are just high school grads, too.

With foresight, the whole labor movement today could have been like the Machinists and the Pilots. But who knew? The Machinists and the Pilots knew, but no one else.

Once, in the 1940s, organized labor almost had a chance to buy up the country. John L. Lewis, the great Mineworkers leader, was the Donald Trump of his day, and when Lewis set up the UMW pension fund, he had the money at last to be a player. The coal industry had no say in running the fund, and Lewis had total control of it. He began using the fund to buy up stock, buy up companies, even buy up a bank, the National Bank of Washington.

If Lewis had continued, and if the rest of labor could have followed, then the AFL-CIO today might own much of the country. There would be no need for Danley strikes. But when the Republicans took control of the Congress in 1946, their first objective was to stop Lewis. The Taft-Hartley Act prohibited the UMW or any other union from controlling a pension fund. It is all right under the law for the *employer* to have exclusive control: it was only *union* control that was made, literally, a federal crime.

The right said that the UMW fund was a "war chest" or "slush fund" for Lewis and that they were only protecting the workers' money. In fact, they were protecting American business from a new threat, the threat of "union capitalism," a labor-dominated economy, with labor leaders like Lewis making the deals. Today, employee benefit funds, or ERISA funds, have enormous assets, the savings of the nation. Without Taft-Hartley, the term "pension-fund socialism," coined mockingly by Peter Drucker, would not be a business school joke. Lane Kirkland would be king of the junk bonds. The New Deal would have lasted a thousand years. And the AFL-CIO would be like Japan.

But it never happened. This is part of the secret history of America. I never think to tell it to anyone, except visitors from China.

Strangely, after Lewis, after Taft-Hartley, the rest of labor did not even seek *joint* control of the new pension funds, which the Act did permit. In steel, for example, as in many other industries, the employer is in total, unilateral control of every pension fund, those giant pots of worker money, the giant, oozing ERISA honey pots. Even this joint control could have made labor an investor, a little bit more of a player, a little harder to bust out of the game. I asked a Steelworkers staff rep what happened. "Why didn't you seek joint control?"

He stammered, "Uh, well, that wasn't an issue for us . . . We, uh . . . there were other things we were interested in . . . ."

Yeah: getting the money up front.

Back then, every act of power sharing was a trick. It was the longest-running mistake in the history of labor, the unwitting, almost Gandhi-like renunciation of power. It was so stupid, and it was just one of a million blunders along the way. It took a kind of genius for labor to get to its current state of weakness.

When I was done, each member of the delegation, almost bowing, made a formal response:

"We found your explanation most enlightening."

"We were, indeed, most enlightened."

"We believe you should come to China and give lectures on this subject."

I probably should go to China to give lectures on this subject. But the Chinese should get other viewpoints, too, about labor, strikes, pensions . . . maybe hear from some Americans who aren't in the mainstream.

Without the strike, and without stock, what hope is there for labor? We can always hope for the Great Depression. I think many people in labor believe: "Hey, that's when our ship'll really come in."

Great. Just what labor needs. A Depression. That would really kill off whatever was left of us.

Besides, labor disgraced itself in the Great Depression. At least, the old AFL did, and now even the CIO unions act like the old AFL. Incredibly, in the 1930s, the old AFL actually *opposed* unemployment insurance. But then, labor has always had a funny relationship with the unemployed. Once people become unemployed, even if they were always good union members, they are out of the labor movement. They become lepers, or untouchables: they become, at least potentially, scabs.

It is easy to see it now in the way labor has kept its distance from the plant-closing movement. It is a movement that started outside institutional labor: unemployed workers, community groups, church groups.

My friend Ann, who is a radical, said to me recently, "The plant-closing thing is so great. It's exciting, it's grass roots. So why doesn't labor endorse it?"

I thought, "Why don't they endorse it? Why don't doctors go to the funerals of their patients?"

Anyway, what can labor do about a shutdown? You cannot strike against a plant closing. You just sit on the ground, chant, douse yourself with gasoline and light a match.

Organized labor does not like this. It never has. It hates the sight of the unemployed, and it hates to see them marching, with Jesse Jackson, etc. They are like the dead, or undead, refusing to stay in their graves.

Yet I often think the paradigm strike of the eighties is not a strike at all: it is a plant closing. It has all the anger, the theater, that used to go into a strike, and it is really the only time when it is safe to throw a brick. People throw bricks, fight cops, disrupt Sunday services in churches, and spill blood all over the floor. There is no labor law anymore, nobody can sue or bust the union or do anything to them now: they are beyond the reach of labor law.

The wildest, most dangerous moment of a plant closing is the moment when people realize that not only will they lose their jobs but they are about to leave the Union, forever. It is their last five minutes in organized labor. Then they will be nonunion: they will be in the rest of America, the other 84 percent. It is their one last chance to be mad.

Just this year, a local I loved, one of the best in the country, disappeared. Local 72 of the Autoworkers, in Kenosha, Wisconsin, with 5,000 members, was gutted. Most of the Chrysler plant was shut down.

Just before that happened, the Union called a rally. They stood outside the plant, and not knowing what else to do, they decided to scream.

It was a scream so loud it could be heard in the Loop, sixty miles away. So a story said in the Chicago *Sun-Times*. It was a scream Edvard Munch could have painted. It was a scream which one day they will commemorate with a plaque, and people will walk past it and remember. And they will think: This was the last scream they screamed before they left organized labor.

Ed Sadlowski, my friend, a subdistrict director of the Steelworkers, a hero of the Danley strike, puts it this way:

"How will labor come back? In a strike. That's not romanticism, that's a fact. It'll start with one plant. One plant. And they strike. And there'll be guys across the street, at a second plant, and they see it, and they think, 'Hmm, maybe we can do that.' And they do it, and they win. Then somebody in Idaho does it, the same thing, independently. And then all of a sudden you're seeing some John L. Lewis again, a leader, but he gets thrown up, he's just riding the thing . . ."

He kept saying, "That's not romanticism . . ."

But it sounds Tolstoyan: nobody planning it, no Napoleon, not even a John L. Lewis. Maybe it happened this way in the thirties, but if it happens again . . . well, I must say, a million things will have to go right.

While the Eastern Airlines strike was on, I ran into M., a

labor lawyer here in town. He is an older labor lawyer, more conservative, but we are on the same side. I asked him about the Eastern strike and I thought he would say the strike was doomed.

He said, "I think it's great, unbelievable . . . For the first time in years, I'm really excited, I think we'll win . . ."

I was surprised to hear this from a labor lawyer.

He said, "Let me tell you something, which may not sound like much, but this week, the groundskeepers at Wrigley Field won a strike."

I remembered reading about it.

He said, "Now get this: the other workers respected the picket line. They wouldn't cross. I couldn't believe it. O.K., it was only twenty-four hours. But they wouldn't cross . . . And I thought, 'Maybe something's happening out there. Maybe we've hit bottom, finally, and maybe we're . . .' "

He seemed to catch himself. "Well, not on the way back, but maybe we've hit bottom finally."

My God, was he serious? He sounded more Tolstoyan than all the rest of us. I had to think about it: first the Eastern strike, and now these guys at Wrigley Field. And maybe somebody was doing something in Idaho.

When I first became a labor lawyer, it is true, I was in it for the strikes, for the "war." I liked the masculine, even macho side of it.

But as I get older, I seem to be with labor now more for the feminine, maternal side of it. I am in it for St. Joseph's Day. I am in it for the side of labor that brings us all together and that wipes away every tear.

It was back a St. Joseph's Day or two ago. There had been layoffs at Joe Romano's local, and more were supposed to be coming that week. I sat with one of the men who expected to be laid off any day. As we ate together, he held his little girl, about four years old: she was very quiet, very sad.

I said, "What'll you do?"

His wife shot him a look.

He said, "She doesn't like me to talk about it."

"Maybe it won't happen," she said, and I could see she was afraid.

"Oh," he said, "we'll get by. The Union'll help us."

I said, almost sarcastically, "How? Financially?"

"Yes. Oh, they expect you to try, but if you can't make a mortgage payment, the Local will do it for you."

I just stared at him. He must be kidding. This Local, right now, was down to 150 working members.

Then I thought about Joe Romano, and the faith people had in him: and the faith they had in each other. They had starved together for nine months. Who knows? Maybe this Local did make mortgage payments.

As I left, I thanked Joe, as I usually do, and we shook hands. "Great food," I said.

And he said, "I'm honored you were our guest."

Later I kept repeating these words to myself, as if they were full of mystery, and had a deeper meaning, on the Feast of St. Joseph the Worker.

CHAPTER 12

Citizens

A few years ago, Lane Kirkland, president of the AFL-CIO, a plodding, moderate man, called for the repeal of all the labor laws.

Blow them all up, repeal them all, he said, and just let labor and management go at it "mano a mano."

Now, Kirkland is a man with about six pairs of galoshes. Those who saw the quote were shocked.

A friend of mine, a journalist, said, "He's bluffing, isn't he?"

"Maybe not," I said.

"Come on," my friend laughed. "Labor wouldn't survive five minutes without the labor laws."

He's right, I thought. We are bluffing.

"These laws protect your right to organize."

"But they don't," I said. "This is what Kirkland's trying to say."

I became excited. I said, "There is no right to organize. No Wagner Act. Nothing. It's gone. Over. No longer exists."

He looked at me and said, "I don't believe you."

I don't blame him. We used to impose sanctions on countries like Poland which didn't let their workers organize. We cheered on Lech Walesa. If labor is in decline, there must be another reason ("It's the culture, look at the Reagan vote," etc.). In high school, we all learned in American history that in the 1930s workers won the right to organize. It is burned into people's brains: "Workers have the right to organize."

On paper, the Wagner Act, passed in 1935, does grandly declare there is a right to join unions. But over the years, the right has become illusory. Against any normal employer opposition now, there's no practical way to enforce the right to organize. It is as unenforceable as a right set out in the Declaration of Independence.

I doubt today if any group of workers can form a union if their employer is truly determined to resist. The main reason is, employers can pick out and fire all the hard-core pro-union workers. They can do this flagrantly, almost admit they are doing it, yet can be assured they face no legal sanction for it, except maybe, *possibly*, having to cough up a tiny sliver of back pay, some $2,000 or $3,000 a body: and this is much later, three or four years from now, long after the drive is over and the union is in ashes.

Union busting now is almost a science. And the science is a pretty simple one: You go out and fire people. And keep firing until the organizing stops. Because at some point it always will. It is like sending people straight into a machine gun, and when the bodies pile up high enough, the drive is over and the employer has won.

"Come on," some will say, "that kind of thing went out years ago, didn't it?"

Actually, it did go out years ago. But then it came back.

When Congress in 1935 passed the National Labor Relations Act, popularly known as the Wagner Act, the new law did prohibit employers from firing workers for supporting a union. It created a new agency, the National Labor Relations Board (NLRB), to certify unions when a majority of the workers wanted them and then to require the employers to bargain with these unions "in good faith."

But the law was fatally weak from the start. The Board, for example, had no power to enforce its own orders. It had to petition for enforcement to the U.S. Court of Appeals, which could be a very time-consuming process. But for a while, this didn't matter, because employers seemed ready to obey the law.

Gradually, by the 1960s and 1970s, however, employers began

to realize that the NLRB was weak. They could violate the Wagner Act, and nothing would happen. A whole profession of "labor consultants" had grown up, to tell them how to do it, to coach them in breaking the law. It was a sort of "cultural revolution," or mass civil disobedience, that began to occur, not among the workers, but among the employers, their bosses. It was like a civil rights movement in reverse.

In 1984, Professor Paul Weiler of Harvard Law School published a chilling study in the *Harvard Law Review*. He then estimated that about *one in twenty union supporters* would be fired in a typical organizing drive. He reached that number by taking for one year, 1980, the total number of cases in which the NLRB had made some award to a worker for an illegal firing in connection with an organizing drive. Then he divided that number (about 10,000) by the total number of pro-union votes cast in all elections that year (about 200,000). The number or ratio that came out, fifty years after the Wagner Act supposedly guaranteed the right to organize, was one in twenty.

Yet even this number, one in twenty, is probably an underestimate. First, Weiler was counting only the cases that end in final awards, and many workers, when fired, do not file charges, or they give up along the way. Second, his figures come from 1980, the last year of the Carter Board, which incidentally was not all that pro-union. They don't reflect PATCO, the Reagan era, or the "new permissiveness," when employers knew they could run wild and fire away, because the NLRB was full of "right-to-work-ers," right-to-lifers, and right-wing kooks. So the true ratio is not one in twenty: maybe it is one in fifteen, or even one in ten. It is really whatever ratio the employer wants.

In other words, if you put on a union button at work, in 1990, it can be shown to a reasonable certainty that you will be fired.

Weiler notes how illegal firings have increased over time. In 1939, for example, when the law was still new, the NLRB had to reinstate in that year 7,738 workers. But from 1939 to 1957, there is a downward trend, as employers came to accept the right of the workers to organize. In 1957, the NLRB reinstated only 922 workers. Then, from 1957 to 1980, as the labor consultants appear, there is a steady upward trend. By 1980, the year Weiler studied in detail, the number of reinstatements and other awards had risen *fifteen* times.

"But wait," some will say, "aren't the workers being reinstated?"

Yes, they can file charges. But the charges on average take over three years to resolve, more than a thousand days:

first, going through the General Counsel,

then to a full hearing before the Administrative Law Judge,

then an appeal to the whole Board,

then up to the U.S. Court of Appeals,

then maybe a remand back to the Board,

then back up to the Court of Appeals,

and then, at last, a final judgment enforcing the Board's order as modified.

Now the worker is reinstated. He has "won." But he has spent three or four years out in the darkness, gnashing his teeth. Also, when he comes back, the drive is over, and there is no union to protect him. Not only can he be fired again, but probably he will be fired again. Weiler found that 80 percent of those who win reinstatement are fired again within a year (oh, for something else, of course).

So if you put on a union button, it's not just that you'll be fired. You're fired and never coming back, ever: and if you try it, you'll be fired again within a year.

As a result, many workers don't file charges. Why bother? Perhaps if the worker could last it out, he could win some back pay, but it's usually peanuts. Under the Wagner Act, no matter how flagrant the violation, the employer can deduct from the back-pay award any other money the worker has earned. Unless the man was a total mope, he probably got another job, so the back pay won't be much, maybe a few thousand dollars. If he couldn't get another job, he probably settled the case a long time ago by agreeing to reinstatement without back pay, so he could cut the three-year wait and get back to work and feed his family.

Breaking the law, i.e., firing people, is absurdly cheap. Like jaywalking. The best deal in America, in cold business terms. There is a famous study, somewhere, that says a union on average will increase a company's wage bill by 20 percent. So let us say, at plant X there are 50 workers who make $25,000 a year. A union at this plant would cost an employer, then, about $250,000 *a year.* I don't even mention fringes, pensions, etc. And the penalty for violating the Wagner Act is . . . what, $3,000 a crack? Paid one time only, three or four years from now? An employer who didn't break the law would have to be what economists call an "irrational firm."

Actually, you don't have to break the law that much. My brother, who worked in personnel, saw a union try to organize his plant, which had about 40 or so workers. He said stopping the union was easy: "Our boss just picked out the two ringleaders and fired them."

That ended it. In any group of 40 people, he said, there are only one or two who make the drive happen. The heroes. So just fire them. This is what the consultants tell you. "Besides," my brother said, "one of these guys was a total jag-off," which is probably true, too.

Then he said to me, casually, "You know, I don't see how labor ever organizes a single plant."

By the way, my brother's employer was a good one. Even breaking the law, it was fairly humane. Most employers, to be on the safe side, would have fired a lot more workers.

Yes, the workers can be reinstated. But while their charges hang fire for three or four years, the company has made its point. And the point is not lost on the other workers, trembling, watching like the chorus. Most of us aren't heroes. We scare easy. And the workers today, the unorganized, who speak to us with their eyes, say, "We're sorry, we're not heroes, we don't want to be fired." They might be brave in a crowd, if they were 200,000 Czechs in Wenceslas Square, but nobody is that brave in a small shop, 40 or 50 workers, where most organizing occurs.

A few old union hands can't accept this. One I know will growl, "I've never believed the Board can win your strike." Then he will clench his fist and say, "The only thing the boss understands is . . ." Then he will take his right fist and pound it, *pow,* into his left palm. But the truth is, there are few union officials like him. The rest of us can dream of the 1930s, have a Yeats-like imagination of an insurrection, read the last stanzas of "Easter 1916," but we're going to wait for the Board to rule, even if it takes thirty years.

So do we really want to fight management *mano a mano*? No, we are bluffing. Yet I feel almost sorry for Lane Kirkland, with his secret, tormenting knowledge that there is no right to organize.

There's no other country (outside the Third World) where it's tougher legally to organize a union. It's getting even tougher than in South Korea.

Once, in the 1950s, before the mass firings began, American unions would win a stunning number of elections, even through the Board. I saw some of the statistics in Michael Goldfield's book *The Decline of Organized Labor in the United States*. In the 1950s, unions could count on organizing a new, additional *1 percent* of the work force annually. They often won over 80 percent of the Board elections. At the present time unions barely organize *0.3 percent* of the work force annually. They lose, many years, over 50 percent of the Board elections. Also, much of the 0.3 percent, the "new" organizing, comes in the public sector, where there are few illegal firings. There was little public-sector organizing in the 1950s, so the decline in private-sector organizing is worse than it seems. Organizing in the private sector has almost stopped.

As a result, the unionized share of our work force drops every year. The share is now 16 percent of the total work force and a bare 12 percent of the private sector work force (which excludes public employees). The new organizing cannot offset even the normal attrition or falloff in union membership, as older unionized companies go out of business or disappear. According to Goldfield, unions can still win a stunning number of elections even now, but only under one special set of circumstances: When the employer does not oppose or delay the election, or commit any legal violations, the unions currently win over *90 percent* of the time.

Otherwise, of course, we're screwed.

So far I have argued as if the Board were useless. Now, if the Board were only useless, that would not be so bad. But the Board is much worse than useless. The NLRB now seems to exist primarily to slow down the union, delay the election, ball things up, so the employer has even more time to fire people. In the extreme case, when the union threatens to win anyway, despite the firings, the Board will often step in and put everything on hold for eight years.

By the way, no country has anything like our NLRB, which can function like a bloodless, bureaucratic death squad. Look at Canada, for example. Oh, they have labor boards, etc. But when workers in Canada want to organize, they just sign cards saying, "I authorize the union to represent me." If 55 percent of the workers sign, there is a union, and the employer has to bargain. No hearings, no further elections, no years of litigation. Just the cards. Doesn't it sound simple, civilized, even fair?

Nothing like that happens here. Here we also collect "authorization" cards. But what is the last step in Canada is just a first, preliminary step here in a long, *Bleak House* type of legal proceeding that can go on, literally, for seven or eight years.

"O Canada," I whisper. Across that border is the free world. Now, I should say that in the U.S. a union needs only 30 percent of the cards to start the election process. But in practice, no sensible union would dare ask for an election without having 50 percent of the cards. So everything I now relate occurs only *after* a majority of the workers have come forth, by name, and said they want to join a union.

For ten years, I've represented the Illinois Nurses Association, or INA. This is a decent, honorable, and competent union, and in theory, the INA should be doing great, organizing like crazy. In the 1980s, everything seemed to fall into place. There was a nursing shortage, which made nurses hard to fire; but the same shortage also meant that nurses would work longer hours, in worse conditions. Nurses were mad, angry, and at the same time, they were feeling their oats. They were ready for a little labor unrest.

But organizing them is a nightmare. I know of Board cases pending for *seven* years. Think of it: Seven years ago, a union asked a group of nurses to sign cards, risk their jobs, and said at the time, perhaps, "Look, this'll go fast." Now, seven years later, the Board and the court are still trying to decide whether one little clutch of nurses should be in a union together—whether they are, in a legal sense, "an appropriate bargaining unit."

What, you say, is "an appropriate bargaining unit"? It means the unit or "election district" in which the group will vote whether to unionize. Should the unit be

(1) registered nurses ("RNs") only;
(2) RNs and licensed practical nurses (LPNs) only; or
(3) RNs, LPNs, and maybe parking-lot attendants, electricians, and the grounds crew?

I list only three possibilities, but there are hundreds, maybe thousands, and a good management lawyer will raise each one. Not just raise it, but brief it, put on witnesses, ask for a ruling, and then do it all again for another permutation. And I, the Union lawyer, have to argue it, brief it, as if we are talking about something serious.

The hospital would like the Board to pick the silliest unit: let's say, RNs, LPNs, and parking-lot attendants. This, they tell the Board, is the only unit that makes sense. Then, if the Board says yes, the hospital will go to the parking-lot attendants and say, "Hey, do you guys want to be in a unit with *nurses*? Is that crazy or what?"

Meanwhile, the hospital is firing all the nurses it can.

And meanwhile, the Board is changing the rules for deciding what is "an appropriate bargaining unit." Since the cases drag on for years, the rules can change two or three times in the course of one case. A few years ago, the Board tried to codify the rules in a decision known as *St. Francis Hospital*, or *St. Francis I*. Then it came up with new rules in *St. Francis II*. Since a federal judge has just thrown out *St. Francis II*, we are now all waiting for *St. Francis III*. And after *St. Francis III*, there will be a puff of white smoke, and we will have *St. Francis IV*, and then one day, *St. Francis V*, in dynastic succession, like a long line of popes. One day, when I am old, and young lawyers are at my knee and asking me about *St. Francis XXIII*, maybe I will shock them by saying, "I remember *St. Francis I*."

Meanwhile, the nurses wait and wait, their hair turns white.

If a nurse is fired, I say to her, "You're going to file a charge, I hope."

"Where?" she says.

"The NLRB."

"THERE? *That* place?"

"Well, where did you think?"

"How long is this going to take?"

"Three years."

She looks at me as if I'm nuts. I don't even tell her the truth, which is that for three years she'll see her name dragged through the mud, with doctors, administrators, even parking-lot attendants coming in to say:

"She didn't change the patient's bedpan."

"I saw her yelling at a patient."

"I saw her flirting with a patient."

"I saw her having *sex* with a patient."

And finally: "She's on drugs."

And the hospital can swing away, since in a hearing it has absolute protection from libel.

Sure she should file a charge. Kafka would file a charge.

So I hate organizing. Oh sure, as a labor lawyer I go around telling unions, "Organize, organize," because we need the business, but I really feel like such a hypocrite. I would never be an organizer. In fact, I wonder if, ethically, we should even be asking people to organize. So I say, "Organize, organize," but thank God, it's not me doing it.

I bet somewhere right now union staffers are meeting and saying, "Yes, we've got to do more organizing." Then everyone looks around the room. O.K., who's going out there?

Organizers today are . . . well, they're professionals, naturally . . . Look, basically, they're outlaws. As a young lawyer at the UMW, I used to walk softly past our organizing department, like a child passing a haunted house. Sometimes I would look inside. Hellooo? Were they in there or out on the road? We, the staff, used to say, "Organize, organize," I think because we felt safer when they were out of the building. As bureaucrats, we felt guilty, too, because we depended on organizers for our little desk jobs. Because of them, we could live like quiet civil servants, drink at the Hay-Adams, and occasionally raise our eyes up to heaven and say, "Oh, where can we find good organizers?"

I would try the terrorist networks of Western Europe. That is what the Wagner Act has reduced us to.

I am being a romantic, though. I would like to think of an organizer as someone who can spend six weeks at a Holiday Inn in Kokomo, Indiana, reading novels like *The Day of the Jackal,* and then going out after dark to organize a ten-man machine shop; who sneaks around on private property; and who, after losing the election, can stub out his last cigarette, get in his car, and then, emotionless, drive down to Terre Haute, as if nothing happened.

But I know a few organizers, and none of them are like this. They aren't this romantic. I suppose to be a good organizer you can't have any imagination. Otherwise, going into a plant, you would feel like a virus or a bacillus, first infecting a lot of healthy workers and then getting them fired. After a while, I would go crazy. You have to recruit them. Get them to trust you. Be a father figure, mother figure, one-person support system. And then have to be perfectly neutral, when they are fired, as they turn on you, scream at you, shriek; and then you see how low and craven the human race can really be.

I could also never be an organizer, because I don't have the eye. I go to a meeting with an organizer, and two or three people are there, and I say, "Gee, this is pretty bad."

The organizer looks annoyed and says, "Actually, this is good."

So we go to the next meeting, and twenty people are there, and I say, "Gee, this is pretty good."

The organizer looks really annoyed and says, "Actually, this is bad."

Anyway, it is creepy to be there, knowing what I do about the Wagner Act, etc., and then to see workers come in, smiling, innocent, wearing union buttons. I think, "My God, take that *off* . . ." and I think of their families.

I look at the organizer, who shows no expression.

When the employer wants to call a meeting, there is a full house. This is the so-called captive meeting. Everyone has to attend. The company president stands up, yells, rants, and, picking up a pay plan, says, "If you elect a union, I warn you, I'll be tearing this in two." Then he rips it up right in front of them. This is all within the law, of course.

Remember, this comes *after* a majority of workers have signed cards saying they want to be in a union. Foreigners, puzzled, will ask, "You mean, after the majority say they want to be in a union, the employer can still make these threats?"

"Yes," I say, "it's their First Amendment right."

"They don't have that right in my country."

"Well," I say, "you aren't a free country."

But we have rights, too. Under certain limited circumstances, which change year to year, we can wait outside in the parking lots and catch the workers as they come out. As people open their car doors, our organizer can say, "Psst . . . over here . . ."

While I may worry whether, ethically, we should even try to organize, at least I am not a management lawyer. I wonder how some of them live with their consciences.

Once I dated a management lawyer. It was a blind date, and I didn't know she was a management lawyer. Besides, she turned out to be pretty, and she was even a Democrat. In fact, she was raising money for Dukakis at the time, more than I was doing.

"Well," I thought, "give her a chance."

We ordered drinks, and she talked about Dukakis. Then she talked about labor law. Since she spoke Spanish, she did a lot of work with Hispanics.

I said, "Do you work with a consultant?"

"Oh yes," she said. "His name is Jorge. He speaks Spanish, and he's very popular right now with the employers around town."

"Why?"

"Oh," she said, "you have to see him. He's tall and very charming. And when he goes out in the plant and talks to these

Latino ladies . . . well, after that, they just can't vote *for* the union."

She laughed delicately. "They just can't vote against a man who's so handsome."

I could just see Jorge, tall and charming, out there on the shop floor, looking for people to fire.

I thought, "I'll finish this drink."

"Look," she said, "I'm not uncritical of my clients. Sometimes I tell them, 'Look, you brought this on yourself.' I have a client who uses illegal workers, and sometimes they have to change their names. If they do, he drops them to the bottom of the seniority list, even though he knows they are the same men. So a man can be working there ten or fifteen years, but have only one year of seniority."

I said, "Do you think that's right?"

"No," she said, "and I told him, my client, 'Look, you better clean up your act.' "

"Don't you think," I said, "maybe there should be a union here?"

She looked at me, and she was aghast. *"That's* no answer."

I admit, once I saw a group of nurses organize at a private hospital in an NLRB election: so yes, even under the Wagner Act, it can be done. But let me explain why it was a freak occurrence.

The hospital was in Fairbury, Illinois, a small rural town not far from Peoria. I remember when I first saw the nurses. I came into Peoria on a tiny prop plane, where the stewardess gives you Beechnut chewing gum for the landing, and the nurses met me. Holding my suitcase, I felt with a slight thrill that at last I was an "organizer," the man from Big Labor, from shadowy big-city Chicago, and here I was, the man who would turn Fairbury upside down. I seemed pretty dangerous. I would organize these poor women.

It turns out, the nurses didn't want me to do that. They were already organized. They just needed a lawyer to sneak them around *St. Francis I*, or maybe by then, it was *II*. Anyway, I never even saw Fairbury but spent all my time in Peoria at the hearing. So the whole story collapses, and I wasn't a hero.

How these nurses had even gotten the idea of having a union, I am not too sure. It may have been the smallness of the town. The nurses of Fairbury knew each other socially. In fact, the "union" had started out as a club, like a social club or a book-reading club. Slowly, month by month, the club, the Fairbury Nurses Society, became a quasi-union. The hospital, horrified, called in a labor consultant. Then the nurses, horrified, called in the INA. This is how the battle of Fairbury, escalating week by week, came to be joined.

From the start, the nurses were "an appropriate bargaining unit," if not legally, then at least militarily. They had a sense of union like no other group of workers I ever knew. There were no class distinctions. One of the leaders, for example, was Bev, who was an LPN. Now, in Chicago, I cannot imagine an LPN ever being a leader or spokesperson for a group that included RNs within it. It is unthinkable. But here, in Fairbury, where everyone knew everyone, it was no big deal. Indeed, some of the younger RNs even seemed to look up to Bev, the LPN, and to take her as a model. This was good, because when two of the younger RNs were fired, this admiration would be tested.

We asked the Board to certify a unit of "all RNs, all LPNs, and all the lab workers." The hospital, of course, objected. The lawyer for the hospital was Mr. R., a tall, gangling man, who, unfortunately, like many downstate lawyers, had a Lincoln complex. He talked so slow, each word so slowly brought out, as if every word he said might show up one day in marble on the Lincoln Memorial. It was like hearing, over and over, on 16 rpm, the Second Inaugural Address. At first, Mr. Lincoln said our unit was too small. Then he said it was too big. In slow motion, he came up with every possible permutation (laundry workers, busboys, etc.).

The hearing dragged on and on. The hospital began firing nurses. The snow began to fall. I would sit in my room at night, at the Père Marquette Hotel, and think, "It's falling all over Illinois." What was I doing here? I had to call up a friend in New York and cancel a trip. "Why?" he asked. "I'm snowbound in Peoria," I said. I had a premonition that my body would be found frozen here, at the end of the hearings, after the last

RN had been fired. It was insane, all this money being spent, all this time, just to decide if thirty women in a little Illinois town should be allowed just to have a *vote* whether to join a union. And here I was, all my dreams of being a great lawyer, Harvard Law School, etc., and all the time it was leading up to this, the 1980s, all these Reagan people in power, and Mr. Lincoln holding me captive down in Peoria, and reading at me over and over, for eternity, the Second Inaugural Address.

I worried about the firings. I thought the nurses would crack. I told them they shouldn't be discouraged, I wasn't.

"We're not," they said calmly.

One day, when we were crammed in a car together, about eight of us, Bev said to me, "We have a question."

I did not like the sound in her voice. I thought, "They're going to fold."

"Go ahead," I said, "ask it."

"It's not just my question," she said. "It's everyone's question."

"Go ahead, Bev, ask it."

"Well," she said, "why is it that a lawyer thirty-five years old still isn't married."

Seven people in the car laughed.

Bev was such a sweet, grandmotherly lady. I used to wonder why they didn't fire her, because if they had, they might have stopped the drive. Either the hospital didn't know this or it simply wasn't ready to go all the way. I think that perhaps, sometimes, an employer tries to do the right thing, tries to start down the path of evil, but then, at the last minute, will stop, as if the president, Mr. A., whom the nurses mocked, didn't have the heart to fire any more.

After all, this was a small town, and a small hospital, with a community board. Everyone knew everyone. In the big city, nurses can be fired and just forgotten, dropped into Lake Michigan with weights tied to their feet. But in a small town like Fairbury, there is no place to dump the bodies. These are your neighbors, you keep running into them, at school, at church, even after they've been fired, like the undead, weightless, rising out of the lake and taking over the town. If you are Mr. A., then, and think of all this happening, maybe you get lost or confused and don't do what the consultants say.

Who knows? It could be the reason. I recall that once in Dixon, Illinois, another small town, the birthplace of Ronald Reagan, we represented fifteen nurses fired from a local hospital, and in the Dixon *Clarion* this story was front page for weeks. Six-column banner headlines, as if there had been an earthquake. Reporters would call us up. Our clients were celebrities. We all needed press agents. This may be the only way that any union, or any group of workers, can win these days, given the legal obstacles: to bring in the whole town, to gather people around and make them *look*, the way Jimmy Stewart or Gary Cooper could gather people around in a Frank Capra movie and make them bear witness, and make the big men like Mr. A. feel like little men and feel a sense of shame.

And here is the final reason we won at Fairbury:

The NLRB. The Board. The federal government. The Ronald Reagan people. In this one case, miraculously, they were on our side.

By dumb luck, our hearing officer turned out to be the head of the NLRB staff union in that region: that is, *he* knew what it was like.

I whispered to the nurses, "Thank God."

Over the weeks, I became certain he was on our side, from imperceptible glances, clicks in his voice, the tiniest rolling of his eyes when Mr. Lincoln droned on about the laundry workers. And Abe himself, I think, when the Board finally ruled in our favor, never knew what hit him, just like at Ford's Theater. When we won, I just whispered, like Booth . . . "Sic semper tyrannis."

No doubt by now the hearing officer has been fired by the NLRB, but he was there when we needed him, to get us past *St. Francis*.

I remember a story that a teacher of mine, Sam Beer, told me not long ago. When Sam was a young man, in the 1930s, he applied for a job at the NLRB, which was a brand-new federal agency. Sam asked the man who interviewed him, "Which side are we on?"

The man smiled. "We're neutral."

"Neutral?" Sam said. "*Neutral?* Neutral in the struggle between the bosses and the workers?"

"Yes," the man said, "but we're neutral on the side of the workers."

Well, that was back in the New Deal.

A few years ago, I read an article, "The Decline of Labor," by Seymour Martin Lipset, who wrote it for *The Wall Street Journal*. Professor Lipset is a neoconservative, and I don't much like his views, although I admire him in a way for even bothering to write about labor at all.

Professor Lipset tries to explain the sharp drop in union membership. He says that with Reagan, there has been a return to "individualism," a "resurgence of traditional values," a "new American patriotism," which has been fatal to organized labor. This is why today, no one wants to join.

And what about "Jorge," who's so handsome that all those Latino ladies simply can't vote for the union?

Now, Professor Lipset may be right. Maybe there is a "new American patriotism," etc., although labor's difficulties in organizing arose long before Reagan. But I take the Lipset thesis seriously, it may *be* the "culture." I go to a shopping mall, or drive around a neighborhood, and people have TVs and VCRs, and no one seems to be starving, and I think, "Lipset is right, maybe these people don't want to be rank and file, and why don't I just leave them alone?" It is the land of Eisenhower, after all. But then on another day, same country, I can drive into a different neighborhood and think, "It's also the land of Jefferson, of Jackson, of the New Deal." So first, I don't know if it *is* the "culture," and second, I don't even know what the "culture" *is*.

In 1989, Nissan Motors, the Japanese automaker, beat back an organizing drive of the UAW at a new plant in Tennessee. On the TV that night, after the vote was announced, some of the Nissan workers stood before their Japanese bosses and sang the company song, "We're the Number One Team."

There may be a new "culture," but I'm not sure I'd call it the new American patriotism.

Anyway, Professor Lipset is a social scientist. Why not conduct a little experiment? Why not change the labor laws and let people decide, freely and without coercion, i.e., without being fired, whether they want to join a union? Then we don't have to argue, we can find out what people want to do. But I think conservatives, like Professor Lipset, don't want to conduct this little test.

We can talk "culture" until we all go mad. But isn't it possible that the law itself may help create the culture? The Jim Crow laws create one kind of culture, and the Civil Rights Act over time creates another. Likewise with the labor laws. If the laws are hostile to unionizing, and if the unions are weak and powerless as a result, then the laws are bound to influence the culture, i.e., the attitudes people hold about unions. In the 1980s, the boss looks strong, the unions look weak, and people identify with the boss and shrink from the union, without knowing why.

Actually, the 1980s should have been a boom time for union organizing. Real wages flat or falling, income gaps between rich and poor getting wider, the sense of class increasing. Yet it seems that the more the sense of class increases, the weaker labor becomes. There is more scabbing, more strikebreaking, fewer people voting to join. Also, the weaker labor becomes, the more (in the U.S. at least) it is resented. It holds up in a few bastions, shrinks into a smaller, privileged elite, where everyone makes $13.00 an hour, and everyone else is cut out. So labor, beaten to a pulp, helpless, in retreat on every front, appears more privileged, more remote, more irrelevant to the working majority. Yet this isn't labor's fault. Labor could not organize these people even if it wanted to. Labor, then, may look "arrogant," but this arrogance is thrust upon it. It does not want to be this weak, shrunken thing masquerading as a privileged elite.

But now I am sounding, like Professor Lipset, as if no one wants to join. The maddening thing is: we can't even organize the people who *want* to join.

Look, I am not naïve. I realize Americans are individualists. I know this is the culture of narcissism, and that community, solidarity, etc., are on the way out. But if the labor laws changed, if we had laws like France or Poland, I think Americans would join unions like crazy, simply out of self-interest, raw, Reaganite self-interest.

Let me give some examples:

1. Baseball players. Look at the pros, the big stars. A bunch of young punk kids, multimillionaires, won't even sign autographs for free. The purest crystallizations we have of the Reagan culture.

But baseball players join unions like crazy. Why? Because they can get away with it, i.e., no one will fire them. And look at the salaries they get. *Unions raise your salary. A lot.*

If you can get away with it, it would be irrational not to join a union. Why would anyone, except Professor Lipset, think otherwise?

2. Canadians. O.K., they're not Americans. But they have the same companies, like GM, the same TV shows. Technically, they're a foreign country, but it's like Minnesota being in NATO. Otherwise, they're just like us.

But Canadians join unions like crazy. Why? Because they can get away with it, i.e., no one will fire them. Canadian workers just sign cards, and bang, they're in a union. It goes so fast, there is no chance to fire them.

So in the last thirty years, while U.S. unions have dropped from 35 to 17 percent of the work force, Canadian unions have risen from 25 to 32 percent. By the way, this fact casts doubt on the service-sector thesis, which says that unions will decline as the service sector grows. In Canada, this has not been true.

But then workers in Canada are like baseball players in the United States.

3. Public employees. Also like baseball players, they're all in unions. Thank God, too. Without them, our share of the work force would be even below 16 percent.

Because federal labor law does not apply, the public sector is the only place where unions can organize without being maimed. It is like crossing into Canada. Here, in the public sector, the U.S. Constitution applies, so workers can't be fired simply for putting on a union button.

No wonder, then, that the Teamsters, the UAW, the Steelworkers, and AFSCME all fight to organize the same little clusters of public workers, battling like eagles over the same little nest of birds.

A Steelworkers officer I know is trying to organize the lawyers for the city of Chicago. I said, "What do you guys know about organizing lawyers?"

He growled at me. "Whose side are you on?"

4. Blacks. No one doubts that blacks want to join unions like crazy. Every poll shows it. But blacks can't join unions, because they can't get away with it, i.e., someone *will* fire them.

Recently, the Supreme Court under Rehnquist has cut back, in some limited, technical ways, the protections afforded by the civil rights laws. I don't like these decisions either, but it mystifies me how liberals get worked up over fairly minor blips in the law and completely ignore the fact that, year after year, blacks are being denied a most basic civil right, the right to join a union without being fired.

If we only thought of the Wagner Act as a civil rights law, instead of a labor law, then maybe liberals would wake up and do something. Maybe one day I could walk around my city and not have the scary feeling that the whole south half of it is like Soweto.

There are two other groups to whom unions would have a natural appeal: Men and Women. I take them up in no particular order.

1. Women. Even now, under the current laws, I keep waiting for women to rise up. What's holding them back? The "new American patriotism"? It seems to me they have to organize, in self-defense, to protect the strange double lives they lead as workers and mothers. Women are so vulnerable, so overextended, both on the job and off the job, that they have no choice.

Of course, I can walk into Barbara's Bookstore, and see fifty books by fifty women novelists, and not one word in any of them about unions.

If only we thought of the Wagner Act as a day-care law, instead of a labor law, then maybe liberals would wake up and do something.

As I write, a friend of mine, a feminist from England, tells me, "In England, there's some feeling that women don't join unions because the unions are sexist. Is that true in America?"

Maybe one day that'll be a reason . . . but we haven't reached that degree of sophistication yet.

2. Men. You'd think they'd do it out of self-respect. What do these guys talk about when they're not in a union? When there is just "the Boss," and nothing but "the Boss"? I am thinking of Nissan Motors. Down at that plant in Tennessee, do they walk around thumping their chests, "Hey, we voted out the union"?

Of course, what do they talk about anywhere? Baseball. Football. I remember working in a nonunion plant one summer in high school, and the only thing we could talk about, really, was baseball: that was about the limit of the right to speak, for the nonunion man . . . Baseball. We'd get dizzy talking about baseball, and at the end of the day, we'd clutch each other like exhausted dancers, still talking about baseball.

By the way, baseball players are not like this. Once, with some corporate lawyers, slobbering "sports," I went to a charity event, and we sat at a table with two major-league players. We peppered them with our questions, and the players would answer, polite but bored. Then one player asked me what kind of law I practiced.

"Labor law."

He seemed to wake up. "Union side?"

"Yes."

The two Sox looked at each other. "Do you know ERISA?"

"Sure."

For the next half hour, the two Sox, one of them a union rep, threw me one labor-law question after another. Most of them, I could field.

The corporate lawyers sat there, polite but bored.

My next summer in high school, I worked in a union plant, and there was a different feel to everything. It was not just "the Boss," and nothing but "the Boss."

What did we talk about? Baseball. All day long. It was exhausting. But it was better, that's all I can say.

By the way, I can understand the Nissan workers, why they voted down the Union. Really, they're already in the UAW, and know it. So long as the UAW has organized 90 percent of the auto industry, Nissan has to match or even beat the UAW deal, and everyone knows it. The Nissan workers, then, can play both sides of the street, having the UAW bargaining for them, in effect, but not having to pay the dues.

Now, here is the new American individualism: getting a free ride, coasting on other people's solidarity. It is a rational enough thing to do. But to me, the Nissan workers should be buried in the bottom circle of hell.

The other day, coming back from O'Hare on the train, I was with an American Airlines employee. Computer reservations. Dallas, Texas. Garish red lipstick.

"I feel sorry for people in unions," she said. "We have such good management at American. We get the same benefits they do in the unions, and we don't have to pay any dues. I think the unions are just ripping people off."

I almost said, "It's not the unions ripping people off, lady. *You're* ripping people off. You . . . you take the union benefits and you don't pay your share of the dues."

I didn't put it quite that harshly, but I said something like it. Incredibly, the woman admitted it. She smirked. She was pleased with herself.

Dallas, Texas. What a jerk.

But I still don't quite understand the Nissan workers. Let's put aside higher wages, pension funds, health insurance, all of which the UAW brought about, because Nissan will match these things to keep the UAW out. Let's put aside work rules, too, and even seniority. I would just like to take up only the issue of job security, and ask this one question: Why would any adult, any sane or mature person, responsible to a family, ever choose voluntarily, rationally, to put himself in a position where he can be fired at any time, for any reason, on any whim?

O.K., I can understand why a twenty-four-year-old investment banker at Drexel Burnham might do it. But a forty-five-year-old autoworker? I don't get it.

I should explain here, for those who may not know, that every nonunion employee in the U.S. is an "employee at will." He can be fired for *any* reason, good or bad, for his tie, for the color of his eyes, or for no reason at all. It is amazing to me how many people, even bright, college-educated people, have no idea this is the case. They come to my office and say, "But I worked there for twelve years. How can they fire me?"

Some even believe that the civil rights laws of the 1960s apply to them, even though they are white males. They think these laws prohibit *all* discrimination, not just age, race, sex, but in the generic sense, unfairness of any kind.

When I try to explain the laws, they sit there in shock and say, "You mean it was just for *blacks?*"

I recently saw a man who was a dispatcher at a trucking company. He was a good employee for many years, and then one day he had a heart attack, and sometime later, "I got whacked, for no reason."

I felt sorry for him and wanted to help. I asked if there was anyone in the company, a fellow supervisor, for example, who could testify in his favor, say that he was a good employee.

No, he said, all his friends were in "management" (i.e., they were dispatchers or foremen), and they could be fired if they were to testify. He sat there, running through the names.

"No, I can't involve him.

"No, and not him either . . .

"Oh, there's T. He'd love to testify for me, but he'd get whacked, too, like me."

"Isn't there anyone?" I said.

He brightened. "Hey, why didn't I think of it? The guys in the *Union*. They can testify for me, and they can't get whacked."

The ones who drive the trucks. Because they were in a union, they couldn't be fired except for "just cause." They, unlike the supervisors, could stroll into court, testify, and just walk past the Boss and wave.

I thought, "Isn't that something? Maybe you're in a union, and maybe you're just a worker, and you should be ashamed. But at least you don't have to kiss anyone's ass, like this guy does. You can just go home at night and kiss your kids. And you know that, if you have to, you can walk into court, testify, and walk past the Boss and wave."

Tell me, Professor Lipset: Who is the real American?

Mostly because of the labor laws, the lack of a legal right to organize, I think we are at the end of the union era. What is to be done? Nothing, I suppose. All we need is a law, just a little law, like a civil rights law. But I know, in my heart of hearts, there will never be a law. We, in labor, sit there, riding low in the polls, and there will never be a law, because no one will ever lift a finger to help us.

Once, as a labor lawyer, I thought I should live in Chicago because it would be the last "union town" in America. But not even Chicago is safe anymore. The other day, I saw a priest, Father Egan, a man in his seventies, who has tried to help the unions for years, and he made this remark to me:

"I can walk down Michigan Avenue now, and see the Nikko Hotel, the Marriott Hotel, and they're all nonunion now, and I say to these union guys, 'How can you let that stand?' But I don't have to tell them. They know. They're scared.

"But what can they do? These hotels know, now, they don't have to let the unions in."

I don't have to walk down Michigan Avenue. I can go down my own street.

Not long ago, out of nowhere, a group of Korean ladies were out with picket signs, in my own neighborhood, just in front of my El stop. They came out of a small brown building, almost windowless, with just a tiny slit or two near the roof. The sign on the door said, "D & L Textiles." And I realized, for the first time, that I had been living next to a sweatshop, like a hundred other little windowless places all over the city, employing Latino, Filipino, and Korean ladies. We pass them all the time and don't even notice.

Sometimes a strike can make you look down a street and really see it for the first time.

All summer the women stood outside with their picket signs, which said, "AFL-CIO." Not even the name of a union. Just signs that said, "AFL-CIO." Meek and humble, like the women who held them.

All summer, I passed the women on the way to the El. All of us did, the lawyers, bankers, etc., on our way to the Loop. It was painful to see them every day. By now it was clear that the women had been fired, and after a while, it was annoying to have this painful thing go on, every single day, right in front of our condos. Even I, a labor lawyer, became annoyed, and I began to think, "What idiot had talked these women into going on strike?"

I knew, we all knew, up there on the El platform, that the women below us were doomed. From a distance, it must have been a tableau, the condo owners above, the women below, and we smiled down on them with compassion, but all of us felt helpless.

I think most of us up on the El were thinking, "The labor laws are supposed to work. Collective bargaining is supposed to work. If something is wrong, it can't be that serious."

No, there is just Big Business, Big Labor, and the Rest of Us. And the Rest of Us are like the Swiss, we are morally neutral, with our Swiss passports. A strike, even in our neighborhood, is none of our business.

These little strikes never make the news. But I can go into any law library, go way back in the stacks, to the old NLRB volumes, and read, in dry legal prose, one horror story after another. Thousands of pages, volumes and volumes, where some women try to pick up signs and then somebody drags them screaming away. I can sit there in the dark of the law library and read story after story.

I do not mean to sound so moral about this. If I were not a labor lawyer, I would be crossing picket lines, too, by now.

Anyway, one day, at the end of the summer, the little Korean ladies were no longer there, and I never saw them again. They probably have jobs now in other sweatshops, and they will never try this union stuff again. In Professor Lipset's phrase, they have returned to "traditional values."

I forgot about them until I was in New York a few months back. I was looking for what was then the fashionable new drink in the city, iced decaffeinated cappuccino. I was wandering around SoHo when a door swung open. For a split second, I could look inside, although it was dark, and I saw two or three women, possibly Korean, kneeling on the floor and sewing.

One of the women smiled at me shyly. I remember thinking, "It's filthy in there."

Then somebody slammed the door, and that was it.
I found the cappuccino, a few blocks away.

I think I would like to live in New York. And here is the part
I dream about: Every morning I could go down in the subway
and see the women reading Nabokov.
And I'd take my own copy of *Despair* and stand next to them
and read.
But there'd be other women all around us.
The ones from Peoria. And still in Peoria.
Down in the darkness, without the right to vote.

Chapter 13

To the Medinah Temple

Sometimes, when the talk turns to politics, I say to my friends that the Democratic Party is missing the real issue: it should live up to its name and stand for more *democracy*. Democratize the workplace, democratize the economy, democratize the whole country, in new ways, as we go into the next century. And people say, "Yes, *yes*," and then they look blank. What the hell do I mean?

I shouldn't answer, really. I should just keep it nice, and vague, and Hegelian. Because if I do bring it down to earth, if I say, "Reform the labor laws," or "Let people join unions, freely and without coercion, without the threat of being fired," I know everyone will groan, and turn away.

"My God, is that what you mean? Labor-law reform?"

"Give more power to Lane Kirkland?"

Yet I can think of nothing, no law, no civil rights act, that would radicalize this country more, democratize it more, and also revive the Democratic Party, than to make this one tiny change in the law: to let people join unions if they like, freely and without coercion, without threat of being fired, just as people are permitted to do in Europe and Canada.

The most shocking thing about this issue is: no one even knows it is one.

•

In theory, this sounds impossible. After all, organized labor is still the core, like it or not, of the Democratic Party. In the elections of 1980 and 1984, it came down to labor and blacks, and it wasn't much different in 1988. So if labor can't organize, then surely this fact would have to be of concern to Democrats.

But imagine how shocking it would have been in 1988 if Michael Dukakis had stood up in Brookline and said to his supporters, "Workers should have the right to organize."

Everyone in the room would have looked absolutely blank. They would say, "Michael, what the hell are you talking about?"

Why pick on them? Even the left in the party feels this way. Here I think of my friend John, a professor. We had lunch the other day at Le Bordeaux.

He said, "The thing that interests me is what the new forms of participation will be in the 1990s, for the poor, for the blacks . . ."

In response, all through lunch, I kept talking to John about the Wagner Act, unions, and letting people join them without being fired.

Finally, John said in exasperation, "Look, I'm trying to talk to you about new forms of participation, and you keep talking about things that are purely historical, like unions."

O.K., we need new forms of participation, etc., but how about the old ones? How about fixing those?

Sometimes, though, I talk to foreigners, people my own age, liberals, on the left, from England or Germany, who, somehow, have stumbled into the Midwest. Often, if we talk, they ask me about American labor, about unions. I mean, *they* bring up the subject. I can't tell you how strange this feels. I'm so used to Americans (my friends) who don't even know what an arbitration is . . . and these people *want* to know.

So I tell them about organizing here. They gasp. I tell them about Taft–Hartley. They're shocked. I stop, but they say, go on, keep talking. I can't believe it. I almost fall into their arms, weeping, and say, "My God, someone understands."

Recently I met one of these people: her name was Lea, from England, and soon I was talking to her.

"Well," she said, with some alarm, "the Democrats, I'm sure, must be constantly trying to change this."

I said nothing.

"Well, *aren't* they?"

Actually, the Democrats did try, once. In 1978, the Carter administration proposed two changes in the Wagner Act:

First, the administrative "judges" would have the power to reinstate workers immediately, if they had been fired for organizing. Cases would then linger for only one or two years, instead of three or four.

Second, employers would pay stiffer penalties for illegal firings. They would owe full back pay, with no offsets for other income that workers earned after they were fired.

This wouldn't have restored the right to organize. It would have still been easy to go on busting unions.

But the bill would have helped a bit. And the two changes were such obvious good-government reforms. How could a business lobbyist, on principle, even argue against this bill with a straight face?

And it lost. No, it was massacred. Now, remember: this was 1978, a Democratic House, a Democratic Senate, and a Democratic administration. And it *still* lost. It got killed, trampled, dismembered. By the time the bill reached the Senate, it wasn't even worth discussing.

The unions fought for this bill, too. Knocked themselves out. And it still lost.

And as union membership declines faster and faster, the Democrats are more and more doomed to being a minority party, permanently.

And do the Democrats care?

No.

Why?

Because the Democrats themselves are doing the union busting.

Well, I exaggerate slightly, but not by much.

Take Robert Strauss, who is the former chairman of the Democratic Party. Not only is he the former chairman, but he is also the man known around Washington, D.C., as "Mr. Democrat." He is on anyone's top ten of the party's statesmen. "Mr. Democrat" and his law firm were on the payroll of Frank

Lorenzo. They helped Lorenzo, who must have been the most hated employer in America, the number one enemy of organized labor, go about busting the unions at Eastern Airlines. Try to imagine, in England, "Mr. Labour Party" going out to bust a union: not mediate, not calm things down, but out and out bust the union, smash the whole thing.

Meanwhile, every four years, the Democrats themselves get busted in another presidential election. And after the election, there is a convention of political scientists somewhere, and someone gives a paper saying (once again) that the cause, the *chief* cause, is the decline in union membership. It may lead to an op-ed piece somewhere, but it's no longer a new thesis. By now, it's the dull, the obvious, the taken for granted.

As an example, take the last election. If in 1988 unions still had about 30–35 percent of the work force, and if those union members voted Democratic at the same rate (which is 15 percent more than the electorate does in general), the Democrats would have won the election, or at least they would have come very close.

Actually, this understates the effect. For if the unions *now* had 30–35 percent of the work force, they would have more of the low-wage, sweatshop part of the work force. They would also have more blacks, more Latinos. Now, in Texas, the Latino vote for Dukakis was over 80 percent, but only 23 percent of the Latinos voted. What if more of those Latinos had been in unions? Probably they would have voted. Unions may be dumb, stupid, bureaucratic, etc., and have no influence on anyone's vote, but even if all this is granted (and I'm not sure it should be), unions are still relatively good at turning out their "pluses," at getting people to the polls, especially important in a low-turnout election like 1988.

Of course, the election junkies know all this far better than I do. They see the connection between labor's decline and the Democratic Party's. But this is where they stop. They assume labor's decline is inevitable (the changing economy, etc.). But the Democrats, if they want it, have it in their power to put themselves back in office, even with a mediocre candidate, like

Dukakis. It would be easy, almost mechanical. No soul searching, no rethinking, no "new ideas." Just amend the labor laws. Have it here like it is in Canada.

It can't be that easy, of course. Otherwise why isn't the "labor party" or its equivalent in power in all the other countries that give workers the right to organize? If you look, however, most of those labor parties are very narrowly based, socialist parties, which, unlike the Democrats, are not true center-left coalitions, but way, way off to the left in a ditch.

Organized labor here in America is the very opposite of what they have in Britain. The British unions, so far as I can tell, have no hope. They hated Thatcher for her effrontery in offering hope. They yearn to be back in the year 1900: they long for 1900 and the common grave. But here in America, we're ready to deal. Even now, when labor is dying, when it ought to be mad, furious, ready for class war, all we can think is: "Cut us in on the deal . . ."

Of course, this is just a pipe dream. We can't even get the Democrats to cut us in on the deal.

I could have been a "new Democrat," too. Once I, too, was headed that way.

In fact, I *am* a "new Democrat." Which means, I go around having the same conversations all the time, how the Democrats are boring, how they stand for nothing. And now that we, the new Democrats, have taken over the party, taken it away from the old ones, the hacks, the New Dealers, as it was right and just for us to do . . . well, everything is now pretty boring.

My friend George is a lawyer in New York. I remember talking to him in 1988, just before the Democratic primary. He mentioned almost casually that he wasn't going to vote.

"George," I said, "I can't believe it . . ."

He said, "I can't, I just can't . . . Dukakis is boring, Gore is boring. I can't even *look* at Dukakis on TV, except early, very early in the morning. At night I just can't look at either one."

He paused. "I switch to the Spanish channel and watch a baseball game from the Dominican Republic."

Then he added, "Why are we deliberately blowing every election? Every time now, it seems to get worse. You know, I look back now on the '84 election, Reagan and Mondale, and to me, that now seems like an *interesting* election."

George is bored, I am bored: we, the new Democrats, are all so bored with ourselves. We want some bright, new and shining thing.

What is it that we want?

To me, though, in the very last moments, every presidential election in the eighties *did* become interesting. Or at least, in what I'd call "the last ten days." Every four years, the same thing happens again: The Democratic candidate stumbles, falls further and further behind, and then, in the last ten days, he seems to give up. Doesn't even try. And he goes around like an old-time Democrat. He marches with the unions. Appears with Lane Kirkland. Suddenly, the election tightens up. The Republicans start to lose their cool and accuse the Democrats of making "class-based" appeals. A few journalists begin writing, "The Democrats should have been doing this months ago." (Of course, if they had, the journalists would have written, "Can't the Democrats come up with any new ideas?")

Now, by this point, the election really is over. Most people are watching ball games from the Dominican Republic. But the race does tighten up.

Yet once the election is over, "the last ten days" are treated as a shameful thing, something we shouldn't have done, as if Dukakis, or Mondale, and some of the rest of us had gone into a bordello or something. When the next presidential campaign begins, no one will have the slightest memory of the last ten days, until everything collapses again, and the next last ten days come around, and we all have to go back into Detroit, Pittsburgh, and Akron, the fleshpots of the old New Deal, and slum around for working-class votes. Shamefully, back into the bordello, with old Lane Kirkland as a kind of . . . well, superfly.

Yet this is the only time, in the last ten days, when it is fun to be a Democrat. The campaign is over, and we've lost, and we don't have to think about "new ideas" now, and we can just go out and march in a big torchlight parade. I know this is irresponsible, maybe even immoral, and as a new Democrat, which I am, partly, I should be home reading position papers on "new ideas," but I figure I can do that for the next 3.9 years. For a day or two . . . why not have a little fun?

So I marched in one, in 1988. The Cook County Democratic Party, which has no shame, had a big torchlight parade for Dukakis, in one of those last ten days. It was all unions, really. Unions and black kids in high school bands. The Boilermakers, the Machinists, they all came out to march. Around 6 p.m., I went up to Wacker Drive and met up with the steelworkers, and I found Ed Sadlowski, Ed's son, Frank Lumpkin, even Carl Alessi, and a few other staff reps and members. Ed introduced me to a few I had never met. Then we started up Michigan Avenue, across the bridge, and past the blocks of elegant stores.

Some people had torches, fake ones, with gummy glow-glop, which I hate, and I gave mine to a child. It was a big parade, much bigger than I would have thought. The Republicans could never, never have a parade like this.

Then the Cook County Democratic Party began to set off fireworks, just over our heads. It was like the Fourth of July. The fireworks must have cost a fortune, and I thought of all the television time that this money could have bought.

As we marched, we passed young fathers and mothers, neoliberals probably, holding their kids up so they could see.

I looked at them, standing on the sidewalks, and I wanted to say, almost in a whisper, "Come join the New Deal."

We, the old Democrats, kept marching, with Dukakis in front of us, as if he were our captive, and we waved our picket signs like spears. We seemed to be dragging him to the Medinah Temple, which was the end of the parade, where he would have to stand in the Temple before us, with all the Cook County Democrats, and swear an oath that he would never have "new ideas" again. I think he might have done it, too. By this point, he would have done anything. I think, marching with all the unions, with the crowd, with the fireworks, Dukakis that night was overwhelmed, stunned, really, as if nothing like this had ever happened to anyone from Brookline, Massachusetts.

I had never cared much for Dukakis before . . . but that night, as we marched, I began saying to people next to me, "You know, he'll make a *great* President."

Because that night I knew Dukakis had changed, and from

now on, he would be changed, changed utterly, and he would go on to be elected. Not that he would stop being a neoliberal or a new Democrat, but that he had become something else as well. We should all be new Democrats, I believe. But everything the new Democrats or neoliberals have to say or to teach, it seems to me, you can pick up in a magazine. But what the old Democrats have to say, or teach . . . well, the only way you can learn it is to walk block by city block and carry a smoking torch.

As we marched, Ed Sadlowski told me this story:

"I was in one of these back in 1960 for John F. Kennedy, except it was two or three times this big. It started way down in Soldier Field, too, so we marched two or three times as far. We had real torches, too . . ."

"Real torches?" I said.

"Yes, yes . . . real torches."

It was startling to think that as late as 1960 John F. Kennedy was being elected by people going block by block, with smoking torches . . . almost like Grover Cleveland.

My friend S., a banker from Boston, had been in town that day on business, and I told her, "Come march in the parade." And so she did. She was with the steelworkers now, and she was holding a sign.

"You know," she said, "I've been going to all these high-level Dukakis things in Cambridge and Boston, but I think this is the most fun I've had so far."

I could see her going back to Boston and telling our friends what I was doing out here.

"Oh God," I said, "don't tell anyone about this."

She laughed. "Tom, don't be silly."

"Just say, 'He's out in Chicago and very active in the Dukakis campaign.' "

And I was waving the sign, up and down.

Once in the late sixties I thought that I would end up in government and that most of my friends would, too. Back then, I thought the whole regime of Kennedy-type liberalism would go on forever: and we would be part of it, and grow old with it. In and out of government, in and out of private firms, doors slamming, people giving little shrieks, just like in a play.

But always, in the end, government service, at some point in our careers.

In and out, yes: only we never got in.

Maybe we never will. But that night, I would have said, to all the "new Democrats" everywhere:

"It's all right, it's all right . . . Come join the New Deal."

If we can just have these parades, with the Boilermakers, Machinists, etc., and a few bankers from Boston, and even make it a little longer, and not even try to explain it or defend it, but just make it *longer*, then we can get elected, and we won't have to have a brain in our heads.

I am a New Deal Democrat, in the sense that I want the Wagner Act all over again. I don't want class war. I just want to make the parade longer. Class? I wouldn't even have our leaders use the word "class," or even "workers" (even that word makes me cringe), but just talk about the right to vote. And this right to vote goes way beyond labor. It's the right to vote, not just in one place, but the right to vote everywhere. Does this sound like class war? It sounds to me like the Fourth of July. And we don't have to throw out a single neoliberal book or article when we give people their right to vote.

And here is the best part: The whole thing is free. It's entirely off budget. It doesn't add a single penny to the deficit.

As we marched, it began to rain. The fireworks may have brought it on. It rained on the union members, the men and women who broke and ran. It rained on the kids in the marching bands. The kids, mostly black, kept marching.

I stood in a doorway, across the street from the Medinah Temple, and from the PAs I could hear the roll call as the party's candidates came up, one by one, onto the stage: "Carol Mosely Braun, next Recorder of Deeds . . . Aurelia Pucinski, next Clerk of Courts . . . and Michael Dukakis, next President of the United States."

That night, in the cold and the rain, Dukakis was so hoarse that he couldn't speak. He could only look at us, marching, and who knew what he thought?

A few days later, he lost the election.

Epilogue

1990

A friend of mine who lives in the East said to me the other day, "You know, you have a very aesthetic view of politics, and that's really *dangerous*."

I think I know what he means . . . as in radical, left, the reign of terror. And I was quite upset when he said this.

I wanted to say: Look, I'm an American, I'm a liberal, and I'm just like anyone else . . . I don't *want* a world where there's solidarity all day long, twenty-four hours a day, endless moral beauty around the clock. Yes, it's true, sometimes I want to go down to South Chicago and hold someone's hand and sing "Solidarity Forever."

But after that, believe me, I want to go home.

But maybe this is my friend's point: I'm not serious about it.

It's even possible that I became a labor lawyer to escape from community, solidarity, and holding people's hands. It seems a little rootless to be a labor lawyer in America, and be for "community," especially in the 1980s. If I wanted to be outrageous in the Reagan era, why didn't I just go to a coffeehouse and wear black? It's as if in trying to be "moral," or "ethical," I was merely being decadent, and proving that in America you could do anything, even be a labor lawyer, and in our culture of individualism, which permits everything, there's nothing, no thrill, that's really out of bounds.

•

It's Saturday night, August 1990, and I'm driving in a car down Lake Shore Drive. The boats are loading tourists, like at the landings at Martha's Vineyard, and the gulls are circling the cops, who circle around the ghetto. I'm driving down to South Chicago to meet with a group of workers who are having a benefit. I'm thinking, "I'll probably never leave Chicago."

This is my post, being a labor lawyer in the Midwest.

"Someone's got to do it," my friend Ric said to me once. "We can't all live on the coasts."

Someone's got to live in the middle of the country.

Oh well, I'm being morbid.

Tonight, I decide to turn off at Hyde Park, because I have some time. I go into the bookstore and browse. I know this is bad. I know time is passing, but I can't move.

I stand there fingering a book, *The Fragility of Goodness* by Professor Nussbaum.

Five hundred pages of moral philosophy.

Then I realize I'm half an hour late. What about these men who are waiting?

I run out to the car and drive to the hall. I feel sick.

And as I drive up, I see a man walking up and down, looking for me as if I'm lost.

I didn't do this deliberately.

Yet no one seems to mind. All through the meeting, I hear people say, "The lawyer's done this . . ." and "The lawyer's done that . . ."

I realize after a while that they don't know my name.

Then I decide, I'm going to go back and buy that damned book.

It's late in the bookstore. I stand in front of a clerk, about twenty, who's dressed in all black.

I give her *The Fragility of Goodness*. And she looks at it, and looks at me, and says, "This is not a happy purchase."

It seems to me a matter of luck, dumb luck, if you end up living a "moral" life. Often people trap themselves into living ethical lives. As in the case of someone who's a priest, and wants to get out and get married, but he can't. He's trapped. Too many people expect him to be a priest.

About a priest one can say, "Well, he started out too young, went in a seminary when he was twelve." But what about a labor lawyer? I was twenty-four when I went off with the miners, like one of the lost boys. And I didn't even know their names. It serves me right to have ended up, as I have, in South Chicago. Oh, come on, what am I complaining about?

I'm lucky the way that liberalism has worked out for me: I can do it, and not drip the acid of it on other people. I can get into some odd places, like union halls, simply because I *am* a liberal, and believe in rights . . . like the right to vote, the right to speak. And incredibly, I'm not tearing anything down. I'm for community, solidarity, and holding people's hands.

The only problem is, I feel like I'm cheating.

Lately, I've been writing this book. I've been writing it on weekends and in the mornings before I go to work, and now that I've reached the end of it, I hate to let it go. Because in writing it, I come closer to solidarity with . . . well, not the workers, but other people . . . than I do in the day-to-day living of my life.

Here's a depressing thought. Maybe in a book, and only in a book, is solidarity "forever."

But there's a great danger in writing a book. I can already see what's happening. I keep some steelworker waiting on a corner, walking up and down. What kind of "solidarity" is that?

That's where the aesthetic view of politics leads. That's why it's dangerous.

That's why when you shut the door and begin to write, someone should ask you, right then,

Which side are you on?

Afterword

It's 2004, and Labor's Even Smaller

If I had any sense, I'd add two things and stop. First, Ron Carey won that election, back in 1991—ah, how long ago that seems. Second, it's 2004, and I'm still a "labor lawyer," which may soon be a term of art for "a lawyer with no labor."

A month ago, I met a gorgeous official from a European consulate. When she asked what I did, I told her. "What an awful job!" she said. "You must always lose!" No, I said. I don't "always" lose; I even win a lot. But it's just that the line of battle keeps going backward. First, it was: Would they be in a union? We lost. Then, would they keep a pension? Lost. Then, health insurance? Lost, either all or part. Now it's: whether they are really "employees" at all or just independent contractors. That's the big one now.

Yes, along the way, we win lots of little victories. (For example, later, against Envirodyne, the yuppie firm in chapter four, we *did* get a bit more money for Frank Lumpkin and Save Our Jobs. In time, I'm sure I could think of another victory, too.)

But with that, I should just stop. Why continue the book? If I try, it would be in a different voice, much grumpier, middle-aged: It's 2004, so of course, I'm a different guy. Besides, if I were to "continue" the book, I'd have to go back and read the damn thing, and besides being lazy, I think it'd be too painful. It would be like long ago, in law school, when some of us would have to type up our illegible answers after exams, and have to writhe, as we typed it up, with no changes: Good God, did I have to say *that*? And aside from the pain of rereading it, I'm terrified I'd come upon this wraith of my younger self, and find out, to my horror, I'm so utterly different—or scarier still, that I'm more or less the same.

Anyway, I can sum up what happened after the book fast enough, at least for labor. At first, everything went right—absolutely right! Then it all went wrong—terribly, terribly wrong. As the good part won't take long, that's where I'll begin.

Carey Wins!

Yes, that's the big thing: Carey won! If you recall, my case for a rank-and-file election had been that it would be enough if Carey came close. So I feel a little silly, that the first time out, we won the whole damned thing. But we won! Even as I write this, years later, I still want to jump up and down. We won! I don't even mind, too much, that he never gave me any legal work. He won! For I'd seen clients walk out of my office, then get beaten up and bloodied. But now . . . we won! Not just Carey, but his entire slate—they all won. Every day, for months after this, when I woke, the sun would shine. The sky'd be blue. For all of the bad guys, at the very top—*everyone* was gone! I recall a TDU member, on the night of the election, being quoted somewhere:

"They're gone! All of them! Boom!"

What it meant, oddly, was that I had nothing more to do with the Teamsters. For now, the suits against the Teamsters just dropped out of my practice. Was I sorry to "lose" the Teamsters from my life? No. Good riddance. I never wanted to sue, or see, or depose a Teamster guy again. Good-bye, IBT. And I was happy enough just to watch the Carey "New Teamsters" at a distance. Well, I guess. Some others in TDU also had to watch, at a distance. Others didn't. Carey brought in some great people, even some of my friends from the UMW. And remember, there were now vice presidents of the IBT who had come from TDU! But Carey took his time to slam in the first trusteeships. The slowness of it made me itchy. First, he did the New York locals, which he knew. It took him years to get to Chicago, and not to Local

710, alas. Still, in the end, with the union's outside Independent Review Board, and the U.S. Attorney in New York backing him up, he bagged a lot of people: the IRB or Carey removed or kicked out over 300 officials.

Though in a few locals, late, the sons have sneaked back into the jobs from which the dads were removed. (See, it's not just in the White House.)

Other bad guys, old, wheezing, decided to "retire." Or they even died. If you start out young enough, you can often win in life just by outliving your mortal foe. But it's more sporting to beat them before they die off. And that was largely the case here. So I'm proud of TDU, my helping a bit: Carey's victory in 1991 was the biggest, best thing I have ever seen in labor. Sure, being an American, I had assumed that "we can change the world," as in the 1960s song, but what a shock to find out, in middle age, that such a thing is true. Kids today may think that it's only by being on the Right they can make a "Big Bang," like in Iraq, but there are other, better ways to shock and awe the world.

I took such pleasure in seeing dozens, hundreds of Teamster rank and file start to win local office. Or see others take staff jobs. Put on suits. And now, instead of loading trucks, they could go off to fund-raisers and sit there with the archbishops and the mayors. And they were not just union, but civic leaders! And the whole freshness of the rank and file getting these jobs, it gave the Teamsters a kind of moral glow.

Carey's win did even more: it changed the whole AFL-CIO. It changed, for example, who was on the Executive Council. Instead of a deadweight like Jackie Presser, the old Teamster boss, there was someone hip, Sadlowski-like, coming from the left. And from the moment Carey came in, I should have known (though I didn't) that Lane Kirkland was as good as gone. Very soon, he was gone. So by the mid-1990s, what I had hoped for with Sadlowski, in the 1970s, happened in my middle age—the AFL-CIO had crept over, a little, to the left. It became hipper, edgier, and even big with college kids. People use the term "New Labor." For who would dream that one day the AFL-CIO, which beat up kids for protesting the war in Vietnam, would come out against our invasion of Iraq? The rise of this New Labor happened for many reasons. For one, the rise of a New Right with which we could no longer cut a deal. Also, the rise of the Service Employees International Union (SEIU), which, to my shock, came to organize over 600,000 workers. It's bigger now than the Teamsters. It was this new SEIU that turned "Old Labor" into a labor movement for the poor, not for CIO-type autoworkers but for janitors and cleanup crews. (The poor, with less to lose, are often easier to organize!) Other reasons? The rawer income inequality, of course. But the Carey win, to me, is still the single biggest reason why labor, at last, started turning left.

As I was still jumping up and down and saying, Carey Wins, Carey Wins, I woke up one day and realized, to my shock, something just as good had happened, namely, that:

Bush Is Gone!

In 1992: Bush was gone! When I wrote this book, I figured that President Bush would be in there forever. And of course, "Bush" still is in there, though in a goofier version. But the point is Clinton came in between. Just as labor was losing three big strikes out in the heartland, all in downstate Illinois, of all places—the strike at Caterpillar, then the one at Staley, then the one at Goodyear—it seemed, oddly, we might come back, not by our strength in the heartland, but by our new clout in Washington.

After 1992, we had a chance for labor law reform, which I never dreamed of when I wrote the book. Even though we were weaker economically, we were, by luck, stronger politically. So if by a law in Congress we got the right to organize, we could start to get back all that we had lost at the bargaining table: in wages, pensions, health, and in endless hours of extra low-paid work. We had the White House—and back then, as we always did, the Senate and the House. In Western Europe, by the way, this is also how labor built its clout in the 1990s. European labor was able to expand works councils into more and more companies, not by its economic but by its political power, because the Socialists were in. And in America I dreamed a new law would resuscitate us, too.

We almost got it, too.

How close did we come? By the whisker of a Senate filibuster!

With a flip of a few votes, we'd have been back! And there'd have been no need for a new edition of this book.

Oh, it is so painful now to think back to that election night in 1992. On TV, Clinton came out, like a rock star, in Little Rock. We had won! We, the Democrats, had won everything, the White House, the Senate, and (as we always did) the House. As a friend of mine said, "We have the keys to the car!"

But some will gasp that I am so gaga for Clinton when supposedly he didn't care much about labor. It's true, he *didn't* care much about labor. But I'd be gaga for Eisenhower if we could get the same share (a third of the private sector, by unofficial estimates) that Old Labor had back under Ike. The point is not whether Clinton "liked" labor. FDR didn't really like labor that much, and probably JFK didn't either. The point is now we had a Democratic House, a Democratic Senate, and not just a Democratic president, but a really smart one. He could not only sell us the encyclopedia, door to door, but come back and give the lectures.

And even if he didn't "like" labor, I liked him for being so smart, Ph.D. smart, and street-smart, and never giving up, and also, I suppose, because I met him at a party, one at which I was not supposed to be. Such a dumb reason, isn't it? I'm supposed to be a labor lawyer, and hostile, but I'd never gotten this close to a guy actually running for president. The reason I, with no money, was at this party or fund-raiser was simple: I have a friend, L., who was connected with the Democratic Leadership Council ("DLC"), and in a gentlemanly way, I think he was trying to "convert" me, though I'm about as likely to marry a Moonie.

Anyway, he thought I might like to hear this new guy, a governor, Clinton, running for president. There was a ticket, free dinner.

No, I can't.

Well, it's there at the door, if you change your mind.

And I did change my mind, because as my friend Kathleen said, "It's a dinner and it's free." So in we came into a huge room of uneaten salads, and we went to a table way in the back, where a young African-American man, in a nice suit, was sitting, at his own table, completely alone.

It looked awful, of course. The only black in the room, and at a table alone? So, we sat next to him. As soon as I could, I said: "Uh, can I ask . . . what attracts you to this guy Clinton?"

He flipped open his badge: CPD.

Oh. Chicago Police Department.

And at that moment Clinton was standing up to speak: "As I look around the room tonight, I see people of all races. . . ."

(As I tell this story, I now realize, sure, of course, Clinton knew he was a cop!)

And while he had a few good lines about the Working Poor, he had more lines about America's Millionaires: "Yes," he said, two or three times, "why, even MILLIONAIRES have come to support my candidacy. . . ." Yes, because of the economy, they were all for Clinton now, and just so sorry they had been for Bush. And while in one way, I wished he would stop with the MIL-LIONAIRES, and I was annoyed with his speech . . . in another way, I was weak with pleasure, because the guy was such a pro. No, no, I didn't trust him. But my God, don't we want to win? My friends think because I'm with labor I want to lose, but no, I want to win!

And I knew we were going to win.

It's not just that he's Elvis's brother, but that he's Elvis's brother AND he got a Rhodes. AND he always kept his cool. Well, maybe I was the only one smitten, or maybe it was just because I wasn't paying for the meal. Anyway, when he stopped, all the lawyers—and they were all lawyers—rose, checked their watches, and stampeded for the trains. Cut off from Kathleen, I tried to go against the flow of lawyers, to get up front, to show L., hey, I had come after all. But it was too hard, and I stopped about halfway and turned, and . . . there was poor Clinton, all alone.

As my party planner friend M. once told me, when we dated: "The easiest person to meet at these events is always the guest of honor." So out of pity, I went up to him to shake his hand. "I really liked your speech," I said, of the speech that had annoyed me. "But I only wish you could have said . . . well, a little something about labor."

So he smiled at me and he was about to say . . . but then he stopped. What did I want him to say about labor? Uh-oh.

I decided to throw him a life preserver. "I'm a labor lawyer," I said, under my breath. "Union side. I'm FOR labor."

He gave me a big grin, and knew I was bailing him out. Then he went dead serious. "I'm in favor of the Striker Replacement Bill." Then he said something about a Position Paper. And I should write away to get it.

The whole subject must have left him as cold as the windchill on the El. He probably hated the Striker Replacement Bill, i.e., the idea that in America of all places, striking workers were the only workers who could not be fired. Damn it, how was he supposed to explain it on television? Oh, I'm sure he wanted labor to come back. As a Democrat, how could he not? But the Wagner Act, striker replacement, all of it—he couldn't wrap his mind around it.

If anyone had the gift to sell it, it would have been Clinton. Maybe no one could sell it. Striker Replacement violates Tocqueville's "Political Rule Number One": In a democracy, it's dumb to propose laws that give rights to some Americans, but not to all Americans. So here we had a "labor bill" that would let every nonunion worker, over 90 percent of the private work force, be fired for any reason, at any time—but not if they were on a strike.

Can you imagine the groundswell for that?

Worse, it was so defeatist. The whole intent was to use Striker Replacement to put up a shield, build a military-type earthworks, establish a kind of Maginot Line around what was left of the Old Labor army, out in the old industries. Yes, it was like France 1940. In theory we could use it to organize, go on the attack. But the main point of it was to defend against busting unions in the old heavy industries. And what was the point, anyway? Even if we got Striker Replacement, Free Trade would sweep them all away in just a few years. Oh sure, I would have loved a Striker Replacement bill. Imagine being able to say: Want to save your job? Tell the boss that you're on strike.

But I have to confess, I still thought we could get it. For a while, after Carey, and then with Clinton winning, I was sure anything could happen. And labor would come back. And all I had to do was wait.

All I Had to Do Was Wait

So even by 1991, I was figuring, with Carey in, all I had to do was wait. A New Teamsters. A New Labor. Which meant, maybe I'd get some paying business. (I'm sorry to obsess on that.) But in the meantime, I had to take a few nonpaying cases. I mean, as a part-time labor lawyer, I had to do a lot of employment law. Cases for ad hoc employee groups, or just individual employees, usually not in a union. As labor shrinks, more and more lawyers drift into this individual, "civil rights" type of employment law. In a country where it's easy to fire people for no reason—none, zero—it's mind-boggling the number of laws that could apply, once in a while, more or less:

Title VII (race) of the Civil Rights Act of 1964, as amended in 1991

Title VII (sex discrimination) of the Civil Rights Act of 1964, as amended in 1991

Section 1981 and 1983 of the Civil Rights Act of 1871, as amended in 1991

Age Discrimination in Employment Act (ADEA)

ERISA (the part that prohibits firing people to keep from paying their pensions)

Pregnancy Discrimination (prohibits firing women for having babies)

OSHA (same with firing people for reporting safety violations)

The WARN Act (firing people without notice)

Every law, except a decent labor law, to protect people, truly, from being fired, without cause. And under Clinton, there'd be more of these antidiscrimination laws. Poor Martin Luther King Jr. marched for laws like these, and now the people who use them most effectively are not the poor, but top salesmen, vice presidents . . . and one day, I suppose, even the MILLION-AIRES when the shareholders push them out. Why do these laws work for the rich? The rich have more expensive lawyers, more lawyers—and more money to make trouble.

Anyway, I had to keep doing these cases, to run out the clock till the labor movement came back. By the way, it's not that I'm against doing employment law. It's just that this law doesn't work if there's no labor movement around.

Let me try to explain. In a civil rights–type case, we have to show that Joe Smith or Jane Doe was fired without "just cause." I don't mean in a formal, legal sense. Indeed, in that sense, it is unclear what we have to show. Even now, forty years and forty million cases later, it's still murky down in the trial courts what we have to show to win a civil rights case. Isn't that amazing? Yet as I write this, our firm has an appeal in a Title VII race case up in the Seventh Circuit, and here's the issue: if a largely black group is being paid less than an all-white group, does race have to be "the" factor? Or does it have to be just "a" factor? And if it is merely "a" factor, does it have to be a "catalytic" factor? Or does it only have to be a "substantial" factor? And if it only has to be a "substantial" factor, can the employer get out of this by proving it would have made the same decision anyway?

And for another century, the law is going to wobble back and forth.

But no matter how it comes out year to year we always have to prove in some real-life way that our client was fired without "just cause." But if there is no labor movement to say what is or is not just cause, there is no standard to which as a lawyer I can refer— since almost every one on a jury now is nonunion, and can be fired for any reason at any time, it's hard to say even in general what is "just" or not. If there's no New Deal labor law to set a standard, or base, of just cause, it makes it much harder to use civil rights law.

And that is even true in what remains of the union world. I did an arbitration for a guy fired for eating pizza when he was working late, while everyone else around him was eating pizza. Reason: "An employee in that classification is forbidden to eat pizza when working overtime, even when working with other employees who can."

Oh, come on! But the arbitrator upheld it! And I have lost other cases like this. Oh, I used to be freaked out to run into a guy in a case like this I lost who is now working as a security guard at the ballpark. I actually stopped going to see the White Sox.

Anyway, I can't do civil rights–type law without some decent labor law behind it. So while I took these cases, I kept waiting, hoping labor would come back before I got into terrible trouble. And in fact, I did get into terrible trouble. I did what I swore, on oath, I would never do. I took a case in Indiana.

The Steel Haulers

In the book, I think I swore on oath that I would never take a case in Indiana, once the Midwest capital of the KKK—the Killing Fields, for any liberal Chicago lawyer. It's flat, because it's easier to hunt us down. No, no.

Not there. Like Chief Joseph of the Nez Perce I have said: I will fight in Indiana, no more, forever.

Then the steel haulers started calling. The steel haulers are the "independent" owner-operators, the drivers who own their own rigs and haul the steel away from the mills. Alas, the mills are now all in Indiana. Now that the mills are all so high tech, the haulers are about the only human beings who get near a bar of steel. As Frank Lumpkin would say, they still need people to pick up and carry things.

Now for all practical purposes the haulers work for the mills, for Inland, USX, for others, just like any working stiff. But legally, the mills just fill out an IRS form 1099 and are done with them. They aren't employees. They're "businessmen." So there's no pension. No health.

And there's no union, of course. So the mills can set the rate, which is like a wage. But it's even easier to fidget with it, move it up and down. Squeeze them. And so one day, like the cab drivers in *Waiting for Lefty,* the Clifford Odets play, the drivers met. They argued. They made motions. Why didn't the mills pay for their health insurance? They decided to form a group. The Great Lakes Steel Haulers Association. GLASHA. What did GLASHA want? Health insurance. Not just for the men. For their kids. For their wives. The mills, their true employers, scoffed. So the men voted. They wouldn't haul a bit of steel.

And . . . BOOM! The mills and a half dozen corporate law firms came blasting into court. After all, these were businessmen. And they were acting "in restraint of trade." They were violating the Sherman Act.

And this was a criminal violation! In theory, they could go to prison. And even in civil terms it was horrific because the mills could get damages for all the profits that they lost while the boycott was going on. Not just ordinary damages: treble, or triple, damages. And worse, they were in the hands of a right-wing Reagan judge.

So first came the temporary restraining order. Then, the preliminary injunction. And the Judge, who was supposed to be a slow judge, had put the case on a fast track. In a few months, which was unheard of, he'd start their trial. For millions in damages. Tripled.

I ignored the calls, on pink phone slips, because the phone numbers started with 219, which is the area code for Indiana. At last I returned a call.

No.

Was it in Indiana? I referred them to T., who was in Indiana, and braver, and is a lawyer I much admire. Would I help, though?

No.

No.

No.

So why did I say yes? Because it was so archaic, so 1920s-like, for workers once again, like in Odets, to be sued under the Sherman Act. Maybe I'd get to quote Felix Frankfurter, my hero. Indeed, to my bedside, at twelve bells, clanking in chains his ghost came to me: "Swear to me, take an oath, you'll carry out my work." And it was the kind of case a Frankfurter, or a Darrow, would have taken in a heartbeat.

And wasn't the situation worse, now? It could be a criminal conspiracy just to ask for health insurance. But they *were* businessmen, yes? Independents, who own their own rigs? "When you subtract the gas," a Teamster local president once told me, "and the insurance, and the depreciation, and all the rest, I doubt they make more than $8 an hour." To him, they were about as "independent" an "owner" as a migrant on a cleaning crew working at a Wal-Mart.

Why didn't it occur to them to form a union, to bring in the Teamsters, or the Steelworkers, whose lawyers knew the pitfalls of the Sherman Act? In part, I think they really did believe, in a sliver of each man's cortex, "I-am-a-businessman," but in part, I think, people in this country don't know what unions are anymore. Labor law, collective bargaining, all of it is becoming a lost civilization.

Maybe I would now start a kind of boutique labor law practice, specializing in the Sherman Act. Maybe I'd go on to represent ball players, the stars, the free agents. But I never got near any of that, though later, I did have a client who was a waiter in a sky box. No, this case was a rarity, one of a kind. For me, what made it so emblematic a case, a paradigm case, a "case of our time," was something else: The risk these poor guys took to get health insurance for their kids. Health insurance! It started with the GLASHA case, and when I look back on the 1990s, it seems every other case had, at the core of it, somebody trying to get health insurance.

Think how desperate these men must have been: Did you know that uninsured people pay two to three times what you and I, as insured patients, have to pay? Many years later—well, now, in fact—I brought a class-action case for uninsured patients because the hospitals gouge them. You and I have Blue Cross or Humana to negotiate for us and lower the prices. The uninsured have no one.

It's not just the for-profit hospitals. The religious, charitable hospitals, tax-exempt so they can serve the needy, pick out the neediest people, and charge them the highest prices. And if someone like a GLASHA driver doesn't pay, the religious, charitable hospital puts it in collection, then sues, then garnishes the man's wages, or levies on the house, or sometimes, in the worst cases, has him put in jail.

Why? Because his kid happened to have asthma.

Imagine how the uninsured must feel. They're working longer and longer hours. But they see you and me, above them, with our health insurance, and with all our miracle drugs, magic antibiotics, and longer lives, so that at age ninety or a hundred we'll be playing tennis and rushing the net, and meanwhile they can't afford a doctor for their kids.

They have nothing, no money in reserve, no extra hours to work since everyone is working. The other day, Edward Wolff, an economist who studies wealth distribution, put out a report that 46 percent of American families have LESS than $5,000 that they can come up with in an emergency, from anything at hand. How many are without health insurance or have deductibles of $5,000 or higher? I know that the consumer confidence survey tells us every month how "upbeat" we Americans are, but it must be, for many of us, a kind of nervous hysteria. One would think, in the bottom 40 percent, all of them would have to be on drugs. Except they can't afford them.

So with the haulers, for the first time it really hit me how desperate people are for health insurance. I don't hear about pensions anymore. Recently Professor Elizabeth Warren at Harvard Law School and her daughter, Amelia Tyagi, made a great point of this in their book, *The Two-Income Trap*. They first note that both parents, Dad and Mom, are working, that people can't work any more hours to come up with extra cash. And the biggest single cause of bankruptcy in America? No health insurance.

It's not just the scandal of no health care for the forty-three million who are uninsured and the millions more who are severely underinsured. Just as bad, there's the scandal of families going bankrupt. And that's why doing labor law, to me, in the 1990s, came to mean tending to a "middle" class hounded by collectors.

But in a case like GLASHA, here's the problem: If they have no money for health insurance, they have no money to defend themselves in court. Besides, these guys were in a perfect squelch given that they were being sued for antitrust "conspiracy." If they even talked with each other about raising money for our case, it was arguably another legal violation!

Did I say in the book that the 1980s were bad? I guess. But in the 1980s, we were the plaintiffs. We were the ones suing the mills. Now they were suing us. And we had no money. No money to pay for depositions. No money for a trial.

NO MONEY.

We didn't have the money to lose the case.

Now the mills claimed they had lost millions. We suspected,

though, the mills actually made money because, thanks to the boycott, they could shut down and just work off their inventory. They lost nothing. But they'd bring in some expert from the University of Chicago who'd swear to some nonsense, and we'd end up screwed anyway.

What to do? Surrender. If the mills dropped the suit, we would promise never to ask for health insurance again. So the lawyers drafted an agreement for me and T. to review.

So, with big shit-eating Mona Lisa smiles, since I'm sure they knew they didn't have any damages, they sent over the terms of surrender, which were more or less that we had to give up our immortal souls.

I had never read such a document before and hope I never do again.

I stared. I read it over and over. Our clients couldn't even meet each other again, ever, and talk about work. What, like even in the parking lot, by accident? As a lawyer I couldn't sign it!

Of course as a lawyer I could sign it, and the men wanted me to sign it. But we had to talk it over. Now that was a tricky thing because under the theory of the complaint it was illegal even to talk it over. We couldn't even meet to give up!

But we did. As I drove down to the meeting that Friday night, I thought, "These guys will have to fight!" And once again, I felt a little high, to be driving past the mills down into Indiana, except there are only a few mills left now. Now I see riverboat casinos lit up the way I used to see the mills. They say the wives of dead steelworkers are over there, maybe tonight, gambling away the survivor share of dwindling union pensions. I used to think: One day, I have to go into a mill. But I never did. Now I think: One day, I have to go into a casino, like Harrah's or Trump's. What's it like? My friend Myer says, "There are little pools of urine, right around the slot machines." (Some people are so intense, there's no time for a restroom.)

By the time I reached the hall I had decided to say: "We're going to have to fight." Of course I had told my cocounsel that I'd say the very opposite. But this was worse than a "yellow dog" contract, the kind the young Felix Frankfurter used to fight. A yellow dog was a contract in which the worker promised not to join a union. This damned thing was a contract in which the drivers said they wouldn't even meet with each other. I opened the door. I was going to give a blistering speech. . . .

Then, it was as if a class of children looked up at me, like I was their teacher, and got ready to take notes.

No haulers. The mills had found out about our meeting (and didn't know that the haulers were just meeting to surrender). So to break it up, they announced Friday night that there were fresh, steaming, just-out-of-the-oven steel to pick up, like hot bagels. "Come and get it!" So that was the end of our meeting. Except some of the haulers sent their kids, older, in high school, maybe twelve to seventeen, to sit and to take notes.

"You want me to talk to these kids?" I said to a GLASHA leader, one of the very few men there. But he said the kids were there to take down what I said.

Well, it wasn't very Churchillian. I lost my nerve and told the kids, everybody, that we really had to sign this. Though I griped and moaned about it in an unbecoming way. I now realize I looked down on these guys for not telling me to fight it, for doing what I, their lawyer, told them.

But then I didn't know how it felt to be hunted as they had been. In my next big case, instead of my clients being hunted, I'd be the one that the big firms would chase. Then I would find out what it's like to be hunted.

Vizcaino v. *Microsoft*

Let me first make one big statement about the 1990s: It was when people at the top of the labor market began to get screwed. If I could put in your cupped hand a Rosetta Stone that would crack the code of all the happy talk about the 1990s, I'd give you the case of *Vizcaino, et al.* v. *Microsoft.*

Read it and weep. Then skip to the next section.

In *Vizcaino,* the lead plaintiff and her colleagues were earnest, post-grad types working at Microsoft. But in a way they were like the steel haulers. They were "independent" contractors, free-lancers, with no Microsoft pension, no health insurance. Yet they did the same work as Microsoft employees. Had the same

Microsoft badge. Parked in the Microsoft lot. Even punched in at the Microsoft clock.

But no health insurance! Not to mention no pension, no profit sharing, indeed, no Social Security, either. They were in a golden kingdom with nothing, while Microsoft made billions. In some respect, Ms. Vizcaino couldn't get what any busboy could in Canada.

Now it's true, when Vizcaino and others sued as a group in 1989, Microsoft refrained from suing them back under the Sherman Act, as in the GLASHA case. Let's give Microsoft credit at least for that. (Maybe, given its own alleged monopoly, Microsoft was a bit nervous about suing anyone under the Sherman Act.) Still, Microsoft fought! But lost, thank God. But why did it fight? If labor markets work the way we learn in Economics One, or reading Adam Smith or David Riccardo and the other classical economists, why did these post-grad types have to go to court? If there was such a shortage of skilled workers, if New Democrats were promising us, "Just skill yourselves up, and you'll be at the top," and if Microsoft was making more money than the European Union, it makes no sense that Microsoft workers would have to fight for:

Pensions
Disability insurance, and even
Social Security!

A bit later in the boom, a writer in *The New Republic* claimed that in St. Louis, kids were applying for jobs in fast-food land, and in terms of wages, the kids could "name their price." Oh? If true, then they had more clout than some of the highest skilled people in the United States.

Or consider the case of the engineers at Boeing. In 2000, the engineers (not the blue-collar, but the white-collar engineers, with graduate degrees from Purdue) had to go on strike against Boeing just to get a raise. Keep in mind that without the engineers at Boeing, with their designs, the United States would have virtually nothing to sell abroad. O.K. I exaggerate, but our balance of trade swings every month, back and forth, more or less on how many Boeing planes we sold abroad. It is hard to imagine the United States economy going on as it has without the Boeing planes.

But the engineers, guys with slide rules who went, for God's sakes, to Purdue, and who like the Praetorian guard defend us in the World Economy, had to go on strike just to get a raise. And for the first time, doctors began to organize!

When Clinton and Gore talked about the Digital Divide, they were as out-of-date as two men in their suspenders and spats. In the 1980s, the income gap opened between high school and college (I should say most high school, and most college). But in the 1990s, the income gap opened up, yaw-like, between college and . . . well, college. That is, while Clinton and others were telling us to look down below us at the Digital Divide, there was another, bigger Divide cracking open above our heads.

How does the Digital Divide explain *Vizcaino* v. *Microsoft*? It doesn't. So what does?

Two things: labor getting smaller. And poorer. And Business getting bigger. And richer. Once they had taken all the money they could take from the high school grads, they came after you and me. It's a culture now, in law, in medicine, at Microsoft, at Boeing, of Winner Take All. In a culture that has no labor movement, there is nothing to put a brake on Winner Take All. Labor is now barely even a presence. In the private sector the percentage is now down to maybe 8 percent. As a lawyer I know said, "If the airline unions disappeared, we wouldn't have anything at all."

And Business *is* getting bigger. It may be true, as they say at the University of Chicago, that size doesn't matter, or that it doesn't affect the market price. Especially in a global economy, some might argue there is no such thing as a single company having power over market price. But I question whether this is true for the labor market. Here, I think, the size of a company can give it power over the so-called labor price, or the wage rate. Was it true that Microsoft is a monopoly, as the U.S. Department of Justice claimed? Here's my test: when Microsoft has to compete enough to get skilled workers that it has to pay their health insurance and pension.

It was bad enough that in the 1990s we had overregulated labor, so as to make it impossible to organize on any large scale.

But did we also have to deregulate Big Business, let it get even bigger still with more power over wages? It seems that one day in America we will have One Company, as in:

One Retail Company: Wal-Mart
One Coffee Company: Starbucks
One Software Company: Microsoft
One Bank: Bank One, Bank Two, changing names every month
One Global Company: General Electric

There's a longer list, but let's just stop.

And the Big Ones are the ones that, in devious ways, don't pay health insurance or other benefits. Now this is contrary to the usual view that it's Small Business that won't pay health insurance but Big Business will. But in America, Small Business is often Big Business in disguise. An example: our suit for the skycaps of United Airlines. Once, the skycaps were the proud employees of the Biggest Airline in the World, but United Airlines decided not to pay their health insurance anymore, which means, because of the terms of group coverage, United had to dump them, throw them out on the sidewalk.

Yes, United fired them! But then took them back, in effect, as employees of much smaller contractors. Indeed, we alleged that United told the contractors: "These are our people, you have to hire them." So they now work for Small Business—with no benefits. But still, at the same time, they are the skycaps of United. So, how is that possible?

Because Small Business, in America, is mostly Big Business in disguise.

Clinton Craters

In the early 1990s, because of cases like this, I became obsessed with health insurance. Alas, Clinton did, too. I wish he had concentrated on Striker Replacement. It was his Health Plan that was his downfall, and may have brought the Republicans to power.

Most Democrats seem to think we can fix the problem with

something other than single-payer, i.e., government-paid, national health insurance. Unfortunately, we can't. Or if we load the costs on employers, they'll simply cut back jobs, or find some new way to spin people off. Indeed, that's why German employers, which pay health insurance, hesitate to hire, while British employers, with single-payer, don't. It's odd to say the U.S. economy has a similar problem to Germany's, or it's at least one reason why we, of late, have had a recovery with few new jobs.

It's not just that health insurance costs so much, it's the uncertainty. Employers hate uncertainty. It's not wages that bother them. It's health insurance. The "defined benefit" pension, which they can't cost out. They don't know what they'll end up paying.

That's why we have labor movements or socialist measures like single-payer.

At any rate, Clinton offered his Health Plan, about 10,000 pages long, but it was mostly a plan to get Small Business to pay. He figured, reasonably, that labor was too weak to help him, but Big Business might help him get the bill through. Why not? Big Business paid health insurance. Small Business did not.

So he and Hillary Clinton, they did a brave thing, to take on Small Business, the Insurance Industry, all the assembled powers. They marched with their Health Plan up to Capitol Hill, turned around, waved . . . and Big Business didn't move.

And the Clintons were demolished. There was nobody behind them. Not labor. Not the country. They failed to grasp why in America we have so much Small Business: As I found out in my own cases, Small Business—not always, but often—is Big Business in disguise.

By the Way, I Crater, Too

Meanwhile, just as the Clinton Administration began to crater, I happened to be melting down myself. As a lawyer, I almost went out of business. Remember that I said I know what it's like to be hunted?

I now know more what it was like to be a steel hauler facing trial, and by the way, I have more respect for Clinton, too. They know what it's like to be hunted. In my own case it happened because I brought a suit against American Airlines whose CEO, Robert Crandall, who seemed to me a smarter, more statesmanlike "Chainsaw Al." I knew it was dangerous to sue American, but I had gotten careless. Over the years no one, not even in Indiana, had really come after me with sanctions.

American did. It's meaner than United Airlines.

I also learned it was dangerous to go on being a "labor" lawyer, and arguing the old labor law that I took in law school. The judges of today see fewer labor cases, and their law clerks rarely take the course in law school. So when I write a brief it can sound like gibberish, in Latin.

Yet, as with the haulers, I thought my clients, a group of younger pilots, had a case hard to resist. The younger pilots wanted to knock out as illegal a "two-tier" agreement between American and the pilots' union. A two-tier agreement sets two different pay scales, forever, i.e., the younger pilots in the "B" scale, no matter how long they work, can never make as much as the older pilots in the "A" scale do.

Normally, a two-tier agreement goes "pffttttt" when the younger B pilots become a majority of the pilots' union. Then the union says: No A, no B. But to stop this from happening, American and the A-scale pilots cut a deal. The labor contract would no longer be the ordinary two-way agreement between the employer (American) and the union. Instead, it would now become a three-way agreement, with three parties signing on:

Employer (American)
Union (all pilots, A and B)
A group of A-scale older pilots with a veto over what the Employer
    and the Union did.

So even when the union became a B-pilot majority, the employer and the union could not lawfully bargain the damned thing away. Three had to agree! So the two tiers could last forever! Now in law school I learned that three-way interference with two-way bargaining is illegal. There's a Supreme Court case, *Emporium Capwell*, directly on this point. So even though I knew it was dangerous to sue American, I told the younger pilots, "Sure, I'll bring the case." Why did I have to worry?

To my shock, I lost. I lost at every level. District Court. Court of Appeals. I cited the right cases. Other labor lawyers told me I was right. The problem? The clerks hadn't taken the courses I had. One clerk, writing for his judge, said my argument "verged on the frivolous."

I LOST! So it was like a duel and I had turned and fired my pistol point blank at American, and now, slowly, American raised its pistol straight at me. . . .

I realized I was going to see a motion for sanctions for making an argument that "verged on the frivolous." American filed it before the same law clerk, or his judge, now in his dotage, who had written these fearful words. How galling that a twenty-something clerk could put me in this danger. And somewhere in this big corporate firm facing me there was another twenty-something lawyer, freshly minted, who was "tasked" to draft the motion for sanctions and to end my career. Do I mean to disbar me? No, but just as bad. I would have to pay the entire legal bill that American had run up, from District Court up to the Court of Appeals—at $350 an hour. How much? Here's my guess: FOUR HUNDRED THOUSAND DOLLARS!

Or slightly less.

Yes, it's a great thing about this country, how I, an individual, can create myself out of nothing. But the bad part is it's easier to be destroyed. What was I going to do? I had to write a brief and pray: Please God, I want to go on being a lawyer! (Which, in a calmer moment, I'm not at all sure I want to do.) I had to explain why my argument, which was right but came from what is now a lost civilization, did not "verge on the frivolous." My real hope was that the old judge in his dotage would now wake up and see what was going on when his clerk brought in the order to impose the sanctions.

"Wh-, what's, what's this? No, no, no. Let the poor boy go!" (Or so he might wake up and say.)

Only, I was unsure if he would wake up. And he might sign whatever the clerk put in front of him! By the way I now realize the judge was dying.

So for weeks, over my head, the motion hung in mid-air, about to drop, and every time I went to a restaurant and started to laugh, and drink wine, I'd remember: The motion! And I'd stop laughing and want to leave. I began to listen to Gregorian chants on a CD as I drove around in my car during Lent and got more and more scared. If only I had been in a bigger firm with more lawyers to surround me, I'd have felt safer. But we were so small.

The young pilots, my clients, were blasé. "Oh, so American is trying to get you?" Maybe to pilots it didn't seem that big a deal. Some had just come back from Operation Desert Storm.

The decision came: "Defendant-Appellee's Motion for Sanctions, DENIED."

That was the whole text. So I could put the Gregorian chants back into the glove compartment and laugh now and go back to being a lawyer. But I had more respect for the steel haulers. And for Clinton when he was being hunted, too.

But now I knew: Unless Congress passed Striker Replacement to bring unions back, it was going to be more and more dangerous for people like me to practice labor law. So I prayed, under my breath, "Pass Striker Replacement!!" Didn't we have the votes to pass it?

Now came the thing I'd dreaded.

We Lose the Keys to the Car

Under the Constitution as it is on paper, we should have had the votes. But it is worth a word to say why we didn't.

While it may have seemed that the Democrats were "in," they were not *really* "in." Didn't we have the White House, the Senate, the House? Yes, but the U.S. Constitution, unnoticed, had a little meltdown in the first two Clinton years. The filibuster, the sixty-vote rule, or the super majority, unauthorized in the U.S. Constitution, now became the rule, and not the exception, on every major bill. (Except the budget, by a special Senate rule.) To do this, as Robert Dole and the Senate Republicans did, was a kind of small scale coup d'état. We had over a hundred of these "super majority" votes in Clinton's first two years. While one may call these votes filibusters, they were not all-night affairs with Huey Long reading his mother's recipes or Jimmy Stewart ripping off his tie. Now, under Robert Dole, they became normal day-to-day things.

I admit, the sixty-vote rule, this wicked thing, was already in place after 1976. But only under Clinton did it become a normal everyday rule for passing any bill. What Dole did, as a minority leader, would have shocked the Founders in at least two ways: First, simply that Dole did it, and no one, no court, stopped him. Second, that the rest of us, the public, the press, no one seemed to care.

So of course Striker Replacement crashed and burned. Still, when it did, I was so furious: Striker Replacement "only" got a majority, with fifty-three but not the sixty votes needed to beat a filibuster. Damn it, damn it, damn it! If only we had a Congress with majority rule, I wouldn't have to write this grieving afterword. By the way, we even lost six Democrats!

And which lost senator's vote would I pick out for honorable mention? Bumpers, Dale Bumpers, from Arkansas. I know, it's Clinton's state: For a moment I was suspicious too. But still, I don't blame Clinton. It seems that Bumpers was about to leave the Senate, but not D.C., where he'd make his fortune as a lawyer. So maybe the vote was to put him in good stead with future corporate clients. Maybe he hates labor out of principle. By the way, in 1999 Bumpers came back to the Senate, as one of Clinton's lawyers during the impeachment trial. "Oh Bumpers!" my friends said. "Did you hear his speech for Clinton?" Bumpers-this, and Bumpers-that, and Bumpers-is-a-hero. And all I could think was:

Bumpers. That's the guy.

Bumpers.

But it was all worse than just losing Striker Replacement. Thanks to the mass use of the sixty-vote rule, we, the Democrats, ended up losing Congress, too, in the 1994 elections. With these filibusters, Dole was able to make Clinton look ridiculous. Worse, it made him look further to the right, and less of a Democrat, than he really was. I mean, everything that Clinton-on-the-right wanted, such as a NAFTA Treaty, which many of us hated, Dole waved through. Everything Clinton-on-the-left wanted, Dole blocked.

Sorry. Only New Democrat bills get through the gate.

At some moments, Clinton looked like a bungler who was blowing every bill, and at other moments, he looked like a closet Republican who only delivered for the right. Dole must have known: Of the two, the latter's even worse. Because Clinton's base would leave him. People on the left began to shrink from him. None of us blamed Dole, the gatekeeper. No, it was Clinton's fault: He was President.

Clinton, that's the guy.

Clinton.

So in the 1994 elections for House and Senate many of the best people in labor scoffed. Why help this Clinton guy? So we sat back, and it now seems as if we were waiting for the Republicans. It's eerie to think back to the fall of 1994. It was as if we knew, and did not know, the New Right was going to come down from the mountains and take over the city square. And we knew that we, on the left, were waiting for the barbarians, but really deep down, it was hard to believe they'd really come.

Newt Gingrich, Tom DeLay, Dick Armey: no, not in America.

Even now, I can't believe they're in. But they are. I think back, to the weeks before in October. I went to a wedding, in the East, and there was a congressman, from the Midwest, and to a little knot of us he was saying: "It's pretty bad for us out there."

"But you don't think, do you, that . . . ? "

Oh no, he said, we've been tied up in Congress. If we Democrats got out there, there'd still be time to turn it all around. So I went back to the wedding party, nibbling the marinated shrimp, but I felt a chill.

My God, I thought. We'd always had the House. They couldn't take the House, could they?

Oh yes, they took the House! That awful November. They took the Senate, too. And poor Clinton, right then, he might just as well have been impeached. Really, why did they wait? But I was even more terrified for labor! The irony is, the wild, far-out New Right had come to power through just the kind of organizing that labor used to do. The New Right was a kind of mock labor movement, a kind of Black Mass version of labor. And Gingrich, DeLay, the Christian Right were the ones who, CIO-like, rang the doorbells, sent the e-mails, and ran the phone banks, too. How long would they let labor, or what was left of labor, hang around? For years they had queued up their scary bills to get rid of overtime pay, even to stop us, maybe, from collecting union dues.

But some of us in labor thought: Oh, we can get back in. It was only because of the NAFTA Treaty that our own angry white males—and others—sat out the election. And there was still the bitterness of the Bush recession, which Clinton had not managed, yet, to take away completely. So maybe the New Right thing was a fluke.

But maybe we had lost the knack of getting out there, door to door, the way the New Right did. Maybe that's why Clinton decided, at the Fairmount and other dinners, he had to court the Millionaires. Didn't labor act, in a certain sense, like one of the Clinton Millionaires too? Not all, but too many AFL-CIO unions would rather write a check than bother to go door to door. Much less organize new members. Yes, it's expensive, but why did we throw so much of it away on Democrats with big hair?

And perhaps it would be a good thing if the McCain-Feingold Act, just passed in 2003, would stop us from spending so much money. Yes, McCain-Feingold unfairly picks on labor, and it may tilt things to the Millionaires even more than before. Yet maybe if we stop writing checks we can spend it organizing new members. I bet there are twenty or so House districts where, if labor targeted them for organizing, we could flip them from the GOP to "us." Is it possible any Democrat will ever have the wit to say: "Skip the money for TV. Just organize in my district!"

The union factor flips far, far more white males from right to left than any thirty-minute "infomercial" at the halftime of the Super Bowl. Yet has there ever been a Democrat who turns down a labor check?

A Footnote Here on 1994: What Might Have Been

Well, that was the Clinton era, R.I.P.

No reform of the Wagner Act. Nothing. And because we blew it, labor is even smaller. It's down now to 8 percent or so of the private sector. Yes, with the public sector, it's a little higher. But

as a labor lawyer friend of mine says, "If we have just one big disaster, like losing the airline unions, that really would be the end
of the AFL-CIO."

He means: There wouldn't be enough "there" there to go on.
Doing nothing, with no organizing, we lost 369,000 members in
just the past twelve months.

And what's more galling, it would take only a few more union
members to put in the Democrats as the majority party. For ten
years I've been haunted by one thought: Weak as it is, labor is so
strong in part because more and more voters are dropping out.
Yes, we may be a laughable 8 percent of the private sector and 13
percent total, public and private. (Off the record, I think it's
less.)

But in the 2000 elections, well over a quarter of the voters
came from "union households." So the very fact of union membership, i.e., just nominal membership, means in the case of a
voter, "V," the following:

V is more likely to vote Democrat, e.g., switch from Bush to Gore.
V's household is more likely to vote Democrat, too.
V and everyone in V's household are far more likely to vote.

Suppose instead of 8 percent, we had a miserable 12 percent
of the private sector, and labor was still flat on its back, economically. I'm not smart enough to calculate the multiplier, in terms
of raising the turnout, flipping votes from Bush to Gore. But if
we came back by just that tiny 4 percent, I like to think Gore's
majority would have gone from half a million to something like
a blowout.

But it's worse than just the fact that we didn't get the extra
members. When there's no labor to bargain for the bottom two-
thirds of America, by household income, we get exploding
inequality. Longer hours. There's no connection anymore between effort and reward. People see the world as arbitrary, unfair. They stop voting. They drop out of civic life.

And the Democrats spiral downward, and things are worse for
them than ever. In a way, with no labor movement, the 1990s
boom made people at the median more bitter than ever. Why?
We had no one to protect us in the boom!

There was no labor to protect the typical, average American family from the coming boom of 1995 to 2000.

What? Did people need a labor movement to protect them from a boom? Sure. I mean the typical family with median income. It took this American family until 1999 to climb back up to the income level it had in 1989. So say Jared Bernstein and other economists in *The State of Working America (2000)*. But this same family at the median now was working an extra six weeks a year.

Six extra weeks of work, for free, no pay. Close up, year by year, in the boom years of 1995 to 2000, it would appear as if people were being paid more. The median family income in fact was going up, say the authors, at more than 2 percent a year. But if we just double the time frame and measure from business peak to business peak, people in effect worked those weeks for free. No wonder we had a New Economy, a Clinton boom. There are three, only three, ways an economy can grow: more capital, more labor, more productivity. If the people of a country are willing to work for free, no pay, nothing in return, then sure, you bet, the economy is going to boom. But in what way is the American family better off? Since it's for free, like a gift, it's wrong to call it a New Economy type of "slavery." But a Chairman Mao or King Tut might have been glad if his own people had done as much.

By the way, these economists take the official estimates of working hours from the Labor Department as if they were canonical. But we now know, from class-action lawsuits, that Wal-Mart and many other firms were working people off the books. And let's add the little franchises for tires, donuts, and the other sinkholes of endless, uncounted hours of the kind Peter Birkeland writes of in his book, *Franchising Dreams*. No one can say if it was six or far more extra weeks of labor, for free, that the American family poured into the economy, which, alas, never gave it back a dime. There is no labor movement to stop it. Long ago, Congress gutted the budget for enforcing wage and hour laws so there is no one in the government to watch it either.

And now, after Bush, the median family income, even after being pumped up with these extra hours, is dropping back again by 2 percent or more the last few years. But now how do we come back? Work-wise now, Mom, Dad, the whole family is maxing out. Now how do we climb back, next time, without getting some kind of raise?

It can seem so murky what is happening, month to month. "Last month, American incomes rose," is a standard on the front page of *The New York Times*. As a labor economist friend told me, "When the *Times* says, 'Incomes rose,' what it means is, last month, most people's incomes fell." I guess. Even I find it hard to keep in my head that the average American man, especially a white man, is now making up to $2,500 *less* a year, income, than he did in 1973, or even in the 1960s. But it's true. It's even in *Fortune* magazine.

So about the time Al Gore was to run for President, it was scary that my friends, or the ones at the top, kept puzzling: Why isn't Gore running on the economy? Tsk, tsk! It's so silly to run as a populist. I suppose we're all so disconnected from each other that by 2000, the post-grad liberals at the top had no idea that the American family, way below, down there at the median, was working extra without pay.

Anyway, at this point in the story, in 1994, there wasn't going to be any labor law reform. The only real Clinton era was over. The New Right was in, and now, labor had much bigger worries than median family income in the coming boom. Ha! We had to worry if we'd be around at all.

And it was clear, the day after, at least one labor leader had to go.

Kirkland's Gone!

Yes, one morning, I woke up, and . . . well, Lane Kirkland, president of the AFL-CIO, was gone. Thank God. Still, I didn't jump up and down about it, especially. I know in the book I may have mocked him. But being older now, I am more sympathetic to these older men. Maybe if he was ineffectual, it was only because he was too much a gentleman. One day, in a kind moment, perhaps a kid will say the same of me. But still he had to go, especially after 1994. There's a story, maybe untrue, about Kirkland on the night Clinton was elected in 1992: that Kirkland watched the returns on TV with his good friend, William Safire, the right-wing columnist for *The New York Times*. Why were he and Safire friends? Same views about Russia. Or maybe they just liked each other. Look, it's O.K. with me if Kirkland had a right-wing pal, but on the night when the Democrats or the "labor" party take power at last, you'd think that the head of, well, the "workers' movement," as Kirkland was, would find someone else to drink with.

Still, for years, the AFL-CIO was such a Kafka-castle place, Kirkland got away with this. But now, with the New Right in, it was like the "Battle of Britain." Neville Chamberlain had to go. Carey was the AFL-CIO Executive Council member who said it first. So did Rich Trumka of the Mine Workers. It's interesting, by the way, that the first two presidents who said "Go!" were the two who'd been elected, directly, by their rank and file.

But it was not just Kirkland who had to go, but the whole Kirkland administration, too. That's why the AFL-CIO presidents passed over his second-in-command, Thomas Donahue, who, by the way, was from SEIU, and might have turned out fine. No, Carey and Trumka and others wanted a whole new kind of AFL-CIO, or at least what would look like a new, further-to-the-left labor.

So in came John Sweeney, who was president of SEIU, the one union that really was New Labor. SEIU! Did I even mention SEIU when I wrote this book? SEIU, the Service Employees International Union, was not truly AFL or CIO. It was not a "trade" or "industrial" union. It was "service," postindustrial. Or even better, post-CIO, even if it is in fact as old or older. John Sweeney was not a leader of plumbers (George Meany), or of autoworkers (Walter Reuther), or even of truck drivers (Ron Carey).

No, Sweeney was the leader of janitors. Cleaning crews. The nice Latino ladies who take the trash out of our offices, who do the laundry in our hospitals. That was the shock: that compared to the past leaders of the AFL-CIO, Sweeney was almost like Cesar Chavez, the saint who led the Farmworkers.

How could the *head* of the AFL-CIO be a man I like? I've never met him. It's just hard for me to resist a guy who got into labor because (says his bio) he was inspired by Dorothy Day, of the *Catholic Worker.* He also knew, as a friend, the two priests I most admire, Monsignor Egan and Monsignor Higgins, old labor priests, both dead now but still alive for me.

Sure, Sweeney looks like Old Labor. Old, white hair, paunchy. Also, from New York. A regular. "Oh, he's part of the clubhouse," some people scoffed. And he *is* Old Labor. But he's New Labor, too. He's with the kids. He helped start "Justice for Janitors," with its Dorothy Day cache. Right before he took over at the AFL-CIO to help organize janitors in Washington, D.C., he had SEIU block a bridge at rush hour. (Imagine Lane Kirkland blocking a bridge at rush hour.) In D.C. traffic is so blocked anyway I wonder if anyone in a car even noticed. But the rest of us in labor did.

Sweeney blocked a bridge!

So while I don't know Sweeney, I sort of felt my "side" of labor had taken over. It was not just Kirkland: all his people went. The new Secretary Treasurer was Rich Trumka. Though I hadn't seen him much for years, once, as young lawyers, we'd shared the same secretary, Georgia Thompson. If a lawyer on the fringe like me can know someone at the top of labor, it can only mean labor is smaller now than ever.

Under Sweeney, there would be seminars at Columbia for "Labor and Intellectuals." (I'd like to e-mail my younger self, "Can you imagine that?")

Under Sweeney, there would be "Union Summers," where college kids sign up as if labor were the Peace Corps. Indeed, under Sweeney, the unions are now all over college campuses. They organize in the college cafeterias, the kitchen crews who know what's inside that "mystery meat" I had to eat. Under Sweeney, there would be a whole new image: a New Labor, which would be a labor of the working poor.

A labor to which I could bear witness.

O.K., but would New Labor bring the labor movement back? And here's the answer, so far: It's 2004 and labor's even smaller.

I'd Still Like to Go Back to 1994

Maybe it was over in 1994. In a way, Sweeney came in because it was clear by then labor's situation was impossible.

I'd like to say Sweeney came in because the Teamsters got rank-and-file elections and had a leader on the left. As I said above, Carey and Trumka led the Kirkland coup. No rank-and-file elections? Then no Carey and Trumka. No Carey and Trumka? Then no Sweeney either. So I'd like to say the reason for the Sweeney era is rank-and-file elections.

And while it's partly true, what's more true is: If the Republicans hadn't come to power, there would not be a Sweeney era. No New Right? No New Labor. In a way, Gingrich, Tom DeLay, while they may not grasp it, are the people who created Sweeney.

I'm afraid the big reason is really the GOP debacle, the rise of the New Right. That's what led us to throw out Lane Kirkland. The question now is: Are we just fighting on without hope? Because after 1994, there was no chance, none, zero, for labor law reform. Not under Clinton. Not under Bush. Not under Gore, if Gore had won.

So as some people like to spin out: How History Could Have Been Different. It's a genre with a new name: "Counterfactual History." How Hitler could have won the war. How the South could have beat the North. Here's my contribution: How labor, in 1994, could have changed the labor laws.

Answer: By giving up on NAFTA. The North American Free Trade Agreement. I bet, from 1993 to '94, labor spent more time and money fighting NAFTA than pushing labor law reform! And ten years later many economists on the right, on the left, doubt, as I did at the time, whether NAFTA even mattered.

As my brother the industrial-machinery rep said at the time, "Anybody who'd move down there for the wages is already down there anyway." Why fight so hard? We were already in a kind of cohabitation with Mexico. NAFTA was inevitable.

And since it was sure to pass anyway, why not get something for it? Labor could have gone to Clinton, to Dole, to senators like Bumpers: We'll let NAFTA through—for labor law reform. No Striker Replacement: No NAFTA. If not attach them literally, that would be the deal. To get labor law reform, we had to give them, Business, the New Democrats, something they really wanted. But no one even tried it. The main objection I now get: "But NAFTA was the worst!"

"Worse than not having the right to organize?"

"Oh, that was impossible!"

But no one even tried it. That's why we deserved our "1994."

Sweeney, Part I: His Previous At Bats

My friend P., a community organizer, told me: "You're so negative! You think people like me are out here doing nothing?" Aside from saying, "I'm out here trying, too," I will try to be positive, for once. There's the growth, after all, of SEIU. First, under Sweeney, up to 1994. Now under a new president, Andy Stern. Just since 1996, SEIU organized 600,000 members. It is now the biggest single union in all of the AFL-CIO. Here, by the way, are the top five:

SEIU	1.6 million
AFSCME	1.4 million
Teamsters	1.4 million
UFCW	1.4 million
AFT (teachers)	1.3 million

It's a puzzle, at first, how SEIU exploded under Sweeney then under Stern. When I came to Chicago, I knew of it as a very decentralized often corrupt collection of locals. Once a labor lawyer here referred me a case—a group of laundry workers, with the help of a friend of hers, had decertified an SEIU local at a hospital. The local had filed an unfair labor practice against the lawyer's friend for helping these poor women when he was arguably in "management."

"O.K.," I said. "I'll help these women." I flipped through the file full of SEIU handouts saying the lawyer's friend was a Communist, and the new local would be Communist.

"Shocking," said my young associate.

"What?" said the lawyer.

"All this red-baiting. Calling them Communist," said my associate.

"Well," said the lawyer, after a pause. "They . . . *are* Communist."

"Oh———!!" I said a four-letter word. "Oh, great—you mean Communism is dead all over the world except with a bunch of cleaning ladies in Chicago?"

But that's how bad the SEIU local out here was. To these women, ripped off, even the Communists looked good. But slowly SEIU was changing. As I said, Sweeney had helped start Justice for Janitors. He and Stern and others went about building up the janitors as if they were the autoworkers. It is easy to scoff that SEIU is kind of like the Salvation Army, compared to the old UAW, and bargaining at the pitiful level of $7.00 or $7.50 an hour. What's the point of being in it, or in other unions-of-the-poor, like the Hotel Workers (HERE), once corrupt, too and now morally purified by all its new organizing? I'd say the answer is: it depends, local by local. Sometimes, it's the fact of getting health insurance. Sometimes the wages, pitiful as they are, do go up a lot in percentage terms. Suppose it is only $7.00 to $7.80 over two years, etc. As a percent raise, it compares handsomely with what in the 1950s and 1960s the UAW used to get. Slowly, city by city, Sweeney got in place a UAW-type bargaining.

How did Sweeney, then Stern, do this when janitors work late in all these many office buildings like a thousand points of light? Because even in this "industry," if that's the word, a few firms would get "super-sized." In each big city, New York or Chicago or L.A., there came to be two or three "janitor companies" that farm the guys out building by building. So it became easier to bargain, and organize, when it might seem at first impossible. So this is a corollary to my law.

Yes, as we deregulate, business gets bigger. Two companies. Then one company. But, in what may seem like a paradox, the bigger business gets, into just three or two companies or even one, the easier it becomes for labor to get hold of it all and bring itself back. Like Samson, blinded, slowly getting back his strength.

So that's one secret to SEIU's strength: They didn't just organize, they also got a big, old-fashioned UAW- or Teamster-type contract. I wish I could explain how important that was. One of the young lawyers we lost (alas!) in our little firm now does this kind of bargaining for the janitors. "A.," I said, "does everybody really sign the same contract?"

"Yes."

"I know the city. But the suburbs, too?"

"Yes, yes, of course. It's the SAME!"

Well, it's not only like the UAW of the 1960s, it means that SEIU is almost like a German union, like I.G. Metall, for the poor. In *The American Prospect* ("A Clean Sweep," June 19, 2000) Harold Meyerson explains this much better than I do here. It seems that SEIU now goes city by city, L.A. to Chicago to New York, or in some such order, getting the "master" contract in place, city by city, across the country.

So, that's one good thing: It's not the Salvation Army; it's also raising wages. But except in New York and L.A., and maybe spiritually even there . . . they're still the working poor.

Anyway, based on this and on the organizing, Sweeney really deserved to be taking Kirkland's place. In fact, it's hard to compare the rest of labor and SEIU as if it were just another union in it. My friend O. who worked for it said to me the other day, "It's really like a separate labor federation."

If any of us stay in labor at all, we all may end up working for SEIU in one way or the other. Perhaps I better say that even I have gotten a tiny bit of money now from SEIU. But maybe SEIU itself, its record (even more under Stern than Sweeney), undercuts my argument, i.e., that people don't have the right to organize. So, how did SEIU do it? Well, I'd defend myself with two points, and then . . . have to admit I'm wrong. So to defend myself.

First, they're organizing not the middle but the poor, who are at the bottom. I hate to put it in military terms, but when a union is drawing on the poor, then it's like Poland or Russia, i.e., it can take a lot of casualties and still keep coming on. Workers with more income are more likely to panic and scatter.

Second, and if the first reason is too flip, now I'll sober up: Something has happened to the American economy and SEIU was in just the right place to get a windfall of new members. I begin with the obvious, that the United States is creating, each year, as a percent or share, more "SEIU-type" jobs. The stats are shocking. Go to www.epinet.org, since any facts I cite will soon be overtaken by much worse ones. But I mean something more here: It's a point I take from James Galbraith, of the University of Texas, in a 2003 paper about the "American Model." It's Galbraith's claim, backed up with hard numbers, that it's federal-and-state-and-county government that, in America, really does create the jobs by injecting tax money, credits, and loan guarantees into the private and not-for-profit sector. Health, education: an economy that is not "private sector" in the sense of Wal-Mart and not "public sector" in the sense of court clerks. It's something he calls "quasi public," and that's where all the jobs are—nurses, cafeteria workers, etc.

And it's this quasi-public sector where, by luck, SEIU was waiting. So it should have done much better than the UAW or the Steelworkers. Indeed, it's where the UAW would like to go. "One day," says a lawyer friend, "UAW will mean 'United Academic Workers.' " Just as, I'm afraid, the UMW really will mean one day with no one laughing "United *Mind* Workers." But it's more than that the SEIU was in the right place. Because quasi public is different in another way in that it is also "quasi mean," a whole lot meaner than state government but maybe not as mean as Wal-Mart when it comes to busting unions. Take Harvard or Yale: terribly antiunion. But are they as bad as Wal-Mart?

Or religious, charitable hospitals: very antiunion, but not quite in the sense of a Bob Crandall or a Chainsaw Al. In the nonprofit world, SEIU can flail away, and . . . it's possible the Boss may blink.

But still, when I look at SEIU, I think: What really made the difference is they went out and just did it. Hired the organizers. Spent the money. Instead of whining about labor law reform and union democracy shouldn't I have just been part of it?

So Should You Sign Up—Work for New Labor?

By the way, New Labor is missing rank-and-file democracy. Or rank-and-file elections of its top officers. Not in SEIU or in HERE or in UNITE (the Clothing Workers and Ladies' Garment Workers). These are the three unions I would call New Labor. Or the two unions, if HERE and UNITE merge. Anyway, I mean the low-wage unions that are out there trying hardest to organize.

But maybe they don't need rank-and-file elections of top officers. Maybe, as Tony Mazzochi (now the late Tony Mazzochi) said, unions don't need this kind of democracy if they can organize new members in droves. Because the organizing purifies the union, washes away its sin. While I disagree, it is odd the way SEIU, which was just mildly corrupt, and HERE, which was once mobbed up, seemed to purify themselves morally. Was it just organizing in itself that changed its moral tone? Was it the graduate students from Yale who came in to organize? In HERE, Ed Hanley and his son and the rest of his family are gone. Now the new head of HERE? It's John Wilhelm, and Wilhelm, by God, really is a graduate of Yale.

But it's not just Yale that's morally purifying labor, it's the newly organized. More new members? Then more new officers. More new officers? Then more people, inside the bureaucracy, who want to go on jihads. Because so often that's what the newly converted want to do.

But being a lawyer, I like things written up in rules: There really ought to be rank-and-file elections. In case one day moral fervor wanes. Besides, if we had more democracy, New Labor might organize even more.

And speaking of lawyers, I'd like to add that several of the "good" unions of the 1990s were "good" because earlier, in the 1980s, U.S. prosecutors began to hound them. Not SEIU, it's true, but HERE and the Teamsters are two obvious examples. So, as a lawyer, I rest my case. New Labor needs more direct democracy. (I don't think John Wilhelm would lose to some unknown who merely had a Hispanic name. If he did, O.K.)

Lately I've been puzzling over a book by Fareed Zakaria, *The Future of Freedom* (2003). Zakaria warns of the excesses of democracy, especially in the Third World: giving the poor the right to vote too soon. Zakaria is not writing about American labor, but perhaps one might say: Just organize the poor for now. Teach them about contracts, filing grievances. Take little steps to self-government. Then later, push on to big national elections.

I've thought about Zakaria in the case of the Laborers International Union of North America (LIUNA). It organizes among low-wage workers, though it has higher-wage workers, too. I was one of the many "deputy" monitors, watching LIUNA's first rank-and-file election. I'm proud of being part of it. But did direct democracy transform LIUNA, the way it did the Teamsters? Not as much as I'd have liked. Believe me, I loved it all, being one of the monitors. I worked with terrific people. I met great LIUNA folks. And others, like X., a union official, now gone, who would hit me in the stomach and say, yeah, he was going to read something I wrote "because when I'm dealing with a guy I like to get under his skin, see?"

But five years after this first election there wasn't even a race for president. My guess is no challenger had money for a big national campaign. It may be, in low-wage unions like LIUNA, members can't afford democracy on a big scale. Maybe it has to wait—until the typical LIUNA member has a savings account with at least a few thousand bucks in it.

Well, that's New Labor, or what I know of it: the labor of Sweeney, Wilhelm, Andy Stern, and others. Am I jealous that while I was a labor lawyer, sure enough, I wasn't really part of it? Sure! It was new, edgy. Believe me, SEIU, HERE, every year they lose lots of members, too, but still they organize enough that they keep growing!

In fact, the mystery to me is: Why did Sweeney leave SEIU to head up the AFL-CIO? Because remember, in the rest of the story to come: The AFL-CIO is Old Labor with a little New Labor in it. And a lot of the low-wage labor of the poor is Old Labor, too.

Take the United Food and Commercial Workers (UFCW): Here's a union, too, which has at least some members who are eligible for Food Stamps. It's got stock boys, baggers at the Safeway, the Jewel. It looks like New Labor, but it's not New Labor at all. Why?

No graduate students from Yale. (I'm kidding!) And too much deadwood at the top. (I'm not kidding.)

It's not New Labor if it's incompetent. I say this in sorrow. There are many fine people, great organizers, in the UFCW. But I think they need a government prosecutor or something to shake them up. (Then maybe they could organize Wal-Mart!)

Still, if there's one union for which I'd like to bring cases, I'd put UFCW near the top. By the way, UFCW is pretty good about farming out cases for people who work off the clock. The one I wish I had . . . I have to digress here . . . well, I really wanted to do a "chicken catcher case." In particular: the "catchers" who work for Frank Perdue. His catchers all have long, long rides out to the henhouses where, under the naked light bulbs, they run around late at night to catch the chickens, and wring their little necks.

But Perdue doesn't pay the overtime for the long, long ride of the catchers in the van. Ah! But some other lawyer in Maryland got to sue.

These were the great suits of the 1990s: for off-the-clock work in the henhouses of Perdue, in grocery chains like Food Lion, on the cleaning crews at Wal-Mart. Often, that's why retail stores with tight margins could nudge into the black, just by a little cheating, off the clock. They'd claim a profit. The Dow would soar. It was this new "productivity," in retail and not just in "IT," that led some analysts to hail a "New" Economy.

Well, I did my own UFCW-type case on kids in high school who work after midnight in the malls and sometimes off the clock. Actually, I sued the Secretary of Labor for not stopping it under child labor laws. But let's skip that damned case since I wrote op-eds and maybe overdid it.

If that gives a sense of what New Labor has to do, let's see what Sweeney did, and how he changed Big Labor.

Sweeney Hits a Homer

Right away, in his rookie year as the head of the AFL-CIO, Sweeney hit a homer. By the wildest miracle, Sweeney's AFL-CIO managed to get Congress to raise the minimum wage from $4.25 to $5.15 an hour. Adjusted for inflation, it was the first true raise in many years. And, my God, we got it . . . from the Congress of Newt Gingrich!

After all, it was enough of an achievement to get Clinton to propose it. Why did he? It was just the kind of dumb, old-fashioned thing that should turn off a New Democrat. After all, what is the minimum wage? A raise by state decree! We think of only Europe as doing it. But many European countries have no minimum wage at all. It is the United States and our friend France that have had such laws the longest.

So why did Clinton do it? Simple. The New Right was in. His administration was in shambles. Why not let Sweeney see if he could get it?

But why did Congress pass it? Ah, it's simple: Somebody in labor said, "Hey, let's go on television!" Labor ran commercials, which freaked out the Republicans. Yes, even in America, people slumped over in their couches thought: $4.25 an hour is pretty doggone low. I wouldn't call it a firestorm, but there was enough of a breeze that the New Right, nervous, bitter, felt maybe it had to pass it.

But I jumped up and down. That measly little raise was one of the biggest things of the 1990s. It probably forced retailers like Wal-Mart to be more efficient. So it raised productivity. Indeed, it may have misled us into thinking there was a New Economy.

And it raised not just people at $4.25 but people who made more. As an EPI economist once told me, "Most employers aren't competing in the world economy." (As I recall, he was referring to Macy's.) "So," he said, "they look to see what the minimum wage is, and pay like three dollars more."

Half the jobs held by high-school grads pay the minimum, plus. Half? That's tens of millions of people who in 1995 got a raise. Is it a coincidence that this is about the time we had a boom?

In a way, in D.C., in the foundation world, raising the minimum wage seemed to be a "new idea." Or maybe, when Democrats are stripped of all their other ideas, they fall back on labor law. I had a small epiphany about all this: In 1996, I was watching a Presidential debate between Clinton and Dole and Clinton was asked to give an issue that really separates him from Dole.

Clinton shot back: The Family and Medical Leave Act—one of the few laws he got through.

What, FMLA? That's the big thing we stand for? As a lawyer, I know what a flimsy thing it is. Basically, FMLA lets a working mother . . . crawl off into a corner and give birth, without pay. Not a penny of maternity leave, which she'd get in any decent country. After she crawls back, she can get back her good "old job," at $7.00 an hour, while I guess Dole would fire her and she'd just walk out and get another $7.00-an-hour job.

Yet it's what Clinton came up with to separate himself from Dole. The epiphany was to see what happens, in extremis, when a Democrat is asked to say: Why are you a Democrat? They have nothing to fall back on, except labor law.

"I have a gun to your head. Quick, why are you a Democrat?" It's always a labor law. It was the FMLA, and the minimum wage, that gave Clinton, as a "Democrat," his program in 1996.

And under Sweeney, the AFL-CIO did much more in 1996: It started ringing doorbells as if it were the Final Days.

Sweeney Hits a Double, but Has to Hold Up at First

In 1996, Sweeney hit up all the unions, in one blow, for $35 million for a big AFL-CIO campaign fund. I was thrilled the way the New Right screamed! But even a liberal friend said: "Look, it's union dues. You take it out of people's paychecks whether they vote Democrat or not. How can you justify that?" It took nerve for Sweeney to take so much from dues in 1996, right in front of Congress.

And go after the New Right. One good thing about the Sweeney era: He had the staff to do it. Steve Rosenthal, the new political director. Richard Bensinger, the chief organizer. Others who had been in the New Left, or SDS, in the 1960s. Already, in the late 1980s, they had big staff jobs in different unions. But now they were at the AFL-CIO! At the top.

They had new ideas on how to spend, to turn out the vote. "Treat members like adults. Tell them what the issues are. Let them decide it for themselves." That was a new idea for labor! (Still needs work.) "One 'contact' per member-voter." Even today, as I write, that's still the goal. And one day: Door-to-door for everybody! If anyone is left. Here's a depressing thought: I couldn't pick a better staff than Sweeney had in 1996. As good, maybe. But not better. And still, labor was getting smaller! But when he raised the $35 million, it made us seem larger. I felt I had a pied-à-terre, in a big Potemkin village.

"How can you justify taking it from dues?" Because when people vote in a union, they're voting for an organization that is supposed to elect the Democrats. If it's not electing Democrats, why have it at all? To lose a pension, like Social Security. To lose a benefit, like Medicare. If my union lost these, I'd sue it for gross negligence.

Besides, thanks to a stupid Supreme Court case from the 1940s, a member can ask for a rebate of any dues that his union spends on "politics." It ticked off Felix Frankfurter, who wrote a strong dissent. As he wrote, it makes no sense to divide a union's "bargaining" from its "lobbying." It's all to get a better wage or benefit.

More than ever, labor has to be on Capitol Hill. And as my friend Y., a D.C. labor lawyer, said: "Very little of what labor does up there is to help labor as an institution. It's to save Medicare, Social Security. Things that help all workers. That's the odd thing about what labor does, that 90 percent of the benefit goes to people who aren't in unions at all." How do you and I justify that? We don't pay any dues, like freeloaders, but we get all the benefit.

It may be the strangest thing about America: the 10 percent who fight for the 90 percent. In a way, it's like France. In France, to my surprise, the union membership is very small. It's like a priesthood. A gladiator class. A small group marches, strikes, shuts down Paris, and the rest of France watches to decide which side it's on.

Anyway, very few members, maybe under 2 percent, a figure I saw for the Communication Workers, ask for the money back. Why don't more ask, if so many vote Republican? Maybe they figure they've covered their bases: "If I've got my union in D.C. to defend me, I'm free to vote Republican."

Maybe that's why we lost.

For in 1996, in 1998, in 2000, in 2002, Sweeney didn't homer. We didn't blast them out. So now it's like a siege: The New Right isn't bigger, but we keep getting smaller. Each year we take more casualties. Why?

For one thing, most of the sixty or so unions spend very little on organizing. Sweeney's been able to get only a "very modest" increase, according to a paper, "Union Organizing Commitment: Rhetoric and Reality." (Industrial Relations Research Association, 2003). And it's also the economy. After September 11, the drop in union membership, just from the hotel layoffs, was staggering. In the private sector, in 2002, labor lost almost half a million members!

For that reason, perhaps, the GOP got back the Senate in 2002. Believe it or not, by bleeding labor, it may have helped Bush to be losing all these jobs. But why can't Sweeney get Old Labor, or about fifty of his sixty unions, to get out there and organize?

New Labor Is Still Old Labor

Of course the big problem is: Americans don't have the right to join a union, freely, fairly, without being fired. So over the years we get a hunkered down, defeatist culture where a lot of unions don't try. It's so awful! But we have to keep doing it to keep from disappearing.

I began to see: Sweeney has no power. Now I realize how little power Kirkland had! Over the years, Sweeney must have noticed: When he left SEIU, he was leaving one labor movement for another, weaker one. Does he ever wonder if he could go back? For SEIU is the real labor movement now.

It's sad, I doubt he could get back in now. So, if he's stuck at the AFL-CIO, how can be make Old Labor go out and organize?

Given it's so grim a thing, all that seems to work is: (1) to hire grad students from Yale, since organizing in fact may now be a kind of rocket science (yes, I'm kidding!), or (2) to put in some rank-and-file democracy, to frighten the hell out of the old hacks (no, I'm not kidding). Otherwise, they don't do anything. And the problem is not just that the "new" AFL-CIO is more or less the "old" AFL-CIO, but that this "old" one just gets worse and worse.

Example? ULLICO. I'd like to think ULLICO would have shocked a Martha Stewart. ULLICO is a union-owned insurance company. Among the board? Ten current or former AFL-CIO union presidents. Who push the insurance. Who then get into "risk-free" trading of ULLICO stock. Who then make huge profits for themselves.

It's unclear if the "presidents" did anything criminal, I should say. But these are elected officials who try to pocket hundreds of thousands of dollars in profits while serving on the board. Say this for Martha Stewart: She isn't supposed to be fighting for the rank and file. But that's not the worst.

The worst thing about Old Labor is: They now cross union picket lines! Or maybe they always did. But even in the Sweeney era! It seems nobody can stop it. Let me tell a story: Out here in Chicago, a big IBEW local had a strike at an electric generating company on the city's South Side. Oh, "IBEW" is International Brotherhood of Electrical Workers. The local IBEW members put up pickets, but the other union members crossed the picket lines.

Who's crossing? Workers from the Operating Engineers. Other building trades. Not to do their own work. But to do the strikers' work. In effect, other AFL-CIO members are coming in to scab, to break an IBEW local strike.

So the two local IBEW leaders, who became our clients—two white guys, by the way—think, "We're losing the strike. What do we do?" They do what I would do if I were really desperate: They call up Jesse Jackson Sr.

HELP!

So Jackson is a busy guy, but his staff set up a meeting. And because it's Jesse Jackson, he gets the top officials of the IBEW, of the state AFL-CIO, to meet in person or on the phone. As he hears the story, Jackson asks the top IBEW officials, including the International President, who is in Washington, on the phone, and the head of the Illinois AFL-CIO: What, you can't stop these unions from crossing your picket lines?

Uh . . . no.

Uh, the International wrote a letter, but they kept crossing.

Jackson can't believe it! Who could? In effect Jackson is supposed to help the AFL-CIO save a strike that the AFL-CIO itself is trying to bust. Does that make any sense? No. But that's the way Big Labor works.

But something did come out of the meeting. The top IBEW officials were so upset that our local IBEW president would have Jesse Jackson call and lecture them . . . well, they decided to fire the local president. And did! Which led to a big lawsuit, now just ending, thank God. So I have a chance to finish up this damned Afterword.

But let me turn to you, the way our guys turned to Jesse Jackson: Do you think it's worth saving the AFL-CIO?

Why Not Start a New "New" AFL-CIO?

Start a new AFL-CIO? Or a new, second labor federation? After almost ten years of the Sweeney era, there's talk of doing so by the presidents of other unions, i.e., the true New Labor ones. It's not my idea. Don't blame me. There's precedent. The CIO started because John L. Lewis walked out of the AFL.

"But why bother?" one might say. "O.K., the AFL-CIO isn't working. But what would SEIU or HERE or the Carpenters get from starting a 'second' labor federation?" Well, I hate to say this in front of the children, but I will: if New Labor left Old Labor, then New Labor could "raid" Old Labor and steal its members and feast on the carcass of these old dead unions. So long as New Labor and Old Labor are in one federation, New Labor has to be nice to Old Labor.

But if there was a second federation? The strong would get stronger by feeding on the weak. Remember, this is not my idea! But it might be one way to save the labor movement.

I saw how UNITE swept into Chicago laundries and kicked out the "company" unions, which were not AFL-CIO. So? Why not do it with old AFL-CIO unions? Nor is the point just to "steal" existing members. So long as there is one AFL-CIO, the hip unions like SEIU or HERE can't say to the less hip unions like UFCW: "Look, you aren't getting anywhere with Wal-Mart. Let us go in and try!"

I don't like the idea of it, to spend the next few years devouring each other. But it's like the Donner party out in the Old West: Even the stronger ones are starving, and we need a fresh supply of meat.

We Can Blame It on the World Economy

And if we resort to this, we can blame it on the World Economy.
Globalization. NAFTA. This has been our alibi for everything.
The right to organize? We don't discuss it much. Union democracy? We NEVER discuss it. If there is one message that Americans get from labor in the Sweeney era, it's this: Blame it on the
World Economy. That's why we marched on Seattle. Fought our
way through tear gas. I don't blame rank-and-file members for
doing it. For what else could be our problem?

The opposite is just as galling: "Globalization is wonderful."
Or: "Globalization is inevitable." Because the World Economy
has landed like a saucer from another planet. It's hopeless; we
can't resist. Sure, the opposite is just as galling: Robert Rubin
and others deregulating financial markets with no thought, no
safeguards. And soon people in Indonesia are starving.

My little point is: Globalization can lead to global regulation,
too. International bodies. International law. Or maybe that's not
my point: I don't want to get into that! My point is: Before we
take up the real issues of globalization, let's solve some of our little hometown problems first. Get the right to organize, etc.
Right now it's hard to say what is truly a problem of globalization
or one we ourselves have made.

But of course, the answer to my point is: You don't understand
NAFTA, the World Economy!

Well, I probably don't. But in fact I did a "NAFTA case," to my
surprise, right after NAFTA was passed. I did it for the Ron Carey
Teamsters. It wasn't a real lawsuit in a court but just a complaint
(or really an angry letter) to the Department of Labor. The complaint of the Teamsters was: Mexico is in violation of NAFTA, or
the so-called labor standards, because often in Mexico, there is
no effective right to join a union.

Freely, fairly, without being fired. Sound familiar?

I was really glad to get this piece of business. But I didn't know
what I was supposed to do. NAFTA itself was a few days old. It
had some words in the back as to how each country should let
workers organize, and one country could "consult" with the
other if there were violations. Who knew what it meant?

At least it was a chance to have a press conference. Get on TV. And we had a good story. A few days after Congress had passed NAFTA, an American company, Honeywell, which was already across the border in the maquiladoras, fired a group of women for trying to organize. So we could say: "See? They wait till NAFTA gets through, then they go out and fire people!"

So, cameras roll. Then we got to the North American Office (or NAO) of the U.S. Department of Labor. If the NAO decides our case is good enough, it might raise it with Vice President Gore. Then, possibly Gore would phone Mexico. What was the chance of this? None. And even if Gore had made a phone call to Mexico, what would have happened? Nothing. So why do it?

Because it was all new, and the NAO guy, or Robert Reich, or Gore might surprise us. Who am I to be cynical? At least we'd be on television. But about this whole case, there was a confusing little thing: The women who were fired at Honeywell were already in a union. But it was an "official" or "government" union, a PRI union. That meant: It was inept, morally corrupt. In other words, it was like some of our American unions. But rather than get into that, what I thought we should stress was: Honeywell let the women dip their hands in acid and didn't give them any gloves.

Because that's what I found out when Ms. M., who was the leader of these women, showed up at our office in Chicago. It was November, a dark and stormy day, perfect for the wreck of *The Edmund Fitzgerald,* and in came Ms. M. She was about four-foot-something, the height of a Virgin Mary on the stitching of an Indian cloak.

I was nervous. It was my first Teamster case. It was also in D.C., and it was weird a Midwest lawyer would be doing it. I knew I got it as a favor. I wanted to prepare her, and then . . . for the first time it hit me: Hey, I don't speak Spanish!

Somehow, in my Midwest stupor, I didn't think of this. And she didn't speak English. So as it ended up, another lawyer did her testimony. Damn it! I sat by as someone else had to interview her. But as I sat and brooded, it struck me, again, what my brother had said: "Anyone who's down there because of the wages is already down there." Honeywell wasn't down there because of NAFTA!

And the wages were low, absurdly low. Or maybe not, for Mexico. Still, the one thing I did know, these women should have had some gloves. Not because it would force Honeywell to come back to the United States. Not because it would mean jobs, jobs, jobs for us Americans. No. It's because they simply ought to have the gloves when they dip their hands in pots of acid. We don't care if it means jobs, jobs, jobs for us. Right? And if we help them, maybe they can help us, as we in the United States try to get our right to organize.

Of course, I believe it is worse in Mexico. But in this case, here's all we alleged: The boss brought Ms. M. into his office. The boss told her, more or less, "You're a great worker. You can go far here. But if you keep fighting for this union, we have to fire you." Would she stop? No. All right. She was gone.

From this, we argued, see how brutal it is in Mexico! They actually told her, "We're firing you because you want a union." Outrageous! To tell her, point-blank, that was the reason!

Yet as I made this argument, aloud, a little voice inside was screaming: "Come on, was Mr. Honeywell so bad? He was treating her with respect!" In the United States, he would have lied, accused her of something criminal. In Mexico, at least, Ms. M. had her dignity. What if she had been organizing at a place I'll call Milan, Milan? It is, or was, a yuppie-type Italian restaurant where no one is Italian, and I represented a group of waiters and kitchen help trying to organize. Milan, Milan picked out Brian, the waiter who was leading the organizing drive, and accused him of being a thief, and fired him.

Just days before the union vote.

Then when another waiter, Jill, went out of town, Milan, Milan put out the word to all the workers: Jill had fled town because the union had made a threat to her. Did that make sense? One of the leaders of the union drive?

Then Milan, Milan hired security, so guards now walked around.

Oh sure, we filed a charge for Brian with the National Labor Relations Board. It took three years to decide. Then, finally, the NLRB ruled in Brian's favor. Then Milan, Milan, or its parent (since the restaurant had now gone French-Vietnamese or something) filed an appeal with the U.S. Court of Appeals, and of course we lost.

So I often asked myself: Would I rather be Brian or would I rather be Ms. M.?

And of course I'd rather be Brian. Why? Because he's in Chicago and has (compared to her) a lot of money, and even as a waiter he could make a lot in tips. And the other waiters were actors, arty types, who take yoga and shop at Whole Foods, and who even in their youth look younger than their age. And Ms. M.? After I met her, the lawyer who spoke Spanish said to me: "How old would you say she is?"

I thought, for a moment. "Maybe her late thirties."

"Yes," she said. "But she's not even twenty-five."

Why Not Nuke Canada?

During our NAFTA case, I kept telling people, "It's Canada that should be complaining." Unlike the United States and Mexico, Canada really does let Canadian workers organize, freely and fairly. Canada is a signatory to NAFTA. Why doesn't Canada complain about Mexico and the United States?

Because Canada was the big winner under NAFTA. As I write this, we have just marked, in December 2003, the tenth anniversary of NAFTA. And in the United States there have been thoughtful pieces, in *The New York Times* and *The Chicago Tribune*, about how America has lost jobs, etc. It's implied we've lost all these jobs to Mexico. Yet it's not Mexico but Canada that has been running a huge trade surplus with the United States. If we've been losing jobs in this sense, as measured by this huge surplus, it's not been Mexico but Canada that is taking far more of them.

In 2002, Canada ran a surplus of $50 billion with the United States. Mexico ran a surplus of $37 billion. But the difference is, we lose lousy low-wage manufacturing jobs to Mexico, while we lose golden high-wage jobs to Canada. For what is Canada's biggest edge except in the auto industry? Canada is taking jobs from what in America we regard as our "signature" industry: cars.

In other words, if we lost under NAFTA, it was more to a country, Canada, that has more unions, higher taxes, more socialism.

How can America expect to compete with a country where labor unions are so powerful? Or taxes so high? And with so many social safety nets? So, because of Canada, let's repeal NAFTA.

Except, the United States and Canada already had a free trade agreement, in 1989, to which NAFTA added little. So to do any good, we should repeal the 1989 agreement, too. But would that do any good?

Because in that event, Canada would be a freak case. But most high-wage, high-tax, socialist-type countries, like Germany, France, Italy, Sweden, Finland, in total, also run a big trade surplus with our country. No, it's not as big as China's, but bigger than Canada's (or Mexico's). And it's the kind of surplus that hurts, causes us more pain, since dollar for dollar, we're losing better jobs.

Or to put it a nicer way: The trade surplus is creating jobs in Canada, in Germany, in Sweden. Yes, it's true, as the *Times* story also says, free trade cost jobs in Canada. As the reporter wrote, it caused stress. Canada had to retool, scramble. At first, over five years, Canada lost about 500,000 jobs. But last year alone, they created 450,000 new ones.

And there's another difference: Canada, with its high taxes, has a real safety net for people who are hurt.

So the moral of NAFTA and of free trade is arguably: the stronger the unions, the higher the taxes a country has, the harder it is for America to compete. I know the reply here: Oh, these are smaller countries, they pick out niche industries. So? Don't we? Auto or IT? No, it's that we hesitate in the middle: Should we compete with China and try hopelessly to push wages down? Or with Canada, and push them up? Which way should we go? Try to cut wages? Or try to be cutting edge?

So we end up losing out to both China and Canada. We think that the only way to save labor standards is to stop competing. Whereas if we competed more we'd actually have to raise them. Instead of making this case, instead of arguing that we should get out of low-wage things and do more high-wage things, the AFL-CIO argues just the opposite. Yes, I complained about this in the book. But somehow in the 1990s all of this got worse.

To me, the weirdest thing was our big protest in Seattle when the World Trade Organization was meeting. Old Labor was there. Sweeney was there. The cops used tear gas. Clinton was there and, though a fanatic Free Trader, seemed to be on our side and felt our pain. (How does he do that?) And if it were about child labor, and Ms. M., I'm ready to go, and even take a tiny, tiny bit of tear gas, but I had a feeling it was really about jobs: not theirs, ours.

And if it's not about Ms. M. but about our jobs, then I'd like to raise two questions before I put on a gas mask: First, where are the European unions? They skip these protests. On the whole, world trade's pretty good to them. Second, since we're up here in Seattle, why not march on Canada? They're grabbing our good jobs. It's funny. We hate to lose jobs to people of a different race. China. Mexico. Indonesia. But we don't mind at all losing jobs to white people.

Not that Canadians are white, entirely. But up there, as my friend T. says, either their first name is Gordon or their last name is Gordon. So we think of them as white. Isn't it a little racist that we don't complain about Canada?

Myself, I think Canada's surplus is good for American labor. If being close to Canada were not important to our auto industry, it would long ago have left the Midwest for the South. And today, the whole industry would probably be nonunion. But my point is, if we want to compete head-to-head with Canada and Europe, we better be more like them. In other words:

Stronger unions
Higher taxes
More government regulation

Why Immigrants Will Save Us

Will labor in America disappear? To be upbeat, I pick as my title *Why Immigrants Will Save Us!* In a different mood, I might pick *Why Immigrants Will Doom Us!* Month to month, I change my mind. But let's start with why they may save us: They joined unions in the 1990s, and as the "working poor," they even raised their hourly wage. Except in the top fifth (and not even there completely), the poor in the bottom fifth were the most notable for getting more for every hour worked. Even if a family at the median had a bigger "gain," it usually came by getting a cut in pay, i.e., less money for each hour.

And the poor who marched the most to do it were Latinos, and yes, immigrants, and even some illegals. Look at SEIU and HERE: They really did raise the wages of janitors and maids, without the indignity of just working longer hours. Now it's true that economists explain it as a by product of full employment. Only, as I keep complaining, they can't explain why full employment didn't help the middle class.

No, it was New Labor, getting the minimum wage and even by striking. And there would have been no New Labor without immigrants and Latinos. Look at the maids in Las Vegas. Look at Los Angeles in general. In L.A., New Labor hit the trifecta, as President Bush might say if he were part of it, for it had three things going all at once:

(1) SEIU and HERE, both heavily Latino, were both on a roll, had a kind of unity,
(2) This unified labor took over the Democratic machine so that labor and the party seemed one and the same,
(3) The Catholic Church, also Latino, gave this unity a kind of ecclesiastical odor, too.

But I have to say, I'm no expert on L.A., and actually I'm jealous. I missed the whole damned thing and just read about it from afar. The point is: Labor did great in L.A., not because it was Latino, as I may seem to suggest, but because if you were Latino, it was hard to tell the difference between the labor movement and your family. By the way, this is how it worked in Chicago and New York in the 1930s, 1940s, when they were the hot union towns and L.A. was not.

One difference between Chicago in the 1930s and L.A. in the 1990s? We didn't have Hollywood stars coming out to support the strikes—or, as Harold Meyerson reports, in Beverly Hills, people came up to give cash to the strikers.

But in a different mood I could have picked the title *Why Immigrants Will Doom Us*. In fact, I was in this mood a month ago. A union friend was saying how, at a plant he'd love to organize, there was a big, mouthwatering minimum-wage violation. "Oh, J.," I said, weak with pleasure, "what can I do to get this case?"

"Nah," he said. "I can't find anyone who'll stand up." As immigrants, they're afraid of trouble.

"In the whole plant? There must be one!"

"Nope. They're all afraid."

After September 11, it may be tougher for New Labor. No, immigrants won't doom us. But sometimes I worry that we'll have to organize them, en masse, in whole cities like L.A. or Las Vegas. There's too much fear now to do it shop by shop.

Why White Males Will Doom Us

My title could also be *Why White Males Will Save Us*. If I were in a different mood . . . but I never am in a different mood. The immigrants are just afraid of the Boss. The white males also seem to be afraid of each other. "You think most guys don't realize they're being screwed?" said my friend D., the other day. "Aw, most of them know!"

"Then why don't they show it?" I said.

"You don't know what it's like in the business world," he said. "In business, in every company, it's like there's some loudmouth, a guy like Rush Limbaugh, yelling about the Democrats and all that. And if you try to say anything, it's like they don't come back and talk about the 'Democrats.' No, they go after YOU: Like, What's the matter with *you*??? You become the issue. So nobody says anything."

A long pause.

"Of course, what these guys don't like . . . is some of the feminist stuff. Especially women going off to these sperm banks and having kids by themselves. They hate that."

What he said about the bully-in-every-company sounds true to me. I admit I don't know. It may not be that everyone is afraid. But let's say it's just one out of five. Not many, right? But if one out of five screwed their courage to the sticking place, it would be enough to bring back the Democrats as a permanent majority party. And if the Democrats were the permanent majority party, then maybe three out of five would start to talk back. Now there's a continuum from fear-of-the-bully ("How I'd love to shut that asshole up!") to a dumb sheep-like stupor, like sleep, from the shock of the pounding of twenty years. I got this idea from a memoir of a French soldier who was at Verdun. The shock of the bombing was such, he wrote, that many of the troops would have to go to sleep.

White men now make less on average than they did in 1973. They have no pension. No pension! So maybe it's shock. But I say it again: I don't get it. It's like reading about Germany in the 1930s: I can read Erich Fromm, Eric Ericsson, Michael Moore, the entire Frankfurt School, and think, "O.K., I get it," but then later after I've put the books away, I don't get it.

But who cares about the reason? All I care about is fixing it. And what I know fixes it is: If a white male is in a union, the fact-of-being-union alone, with nothing else, tends to flip him from Bush to Gore. I base this on an AFL-CIO claim, which may be shaky: Bush won nonunion white men by 41 points, but *lost* union white men by 24 points.

Let's assume the AFL-CIO claim is true. The way the press treats this is to say "Look at all the union guys who vote for Bush. Look how weak the unions are. They no longer swing their members." Some Republican would be quoted: "Unions have lost their clout. Their members vote Republican," etc., etc.

That's what the press (still) thinks is the story. But isn't the story just the opposite? Steve Rosenthal and his wonderful work aside, I can testify, after many years of being a lawyer, how tiny, how pitiful each contact with a member is. When I see the AFL-CIO claim, I am dumbfounded. "How can the flip to Gore be so great?" Now if this were France, I would understand. There every member is a volunteer. "Excelsior!" There is no U.S.-type Wagner Act, with shop-by-shop bargaining, so some people are in a union whether they like it or not while others who want to join can't get in at all.

So if our members aren't the true believers but come out of the same big pot of white males who vote for Bush, what is it that makes them flip? Let me toss out three reasons.

The first is: They don't come from the same big pot of gray white-male mush. That is, the union white males tend to be public employees, and they're not from the South. But who are these white males in the public sector? Prison guards. Cops. Firemen. All of them sensitive, metrosexual guys. And as to a regional bias, I'd say labor has pretty much collapsed everywhere. So much for the first reason.

The second is: In a union, someone TELLS you what to do. While I don't like this one either, it may be partly true. Because Sweeney hands out one brochure, how can that overcome ten million TV commercials? Well, it's a nicer one. But Bush has nicer ones, too. But we go door-to-door sometimes. But so do they. Still, it's rare for someone in authority, looking out for your best interests, to tell you: Vote for X. So taken am I with this idea that I got into an argument about the African-American vote in 2000. "Well, you know," said a friend, "just by being black who you have to vote for." But I disagreed. What is different about being black is that there are people in authority, black ministers, black lawyers, Jesse Jackson, who are telling you: Watch out for this guy; trust this guy.

In that sense, the black vote is a more "educated" vote, in the literal Latin root sense.

"That's total nonsense," said my friend. And he more or less destroyed my argument. So now I don't believe it either.

But this third and last reason is the one I believe: that the "effect" of being a union member is that it removes or cancels out all the other effects. Now, instead of someone to tell-you-what-to-do, there is no one to tell you what to do. In a unionized shop, there may be a Rush Limbaugh yelling. But now a union steward or someone else is more likely to be yelling back. Now, when there's a question: "WHAT'S THE MATTER WITH YOU???"

There's an answer: "GO FUCK YOURSELF!!"

So, there is a dialogue. And if white males in this kind of shop really go 59 percent for Gore, it's not because either Rush or the union have any real effect, but because this is how white males would vote in general if they were simply left alone.

How Big Business Could Save Us

Over and over I keep agonizing how labor could come back, without an effective right to join a union. One way: People get desperate. They rise up. It's not such a silly argument. Robert Shiller, the Yale economist, noted recently: In 1979, the bottom 40 percent of two-parent American families (not households, who are single, drifter-types, but families) took in 18 percent of the national income. Now, they take in 14 percent. Soon it could be 10.

Ten percent! In a democracy, wouldn't people rise up? Maybe, but in the case of America, these people have already stopped voting. So what would bring labor back? Maybe more strikes, like the one at UPS.

While many good things happened in the Sweeney era, I'd say the single best thing was the strike at UPS. As you may recall from the book, I am a student of the way UPS likes to fire people—not just fire but kick them around. So I took a special pleasure in the fact the Teamsters, the Carey Teamsters, beat them. Also, in the 1990s, it was nice to win a strike that, for once, did not involve janitors or maids.

That's always been my unease with New Labor. In a way, I'm glad that as a young person I came in with the Old Labor: the old $25-an-hour labor, going up to $30, instead of the $8-an-hour labor, going up to $9. It was easier to hang out, class-wise, with Old Labor. I could go out to bars with the sons of steelworkers, and peel the labels off the Buds, and let them pick up the tab, and talk, for a long, long time in a way I wonder if I could really do with janitors or maids.

Believe me, I like bearing witness to the poor: Morally it's better. But I also like the labor that can take you out to dinner, even at Milan, Milan. *That's* the labor which is really on its back. But it won at UPS.

How could the Teamsters win such a huge nationwide strike, when strikes, like at Caterpillar, were supposed to be obsolete? Indeed, in the Sweeney era after 1994 labor tended not to lose but to win the big strikes. But still, the press and others had bet on UPS. So why did it lose?

Because it got too big.

Let me explain. The strike was over many things, but mostly pensions. UPS hated, just hated paying into the multiemployer Central States Pension Fund. UPS argued that if it had its own fund, it could pay more to the UPS drivers. To an economist,

UPS is absolutely right. But if I may say, economists are disciplined to be idiots about many things. If UPS pulled out, it could weaken the Teamsters as an institution: That's the real goal. And if the Teamsters were weaker, then in the long run, as UPS knows, it may not be paying anybody a pension at all.

But is any American sophisticated enough to grasp this? Well, they are at UPS. So the rank and file went on strike. Only it was not like at Caterpillar, where only 12,000 workers went on strike and Caterpillar kept going. At UPS, over 180,000 workers went on strike. The whole "UPS nation," if I may put it that way. Not just Atlanta. Not just Chicago. But everywhere, across the nation. So in a way, it was "like" a 1958-type Steelworker or Auto Worker nationwide strike.

That, I think, is why it worked. In the new world of Super Business, a single company can be the equivalent of a whole industry. UPS, though it competes with FedEx in some things, is truly now an industry employing not a normal workforce but a virtual nation. Unlike the strike at Caterpillar, the strike at UPS was, by necessity, cataclysmic: The fact that UPS was so colossal was the very thing that made it weak.

So labor could come back? But now a new thing may doom us.

How September 11 May Doom Us

Personally, I'm tired of liberal whining about September 11 and how the Constitution is in a meltdown. Things are worse, but not that bad, in terms of our civil liberties and rights. It's been much worse for labor, but no one seems to notice.

For one thing, labor took such a big whack in tourism, hotel, and travel. We can't afford to lose any more members, and worse it put one of our best unions, HERE, temporarily out of action.

So as a result, after September 11, labor became much more dependent on the public sector. But September 11 gave the New Right its first chance ever to outlaw labor in the public sector altogether. In real-world practical terms, the biggest thing Bush has done to fight the war on terror is to set up the Department of Homeland Security and then to prohibit any of its employees, over 180,000, from being in a union. It's a first. The Coast

Guard, Immigration, other agencies now have ditched the unions. And if it's necessary to get unions out of Immigration, then all the more so in Justice, Treasury, the Defense Department as a whole. Next will be the cops, firemen. The New Right may not have the clout to do it now. But if there is another 9/11? Even the cop unions may be gone.

I can see why our leaders in top office would want to get rid of unions. In the United States, most of our managers don't know how to manage, except to say, "You're fired." To manage as European business does, to get consensus, to get a staff to accept, then to embrace a goal or mission—to manage like this in America is rare. So when we bring our CEOs from private business into government and they come up against a union for the first time, they don't know what to do. They panic. All they know how to say is: "You don't do it my way? You're fired!"

What if there's someone who speaks up? In Minneapolis, before 9/11, there was an FBI agent who saw what al Qaeda was up to. She wrote memos. She tried to warn her managers. They ignored her. And in the end, in front of Congress, she embarrassed them. I admit, since she was the manager of the FBI office, she was probably not in a union. But what if she had been? The next time someone in the ranks warns us of al Qaeda, we want to be able to move faster to fire her.

Maybe I'm overdoing it. Maybe I make too much of this aspect of 9/11. Maybe we make too much of all the aspects of 9/11. And anyway, something happened after 9/11 that, at least as far as labor goes, gave me a bit of hope. It was the fight in Congress, by some Republicans like Tom DeLay, to stop a federal government takeover of airport screeners. Against all my inclinations, I have decided that Tom DeLay really cares about our country. So I believe that deep in his heart he knew the feds had to deputize the screeners and make them employees. So why did he fight it? Because he knew that these private screeners, once they were in the public sector, would immediately join a union. They'd flip, on the whole, from mostly voting Bush to mostly voting Gore. Same people. No difference. Except, he knew, every Republican knew, within minutes of being in the public sector, they'd be in a union. (That's why later they set up the Department of Homeland Security—to stop it.) If Tom DeLay and the most hardened ideologue on the New Right know this, know it in their bones, it seems crazy for you or me to doubt that labor, any minute, in this country, could come roaring back. So it could come back, should come back, I ought to feel upbeat.

But the reason I can't be is a story that affects me personally, and it's too awful to tell. I suppose the simplest thing is just to say:

Carey's Gone!

Ron Carey's gone.

If this Afterword is too long, it's because I hated coming to this part.

In 1996, Ron Carey, the reformer, our candidate, went up against, one-on-one, the candidate of the Old Guard, and by a close 52 to 48 percent, Carey actually beat a Hoffa—James Hoffa, the yuppified lawyer son of Jimmy Hoffa. Both sides spent millions.

But then began the investigation—of Carey! It went on for years, through the UPS strike. And in the end, the monitors expelled Carey. Kicked him out of the union for taking campaign money that looked like a kickback. But did nothing to Hoffa, whose own money came from mysterious sources that no one explored. Now there was a rerun and the TDU candidate, Tom Leedom, was a good guy. But a svelte and polished Hoffa, who outspent him ten-to-one, swamped him. So Carey's gone.

The Old Guard rules! Though it rules with a different, more velvet hand and works out at a health club. Indeed, the Old Guard had to put up a Hoffa who was a lawyer, sneak him in as a "member," precisely because with rank-and-file elections, they had to put up someone more, uh, presentable, with a smile and a degree and a family name, than the Old Guard would have had to do before, when they just met in a back room in Vegas.

Yet even against Hoffa: Carey had won! Then Carey was gone. So what did Carey do? Near the election, the IBT was paying out large sums, roughly $700,000, to various public interest groups, mainly one called Citizen Action. In itself, this was not a bad, and even a good thing, since Citizen Action was a group that fought New Labor's battles on Medicare and Social Security. It reached out to all citizens, not just union members. I would call it New Labor's "civilian" arm.

But . . .

Supporters of Citizen Action stupidly kicked in a chunk of their cash, about $200,000 to Carey's campaign. So the question became, did Carey use the IBT's contribution to Citizen Action as a quid pro quo to get their contributions to his campaign? I can understand why Citizen Action and its supporters might be desperate to help. It seemed, in 1996, that the Carey-Hoffa race would decide the very future of the Sweeney era. On the left, everybody in the AFL-CIO wanted Carey to win. Wasn't he responsible for Sweeney taking over, after all? No Carey, no New Labor. And if, in 1996, Carey would have been supporting Citizen Action anyway, what was the problem?

First, it looked bad. The IBT gave the money to this *one* liberal group. Second, and even if "they-all-do-it," the left seems to do it a lot more crudely. And in fact, there *was* a mid-rank Carey guy who was guilty of money laundering, though on a smaller scale, up in Boston.

But to be more technical, Carey's gone not so much because he took money from Citizen Action. One could say that, tut tut, in D.C. it happens all the time. (Does it?) No, Carey's gone because he said under oath that he, Carey, did not know of or approve the IBT's huge payment to Citizen Action. Oh, come on, even his defenders had to groan. How could he not know? As Bill Clinton might have told him, it is stupid, in general, to lie under oath, especially in a hyper-public case. But it is even stupider to lie to a prosecutor, under oath. Remember, if you ever hold a high office: Don't lie to a prosecutor under oath!

Whether Carey did or not, now Carey's gone.

I suppose the only good thing is that he had enough time, while his case went on, to win the UPS strike. How odd that, under a cloud, he had so great a glory—to win at UPS. But then, he left disgraced. Ah!

Well, I've often brooded: Why didn't Carey just say, "Sure I gave the money to Citizen Action! Did I expect them to support me? It's Washington! Of course!" But then, maybe it *was* like money laundering. (Remember the guy in Boston.) Ah!

I'd been so sad not to be in D.C., to work for him. Now I thought: I'm so lucky not to be in D.C., with the prosecutors all around.

While I mostly blame Carey, I also blame the way the prosecutors handled it, too. "It's amazing," said a lawyer after Carey went off, "maybe someday they'll write a history of the fed's oversight of the Teamsters and call it 'Hoffa to Hoffa.'" My gripe was: If Carey deserved to go, they should have kicked out Hoffa, too. For in the election of 1996, Hoffa raised over $3 million. Carey raised over $1.6 million. But did Hoffa accurately report his contributions? The Carey forces scoffed at Hoffa's claim that he got a tsunami of tiny contributions, under $100, from people he did not have to list.

Of course, that's no excuse for Carey. But he must have thought at least once or twice, "Doesn't the monitor or election officer see what's going on?" Besides, Hoffa was raising his cash because of what the government itself had made Carey do. Carey came in. Threw out of office the Tuxedo Teamsters, who made over $150,000 or $200,000. So they left—but rich, vengeful, and still with all their "walking around" money, from years of soaking their Teamster local treasuries.

And where did this Tuxedo-Teamster money go? One way or another, I believe, into Hoffa's campaign: albeit much of it indirectly, in local union efforts and such, into Hoffa's campaign. So Carey, watching Hoffa get support from the very bums the U.S. Attorney had pressed him to kick out, may have wondered: What! Am I being set up?

THREE MILLION DOLLARS. And that's only the direct money Hoffa had to report. How was Carey going to match that money, simply from the rank and file?

The monitors politely looked the other way. Carey may have wondered too why they let James Hoffa the Lawyer slip in, without even a cup of coffee, as a so-called union member. Remember, the government was supposed to ensure the laboratory conditions for this new, infant Teamster democracy. In 1917, Lenin at least had to go into Russia in a sealed boxcar. Not James Hoffa, into the Teamsters. The government just waved him through.

So, in the end, the feds pounced on Carey, after he'd done all their dirty work for them tossing out the mob. Part of this federal investigation got truly nutty. In New York, the U.S. Attorney hauled up one Carey supporter after another on the wildest stretches of Landrum-Griffin law. Example: You tell a friend, "You ought to help Carey." If you were an "employer," i.e., someone who employed not a Teamster but just anyone, like a secretary, the U.S. Attorney might say: That's a matter for the grand jury. *Why?* Because you, as an employer, of just a secretary, not of a Teamster, or even a possible Teamster, were giving a "benefit," an intangible asset, to a union officer, Carey. How? By saying: "Help him."

But once the investigation starts, anything goes.

Yes, it turned into a witch hunt, not just of Carey and his staff, but of anyone who supported Carey, or anyone in SEIU or HERE or the AFL-CIO or just anyone on the labor left. Thank God I missed that. In fact, since Carey left, the Hoffa era turned out to be good for me: I'm back suing Teamsters. Also, for a while, I even had a small pro-reform Teamster local as a client—far more business than I ever had under Carey. But still, it was depressing. While the end-of-Carey was not the end-of-the-Sweeney-era, the era (and maybe New Labor as such) felt a bit more muted after that.

But TDU, thank God, fights on.

By the way, Mary Jo White, the U.S. Attorney, couldn't stop chasing Carey even after he'd been kicked out. She went on and did a big prosecution of him for perjury. But a jury acquitted him. I guess they didn't buy her case. Or maybe they figured: He's gone. It's over. He suffered enough.

After Carey

And then, after Carey, Clinton was gone. Now Bush is in. But am I really discouraged?

You bet I am. In fact, I have been trying to do more and more non-labor cases. In our little firm, we helped file a big suit against handgun manufacturers. And we sued a big payday loan outfit for usury.

I'm trying to think of something other than labor law to do.

Alas, every big problem in the country has to do with the decline of labor. I can think of other causes, but deep down I know these wouldn't be such causes if somehow we got a labor movement back. Whether it's AIDS in Africa or lack of health insurance here, or even such a thing as the Kyoto treaty, it's all the same. If we had a labor movement back, we'd be more of a social democracy. And if we were, we'd be halfway to defeating all the demons in the world. Want to really help the poor in Haiti? Then go out, now, and organize for labor, at a Microsoft or a Wal-Mart.

"But how?"

It's true, for a long while we aren't going to get any labor law reform, though it's the only answer. Yet, if I may draw on a few ideas from Barbara Ehrenreich and sneak in one or two of my own, I can think of a few things to tell the labor movement and myself—things in our control, that *we* can do.

1. *Individual* memberships. Yes, let people, individually, one by one, sign up as union members, not as part of a bargaining unit. One by one. In Europe, that's how people join. For years, Europeans I know have said to me, "Why don't you let people join up individually?" For example: you, the reader, if you aren't in a union. And for years I would tell the Europeans, "Well, you don't understand. Under our labor law, you have to come in as part of a bargaining unit. All we do is bargain for a group. You don't understand."

For years I'd say, "You don't understand." Then one day I realized: Maybe *I* don't understand. Maybe even here, people could join up individually.

But we can't just give them a credit card like at AARP (Sweeney tried this). No, if it's going to be a real membership, we have to give them a "union-type" service. And since we can't give them collective bargaining, what do we give them?

My idea: a free lawyer, or two free hours of legal advice.

Out there, in the nonunion world, people in sales, the freelancers, the techies, even maids, are being fired all the time. Everyone in this country gets fired. Or laid off. Two, three, up to seven or more times in a working life. "What are my rights?" they want to know. And with all the civil rights laws, which we have multiplied in part because we have no real labor law, it is very hard to say when a firing, or demotion, does violate one or other law.

So, give the individual member the right to free consultation with an "employment" lawyer. I mean, for example, one of the many lawyers who are part of the National Employment Lawyers Association (NELA), of which I am a lowly member. But who would want this kind of help? Millions! In federal court here in Chicago, a magistrate judge told me that 40 percent of the cases now are employment cases of this kind. *Forty* percent. And then look at all the people who file at the Equal Employment Opportunity Commission or other agencies but never take it further. And then think of all the people, driving around, wondering, "If only I knew a lawyer I could talk to!"

Labor ought to have a union for these people. "I'm skeptical," said a friend, "it would only appeal to a few." Fine. How about one in ten? That would double the size of the labor movement. And at least people would feel part of something union-like.

In a book like this, I should not be so crass as to go into mechanics. But what about a service plan, where the "individual" member signs up for twenty-four months. It'd be like a contract for a cell phone—and, again, with a right to two free consultations, at any time the member wants.

And if we sign these people up, shouldn't we give them some meetings to attend? That's the next idea.

2. Set up "state" bodies, or "state" unions, for all these new members. Let them join individually, but then group them state by state. Why, if they can't bargain?

To change the "labor" laws of the state. Forget the United States as a whole. Forget the U.S. Senate and the House. At least the state legislature is based on one person, one vote. In other words, the unions have to reach out and start citizen movements, state by state, to change the state "labor" laws, which don't relate to collective bargaining. Yes, Alabama, Alaska, Arkansas . . .

What a slog, it seems. Yet, as tort or personal injury lawyers who bring class actions state by state know, it's not as hard as it looks. If we were to succeed in just five states—say, in California, Florida, Texas, New York, and Illinois—that'd be about a third of the country. But what can states do about the Wagner Act or the right to organize?

Nothing. If they try to tip the balance to unions, it is even illegal. There is a doctrine known as "preemption" that warns a state: Touch not the federal law. So why bother with state law? Because, in general, states can change the way we hire-and-fire. And if we changed nothing else, at least we'd have new state-by-state political movements, which New Labor could fire up on election days.

But the states could change everything, as I will try to explain.

3. Let the states bring back labor. O.K., how?

Pass a law in each state stating: "Nobody can be fired, except for just cause." That is, in each state, get rid of the old common law rule of "employment-at-will," which means "I can fire you for any reason at any time." It's not in the Constitution, after all. Every civil rights law just makes a modest rollback of employment-at-will. Some may say, "But isn't that the kind of thing a union is for? To end 'employment-at-will'? So you can't be fired except for just cause?"

It's true, in the past, unions in America have had that as *a* purpose, because we don't have laws prohibiting employment-at-will. But even in America, that's not the real purpose of a union. What is the real purpose?

Higher wages.

Higher wages.

Higher wages.

Not to mention: pension, health. And maybe even a vacation. How does it hurt labor if some government law knocks out employment-at-will? It doesn't hurt labor in Europe. In a way, we've done it backwards over here in America. We think: We'll organize, then no one can be fired except for just cause. But we should think: If we get a law that no one can be fired except for just cause, then . . . my God, we can organize like crazy.

In other words, a state law like this could be better than striker replacement. How?

Simple. It bulletproofs the people who want to join a union. If Norma Rae is fired, she goes to a state court. Gets a jury. Damages. Injunction. No NLRB, nothing. If no one can be fired except for just cause, it is irrelevant whether the boss is busting a union or not. Who cares about motive? It's just not "just cause."

Of course, this ought to be the law-of-the-land. I'm sick of proving a labor motive. Or an age motive. Or any motive. Just: Is there just cause? Don't tell me the country would collapse. Because when people were in unions and we had just cause, the country was in its glory.

And we could use state laws to give people other collective bargaining–type benefits, like severance and vacation pay. Federal law doesn't prohibit a state from requiring, say, two weeks vacation.

And the biggest benefit of all? We could bring back the Democrats.

4. Get the Democrats to promise collective bargaining–type benefits.

Not by federal law. No, the way the Constitution is set up, even if the Democrats control everything, they can't do that much. So why bother to elect them? To keep the New Right from destroying labor.

For the Democrats the problem is: It's hard to win as the labor party, which is what they are, if the country doesn't know there even is a labor movement. Somebody, visible, seeking high office, has to tell them. Somebody has to say, yes, people in this country can get:

Vacations.
Pensions.
Higher wages.

Just say it. "More." And say, "If we can't get it at the federal level, we'll get it at the state level." Instead of over-promising, we don't promise people enough.

At the next Democratic Convention, it would be nice if for once the nominee would say: *"We've had whopping growth. Huge productivity gains. Year after year. But you, or most of you, haven't gotten a dime. So what I'm going to propose tonight is something like a minimum for the middle class.*

"And here's the minimum, all across the country: If you're laid off, one week's severance pay for every six months of work.

"Ten days' vacation for everyone in this country.

"One month maternity leave, paid, *for every woman who's worked one year at a company.*

"And you have no right to be fired except for just cause.

"I know very well that this does not go far enough. For I believe every working person should have a pension. But let's make a beginning. It is time for all Americans to realize we are in this together, and we have to help each other.

"We can't rely on Big Government anymore. People have a right to a pension, to health care, to time off with their children. If they work hard, they have a right to expect these things from work.

"If we can get these things at the federal level, we will. If not, we will get them state by state. But ask not that our party, or any party, get all these things for you. You must also ask for them yourselves."

So that's what we promise. Not a word about taxes. There's no need. Not a word about "labor." We just pass the laws.

But probably not at the national level. We put them in state by state. New York can pass such laws. California can, by referendum. One day, if they ever stop obsessing about Castro, Florida may, too.

Let the thing build. The Democrats can't, literally, be the labor movement. But if they talk like a labor party, they might bring labor back. And come back themselves, by promising the very things a labor movement promises.

5. Finally, don't forget the little things. Oh, there are all sorts of little technical fixes, which I might put in a memo but I suppose not in a book. I'd change the state laws for not-for-profit corporations to make them more community- (and labor-) friendly. Why should charities and not-for-profits engage in union busting?

I'd have labor run more community colleges where graduates, if they pay dues to cover costs, could keep coming back to improve their skills.

And most of all, I'd push state attorneys general to bring cases against Wal-Mart and other companies for working people off the clock or injuring them at work. And to require them, yes, even at Wal-Mart, to let the workers elect committees, to make employers follow state laws.

But none of that belongs in a book. Indeed, so that this Afterword does not require an Afterword, I'd better end it here. And if you're thinking nothing will come out of any of these ideas, or anyone else's, I'd have to guess you're right. Everything is against labor. The culture. The Constitution, too—the lack of any real majority rule.

And the individualism! It is no longer something that makes us strong so that it might help labor. It is now something that is too strong for us. It makes us weak now, and afraid. In the past we never had to be so much on our own, or make ourselves up with so little family, community, nothing, but more or less from scratch.

It would seem too hard, in such a country, for labor to come back. But that's the good thing about this country. It's so loose, so unsettled: Anything may happen.

We may still end up drifting, warily, into one another's arms.

January 2004
Chicago